INVESTING IN REAL ESTATE

INVESTING IN REAL ESTATE

Second Edition

ANDREW MCLEAN
and
GARY ELDRED, Ph.D.

JOHN WILEY & SONS, INC.

New York • Chichester • Brisbane • Toronto • Singapore

Copyright © 1996 by Andrew McLean and Gary Eldred
Published by John Wiley & Sons, Inc.

This publication is designed to provide accurate and authoritative
information in regard to the subject matter covered. It is sold
with the understanding that the publisher is not engaged in
rendering legal, accounting, or other professional services. If
legal advice or other expert assistance is required, the services
of a competent professional person should be sought.

Library of Congress Cataloging-in-Publication Data:

McLean, Andrew James.
    Investing in real estate / Andrew McLean and Gary Eldred. — 2nd
ed.
        p.   cm.
    Includes index.
                              ISBN 0-471-15398-2
    (pbk. : alk. paper)
    1. Real estate investment—United States. I. Eldred, Gary W.
II. Title.
HD255.M374   1996
332.63' 24—dc20   96-13042

Printed in the United States of America

10 9 8 7 6 5 4 3 2 1

CONTENTS

INVESTING IN REAL ESTATE

1 INTRODUCTION: WHY YOU SHOULD INVEST IN REAL ESTATE

Do you want to achieve financial security and financial independence during the coming 10 to 15 years? Yes! Then you've got no better way than real estate.

More specifically, by real estate we primarily mean rental housing: single-family homes, duplexes, fourplexes, and perhaps later on, larger properties in the 12- to 24-unit category. Of course, rental homes aren't your only real estate possibilities, but in our experience, these properties offer the safest and surest route to wealth for the largest number of investors.

EIGHT GOOD REASONS RENTAL HOMES CAN MAKE YOU WEALTHY

Although every type of investment has its advantages and disadvantages, here are eight reasons rental housing can make you wealthy—especially as contrasted to corporate stocks.

1. You enjoy personal control over your real estate investments.
2. Relative to other investments, rental housing yields high income.
3. Over time, your original real estate equity will multiply by a factor of 10, 20, 50, or more.
4. Tax law permits you to shelter some of your rental income and gains from appreciation.

5. You can get started with little or no savings.

6. Anyone of average intelligence can learn how to invest successfully in rental housing.

7. You can't easily liquidate your real estate investments.

8. The economic fundamentals of the United States point to a more prosperous future.

Personal Control

Nearly everyone talks about stocks and real estate as if they are just different types of investment. But, in fact, buying stocks is much more like playing the horses at Pimlico or rolling the dice in Las Vegas.

When you buy a stock, all you get for certain is a "piece of paper" that you hope you can later sell to someone else for more money than you paid for it. Except when you're buying into an IPO (initial public offering), the company you're "investing" in doesn't see a dime of your money. You're simply betting on the chance that you've picked a winner. As a practical matter, you can do nothing to enhance your returns with stocks; market forces control.

In contrast, when you own rental housing, you call the shots. You choose what tenant market to aim for, what improvement strategy to adopt, what rents to charge, and what operating and capital expenses to incur. When you invest in real estate, your decisions influence the amounts of cash that flow in and the amounts of cash that flow out. By tailoring your investment and operating strategy to market conditions, you can make money in any type of market.

People who think negatively often view these property investment and managerial decisions as "headaches"; smart investors recognize them as entrepreneurial opportunities. Accordingly, we've written this book for smart investors who prefer to control their financial future rather than gamble it on the hoped for performance of the stock market.

Rental Housing Yields Higher Income

Let's assume for the moment that you've decided to put $100,000 into the stock market. How much income (dividends) will those stocks pay you each year? Naturally, it will depend on which stocks you buy, but in general (before tax) dividend yields for stocks range between zero and 8 percent, with the average falling into the 2 to 5 percent range. In other words, for every $100,000 you accumulate in stocks, you can expect to receive annual before-tax cash returns of $2,000 to $5,000 per year, maybe less, sometimes more.

In contrast, with rental housing valued at $100,000 your net rents (after expenses) of say $650 to $850 per month would give you an income of $7,800 to $10,200 a year. Although you can play with the numbers and come up with varying results, the general principle holds: for each dollar of value, rental housing typically yields higher income than stocks. In addition, look at Figure 1.1 to see how you might expect your rental housing income to increase over time.

Equity Buildup

As you look into the future, your original equity investment in rental housing will multiply itself by 10, 20, 50, or perhaps even 100 times. And no, these multiple returns do not depend on double-digit rates of inflation.

Look at Figure 1.2. Using property appreciation rates of just 3, 5, and 7 percent, you can see that over extended periods, your beginning real estate equity of $10,000 can easily grow into hundreds of thousands of dollars. Even better, if you improve your property, pick a hot (fast appreciating) location, or pyramid your wealth by trading up to larger properties, you can grow your real estate wealth larger and faster (more on these techniques in later chapters).

Next, let's compare these real estate equity buildup returns to stocks. If you wanted to grow a $10,000 investment in stocks to say $100,000 over a 20-year period, what rate of price appreciation would you have to achieve? The answer: 12 percent. If over the same 20-year period you were to grow your $10,000 stock portfolio into $300,000, you would need an annual appreciation rate of around 19 percent.

In light of the big run-up in stock prices since the 1987 "crash," stock price gains of 12 to 30 percent per year may not sound unreasonable. But in 1988, sustained home price increases of 10 to 30 percent a year didn't seem unreasonable to property owners in San Diego, Boston, Washington, DC, or Honolulu, either.

The truth of the matter, though, is that whether we're talking stocks or real estate, long term, double-digit price increases are not to be expected. Enjoy these short-term gains when you can get them, but don't count on such heady price increases to continue for 15, 20, or 30 years. It won't happen.

In fact, in 1972 the Dow-Jones Index broke 1000 for the first time in history. But it did not break the 1100 mark until 1983. During the entire 18-year period of 1964 to 1982, the Dow-Jones Industrial Average primarily fluctuated within the 800 to 1000 range, dropping at times to the 650 level. Throughout history, bear markets have always followed bull markets.

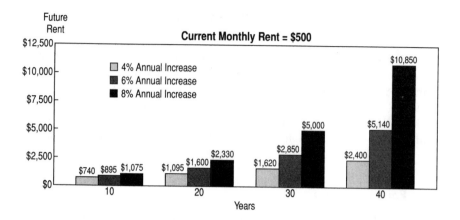

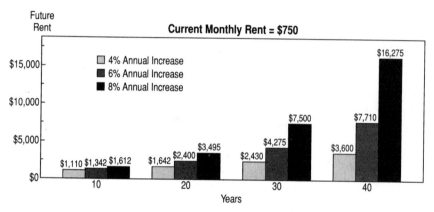

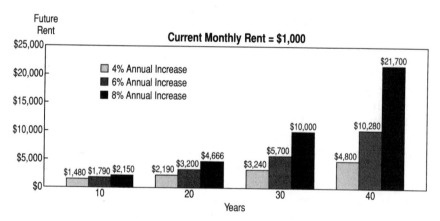

Figure 1.1 Increasing Monthly Rents

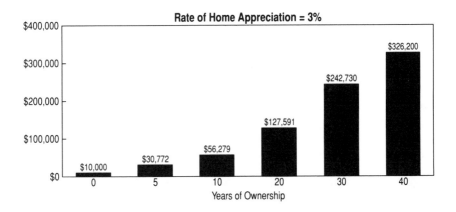

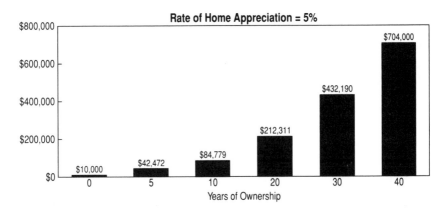

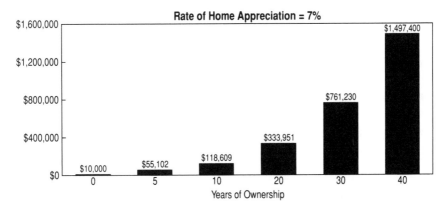

Note: Assumes an original $10,000 equity (down payment) on a $100,000 home financed over 30 years at an interest rate of 7.5 percent. Home equity is created both by paying down the mortgage balance and by price appreciation of the home.

Figure 1.2 Building Wealth through Growing Equity

So, the first rule of successful investing is never deceive yourself into believing price increases (stocks or real estate) of 12 to 20 percent a year will last forever. The good thing is that in real estate you don't need such large price increases to build your fortune. By using leverage (financing) and paying off your mortgage from rent collections, even modest price increases of 3 to 7 percent a year can make you financially independent and secure. Depending on where you live, owning just 5 to 10 rental housing units over the next 15 to 20 years can easily earn you a net worth of more than $1,000,000.

Income Tax Savings

We'll show you in Chapter 13 how the income tax law favors investors who own rental properties. For now, we want to make two major points. First, in contrast to the dividends you receive from stocks, you can shelter some of your rental housing income from state, local, and federal income taxes. Similarly, through what is called a Section 1031 exchange, you can sell one rental property (even at a large profit) and trade up to another property without paying income taxes on those profits (capital gains).

On the other hand, if you sell a winning stock at a profit so you can move your money into another stock (or mutual fund) that now looks more promising, you'll lose a big part of your profits to the IRS (with an IRA, 401(k), or other tax-sheltered retirement plan, you may be able to avoid some of these taxes on trading profits; but numerous rules, regulations, and restrictions apply to these plans). Since you can avoid these types of income taxes in real estate, you get to keep your entire accumulated real estate wealth working for you for as long as you own properties. In addition, through refinancing or installment sales, you can even pull money out of your real estate with little or no payment of income taxes.

Little or No Savings Required

As we demonstrate in Chapter 2, you can get started in real estate with little or no cash savings. Seller financing, government-backed loan programs, mortgage assumptions, and various types of creative financing all permit you to buy rental homes without a big down payment.

Naturally, if you can come up with $10,000, $20,000, $50,000, or more in cash (either by yourself or with a partner), you dramatically enhance your investment possibilities. Plus you face less risk when you have a financial cushion to soften any unexpected setbacks. But a big pile of cash is *not a requirement.* And in the real world, most people who get started in real estate scrimp, borrow, stretch, and cajole themselves into their first property. In real estate, you don't need money to make money.

Unlike buying stock, you can control $100,000 of real estate with less than $10,000. To purchase $100,000 of stocks you'll have to come up with at least $50,000 in cash. Then, if your stocks fall in value, you'll get a margin call. If you can't meet the minimum maintenance requirements of your account rules, your brokerage firm will sell you out and you'll be stuck with the loss. In real estate there's no such thing as margin calls. Even in a down market, your mortgage lender can't require you to put more cash into your property to reduce your loan-to-value ratio.

In other words, not only can you buy rental property with much less cash than would be required to buy an equivalent amount of stock, financing real estate is far easier and much less risky than financing stocks.

Anyone Can Learn to Make Money in Real Estate

Although successful real estate investors need education and knowledge, you can learn all you need to know by reading practical books such as this one and studying your local markets. In fact, the big losses of many real estate developments in the 1980s resulted because high-tech financial analysts spent too much time with their PCs and Lotus spreadsheets and ignored common sense and long-standing principles of sound real estate investment.

Since the excess building of apartments and condominiums in the 1980s has now been absorbed in most markets, vacancy rates have fallen, and rents are increasing. Whereas the stock market may be approaching its peak and "correction," the rental housing market is still positioned on the upward slope of the next real estate cycle.

Apply the lessons we illustrate in the following chapters and you should go a long way toward achieving your financial goals. You won't need an MBA and you won't need experience. You need perseverance, commitment, a willingness to learn, and good knowledge of your local neighborhoods and properties.

Real Estate Is Illiquid

In comparing stocks to real estate, most "experts" say stocks are better because of their liquidity. Whenever you need cash, you can easily and cheaply sell off some of your stocks to raise whatever amount of money you want (limited only by the amount you have in your brokerage account). In contrast, real estate is more difficult and expensive to sell.

Now ask yourself, if your goal is to build wealth and financial independence, is liquidity really an advantage? Or is it a disadvantage? Here's what multimillionaire real estate investor David Schumacher says in his book, *The Buy and Hold Real Estate Strategy:*

> When I was teaching real estate courses at UCLA Extension and Los Angeles City College, I used to invite a stockbroker as a guest speaker to tell the class how fabulous it is to own stocks and bonds because they can be sold in two minutes. Then, after he would leave, I would emphasize to the students how it is even more fabulous to own real estate precisely because you *can't* sell it in two minutes. You can't sell real estate to solve your immediate financial problems because real estate is not easy to sell. You have to find another way to solve your problems. Some financial advisers think that it is a disadvantage.
>
> But I think it is a terrific advantage because it compels you to think things over before you make the decision. Suppose you have a diversified investment portfolio and own both stocks and real estate. Suddenly, a crisis occurs and you need $50,000. The first thing you would sell is the stock. If you didn't have any stock you would figure out another way to solve your dilemma. You might borrow some money on your real estate or you might figure out another way to obtain a loan, but you aren't going to get rid of your real estate because it usually takes a period of time—weeks, months, or even years—to sell.
>
> So you think of other ways to solve the problem. To me, that is a tremendous, built-in advantage of investing in real estate. It forces you to hold on to the property and, rather than receive a small profit, gives it time to appreciate. Maybe your dire financial situation or problem will pass. Once you get over that hurdle, you'll still be left with the property. If you hold it and keep it for the long pull, you'll be much better off. (John Wiley & Sons, 1992, p. 296)

Who is right: the stockbroker or David Schumacher? We think you'll agree that the weight of the evidence goes to David. Very few people of average incomes have built wealth by investing in the stock market. Apart from the uncertainties and speculative nature of stocks, the money is just too easy to get and spend (or to fritter away in ill-fated market-timing schemes). To build wealth, you want to lock your money up. Viewed from that perspective, illiquidity stands tall as an advantage.

The Economy Is Growing

For at least the past 15 years since Ezra Vogel wrote his best selling book, *Japan As No. 1*, the media has fed us a continuing diet of bad news about the American economy. We have been told that the United States is in decline, that we're failing to generate jobs, that we can't compete, that productivity is falling, that incomes are stagnant, that "Generation X" won't be able to live as well as their parents.

Obviously, if the United States is in decline, if the economy is stagnant, and if the outlook is bleak, then maybe you shouldn't invest in real estate (or anything else—simply hoard gold and fill your storage areas with survival rations). But as a matter of fact, the recurring alarmist pronouncements are hogwash. Despite all the drumbeating and hand-wringing, you can put away your worry beads. Although not as strong as it could be (if we had lower taxes and less government), the U.S. economy is (and always has been) on a sustained path of growth and increased living standards.

Just since 1980, the United States has created 25 million new jobs, the gross domestic product (GDP) has increased from $2.7 trillion to nearly $7.0 trillion, and exports have risen from $279 billion to approximately $700 billion. As these figures indicate, the U.S. economy is hardly anemic. In direct contrast to Al Gore's pessimistic lament of several years back, nearly every key economic measure that's supposed to be down is down (inflation, interest rates, unemployment rate, oil prices) and most key measures that are supposed to be up are up (population, incomes, exports, productivity, employment, housing affordability, housing prices, gross domestic product, corporate profits). Although some may believe it smart to sell America short, the economic facts do not support their position.

For a secure and financially prosperous future, now is a great time to invest in rental housing.

2 FINANCING: HOW TO GET THE MONEY YOU NEED

Once you've decided to build wealth through ownership of rental properties, you first must think about financing. If you're like most real estate investors, you'll probably borrow a large part of the money you need. As a result, you'll have to address five major issues: (1) How much should you borrow? (2) What types of financing are available? (3) What underwriting standards apply? (4) What kinds of loan programs make financing easier? and (5) Where can you borrow the money you need?

LEVERAGE: HOW MUCH SHOULD YOU BORROW?

In Chapter 1, we briefly talked about buying rental homes using relatively little of your own money. For most new real estate investors buying with little down is a necessity because they haven't yet saved much money. But even if you've got a pile of cash to invest, you'll still want to decide how much of your own money you should invest in any one property and what percentage of your purchase price you should borrow. In other words, you'll want to decide how much you should *leverage* your purchase.

Through leverage, you can magnify your financial returns and build wealth much faster than if you paid 100 percent cash for your properties. On the other side of the coin, though, lies risk. Highly leveraged purchases tend to expose you to greater potential loss. Let's first look at returns, then we'll discuss risk.

LEVERAGE MAGNIFIES RETURNS

Essentially, through leverage you use a relatively small amount of cash to acquire and control a property. Assume you plan to buy a $100,000 rental home that produces a net operating income of $10,000 a year. If you finance your purchase with $10,000 down and borrow $90,000 (a *loan-to-value ratio* of 90 percent), you have a highly leveraged purchase. You own and control a property; yet only 10 percent of the purchase price has actually come from your pocket. In contrast, if you paid $100,000 cash for that property, you would not have used any leverage (other people's money) at all.

Now, let's see how different degrees of leverage can magnify your returns over paying cash. In the following four examples, we calculated rates of return based on alternative down payments of $100,000 (an all-cash purchase), $50,000, $25,000, and $10,000.

1. $100,000 cash purchase

$$\text{ROI (return on investment)} = \frac{\text{Income}}{\text{Cash investment}}$$

$$= \frac{\$10,000}{\$100,000}$$

$$= 10\%$$

In this first example, you receive the full $10,000 of net operating income (rental income less expenses such as insurance, repairs, property taxes). However, when you finance part of your purchase price, in addition to property operating expenses, you also will have to pay a mortgage payment on the amount you've financed. If we assume you find financing at 8 percent for 30 years, you will have to pay your lender $7.34 a month for each $1,000 you borrow. So, using various degrees of leverage, here's how you can magnify your *rates* of return over paying cash:

2. $50,000 down payment; $50,000 borrowed. Yearly mortgage payment equals $4,404 (50 × $7.34 × 12). Net income after mortgage payments (debt service) equals $5,596 ($10,000 NOI less $4,404).

$$\text{ROI} = \frac{\$5,596}{\$50,000}$$

$$= 11.1\%$$

3. $25,000 down payment; $75,000 borrowed. Yearly mortgage payments equal $6,606 (75 × $7.34 × 12). Net income after mortgage payments (debt service) equals $3,394 ($10,000 NOI less $6,606).

$$\text{ROI} = \frac{\$3,394}{\$25,000}$$

$$= 13.6\%$$

4. $10,000 down payment; $90,000 borrowed. Yearly mortgage payments equal $7,927 (90 × $7.34 × 12). Net income after mortgage payments equal $2,073 ($10,000 NOI less $7,927).

$$\text{ROI} = \frac{\$2,073}{\$10,000}$$

$$= 20.7\%$$

Under the assumptions in these examples, the highly leveraged (90 percent loan-to-value ratio) purchase yields a rate of return double that of a cash purchase. In principle, the more you borrow, the less cash you invest in a property, the more you magnify your returns. Of course, as you may have figured out, the *actual* rate of return you'll earn on your properties will depend on the actual rents, expenses, interest rates, and purchase prices that apply to those properties. You will need to work through the numbers at the time you buy to see how much you can gain (or lose) from leverage. Yet, before we get into the subject of potential losses (risk), take a look at another (and even more important) way leverage can magnify your returns and help you build wealth faster.

In addition to annual income, your rental properties also should pay off in terms of gains from appreciation. If that $100,000 property we've just discussed appreciates at an annual rate of 3 percent, you'll earn another $3,000 a year. If it appreciates at an annual rate of 5 percent, you'll gain another $5,000 a year. And at a 7 percent annual rate of appreciation, your gains will hit $7,000 a year.

So, considering both annual rental income and annual appreciation, here's the total returns from each of the previous examples:

$$\text{Total ROI} = \frac{\text{Income} + \text{Appreciation}}{\text{Cash investment}}$$

1. $100,000 all-cash purchase and (a) 3%, (b) 5%, and (c) 7% rates of appreciation:

a. Total ROI $= \dfrac{\$10,000 + \$3,000}{\$100,000} = 13\%$

b. Total ROI $= \dfrac{\$10,000 + \$5,000}{\$100,000} = 15\%$

c. Total ROI $= \dfrac{\$10,000 + \$7,000}{\$100,000} = 17\%$

2. $50,000 down payment and (a) 3%, (b) 5%, and (c) 7% rates of appreciation:

a. Total ROI $= \dfrac{\$5,596 + \$3,000}{\$50,000} = 17.2\%$

b. Total ROI $= \dfrac{\$5,596 + \$5,000}{\$50,000} = 21.2\%$

c. Total ROI $= \dfrac{\$5,596 + \$7,000}{\$50,000} = 25.2\%$

3. $25,000 down payment and (a) 3%, (b) 5%, and (c) 7% rates of appreciation:

a. Total ROI $= \dfrac{\$3,394 + \$3,000}{\$25,000} = 25.6\%$

b. Total ROI $= \dfrac{\$3,394 + \$5,000}{\$25,000} = 33.6\%$

c. Total ROI $= \dfrac{\$3,394 + \$7,000}{\$25,000} = 41.6\%$

4. $10,000 down payment and (a) 3%, (b) 5%, and (c) 7% rates of appreciation:

a. Total ROI $= \dfrac{\$2,073 + \$3,000}{\$10,000} = 50.1\%$

b. Total ROI $= \dfrac{\$2,073 + \$5,000}{\$10,000} = 70.1\%$

c. Total ROI $= \dfrac{\$2,073 + \$7,000}{\$10,000} = 90.1\%$

When you combine returns from annual net rental income and appreciation, you can see that highly leveraged properties *may* produce phenomenal annual rates of return—even without high rates of inflation. That's why over the years, so many average income investors in rental homes have been able to build net worth that runs into the millions of dollars. When you own rental properties, slow and steady rent increases and appreciation can turn acorns (relatively low down payments) into oak trees (a property worth hundreds of thousands of dollars). As the years pass and you pay down your mortgage balances, your portfolio of just 5 to 10 rental homes can build enough wealth to guarantee you a secure and prosperous future.

You Must Manage Your Risks

During the 1980s, the low-down, nothing-down gurus of "get rich quick" real estate schemes failed to warn their students that highly leveraged real estate magnifies risks as well as returns. Consequently, many real estate "investors" (actually speculators) lost their shirts. Many of these buyers simply assumed that their properties would appreciate at rates of 12 to 20 percent a year. They lost touch with reality.

In fact, many investors barely cared what prices they paid or how they financed their properties because they "knew" they would be able to sell them in a few years for twice the prices they had paid.

One such investor, for example, bought a $300,000 fourplex with a down payment of $30,000. After paying property expenses and his mortgage payments, the investor faced a loss (negative cash flow) of $1,000 a month. But the investor figured that $1,000 a month was peanuts because he believed the property would continue to appreciate at 15 percent a year. Based on this appreciation rate, here's how this investor calculated his total expected annual returns:

$$\text{ROI} = \frac{\text{Income} + \text{Appreciation}}{\text{Cash investment}}$$

$$= \frac{-\$12,000 \ (12 \times -\$1,000) + \$45,000 \ (.15 \times \$300,000)}{\$30,000}$$

$$= \frac{\$33,000}{\$30,000}$$

$$= 110\%$$

As it turned out, this investor, like so many others, was unable to keep feeding the alligator (covering his $1,000 a month negative cash flow); he fell behind in his mortgage payments; as the market slowed, he was unable to sell the property; the lender foreclosed and the investor lost the property, his down payment of $30,000, and the $18,000 of negative monthly outlays he had made prior to his default.

What lessons can you learn from this investor's sad experience? Here are four:

1. Never assume that the price of real estate, stocks, gold, antique automobiles, Old Masters, or any other type of investment will increase 10, 15, or 20 percent a year for extended periods. The larger the rate of appreciation you need to make your investment look attractive the greater your risk.

2. Beware of negative cash flows. If your investment won't pay for itself through the annual income it produces you're not investing, you are speculating. That's okay if that's what you want to do. Just recognize that speculating creates high risk.

3. Don't overextend yourself. High leverage (a high loan-to-value ratio) usually requires large mortgage payments relative to the amount of rents a property is producing. Even if you don't immediately incur negative cash flows, unexpected vacancies, higher than expected expenses, or generous rent concessions to attract good tenants can sometimes push you temporarily into the red.

Over the long term, owning real estate will make you rich. But to get to the long term, you may have to pass through several downturns. Without financial reserves to cushion setbacks, you run the risk that you'll have to fold your cards without being able to play out your hand.

4. Even when the financing looks "good," never substantially overpay for a property. Too many investors are lured into buying overpriced properties with little or no down payment deals. In the preceding example, the investor agreed to pay $300,000 for his fourplex not because $300,000 was a reasonable price based on the rents the property was producing. Rather, he paid $300,000 because he was excited about his 10 percent down financing and the $300,000 price looked cheap compared with the $600,000 price at which he expected to sell the property in four or five years.

By pointing out the potential risks of high leverage financing, we most certainly don't want to discourage you from low down payment financing. But we do want you to anticipate possible setbacks. In addition, you can successfully manage the risks of high leverage financing by following these six investment practices:

1. *Buy bargain-priced properties.* You build a financial cushion into your deals when you pay less than market value (we'll show you how in Chapters 4–7).

2. *Buy properties that you can profitably improve.* The best way to build wealth fast and reduce the risk of leverage is to add value to your properties through creativity, sweat equity, remodeling, and renovation (see Chapter 4).

3. *Buy properties with below-market rents that you can raise to market levels within a relatively short period (6 to 12 months).* As you increase your rental income, you will reduce the fiscal strain of high mortgage payments.

4. *Buy properties with low interest financing such as mortgage assumptions, adjustable rate mortgages, buy downs, seller financing, or other creative financial techniques.* Low interest (or creative) financing can significantly boost your ability to safely handle high loan-to-value ratios (relatively high debt).

5. *Buy properties in up-and-coming neighborhoods that are soon to be revitalized.* Revitalization efforts can easily lift property values by 20 to 50 percent over a 3- to 5-year period.

6. *When all else fails to reduce the risk of high leverage to a comfortable level, increase your down payment to lower your loan-to-value ratio and your monthly mortgage payments.* If you don't have the cash yourself, then bring in a money partner. Don't be penny-wise and pound-foolish. It's better to share your gains with someone else than to risk losses that could take you out of the game.

What Are Your Risk-Return Objectives?

As we have already stated, financing creates great opportunities for you to magnify your returns. Through smart use of leverage, you can quickly build your real estate wealth. But the more you borrow (all other things equal), the larger your risk. When you're highly leveraged, small declines in rents can push you into negative cash flows. Relative small declines in a property's value can sometimes mean you owe more than a property is worth.

Therefore, it's up to you to work through the numbers for the deals that come your way. Only you can decide what profits are worth pursuing and what risks are worth taking. But remember, not owning real estate also creates risk. Without investment real estate, most Americans may have to accept a significant decline in their standard of living as they get older and move into their retirement years.

Are you willing to bet your future financial well-being on a company pension plan or Social Security? Even if you're accumulating significant savings in stocks or a mutual fund, be cautious. Who knows when the next bear market will hit and how long it will last? Who knows whether, 5 or 10 years from now, we'll again see inflation rates of 10, 12, 15 percent or greater?

For these reasons, we believe everyone should include at least several rental properties in their investment portfolio. Regardless of what happens to company pensions, Social Security, stock prices, or inflation, your rental income will give you financial security and prosperity.

WHAT TYPES OF FINANCING ARE AVAILABLE?

In addition to deciding how much leverage to use when you finance real estate, you also must decide what type(s) of financing might work best for your purchase. There's no simple and easy way to classify all the types of real estate financing that you might use. The categories often overlap and some purchases involve several different types of financing.

As a start, though, we will introduce you to the basic types and terminology. Then in later chapters we will further illustrate various financing arrangements through a variety of examples.

Mortgages and Deeds of Trusts

Mortgages and *Deeds of Trusts* are the basic types of real estate financing that create liens against real property. These liens mean that, should the borrower default on the loan (fail to make payments when due), the lender has the legal right to sell the property to satisfy the loan obligation in a foreclosure sale.

Two parties are involved in a mortgage: the *Mortgagor,* or the borrower and property owner, and the *Mortgagee,* or the lender. There are also two parts to a mortgage: the *Mortgage Note,* which is evidence of the debt, and the *Mortgage Contract,* which is the security for the debt. The note promises to repay the loan, while the contract promises to convey title of the property to the mortgagee in case of default.

Trust Deeds are similar to mortgages except that an additional third party is involved and the foreclosure procedures are more simplified. Under a trust deed, the borrower, or the owner, is called the *Trustor.*

The lender is called the *Beneficiary.* The intermediate third party, whose responsibility is to hold title to the property for the security of the lender, is referred to as the *Trustee.*

Under a trust deed, if the trustor (borrower) defaults on the loan obligation, the mortgaged property will be sold at public auction by the trustee through provisions in the "power of sale" clause contained in the trust deed, without court procedure.

Foreclosure is initiated by a notice of default, which is recorded by the trustee with a copy sent to the trustor. If after a specified "grace" period, the trustor does nothing to remedy the situation, a notice of sale is posted on the property, and advertisements of the pending sale are carried in local newspapers. If during this period the trustor fails to pay the beneficiary sufficient funds to halt the foreclosure, the sale will be conducted by the trustee. Proceeds from the foreclosure sale are first disbursed to the beneficiary, then to any other lien holders according to their priority.

Foreclosure under a mortgage instrument, as opposed to a trust deed, is notably longer (periods in excess of a year are common). For this reason, more than half the states in the United States prefer the trust deed over a mortgage instrument.

Second trust deeds and mortgages are similar to firsts, except that they are second in priority to a first loan with respect to security and their ability to claim any proceeds through a foreclosure sale.

Assumed and Subject-To Mortgages

There are important differences in the meaning of these terms. An *Assumed Mortgage* occurs when the borrower assumes the legal obligation to make the loan payments and the lender releases the previous borrower from the liability. Bona fide assumptions can only take place in the absence of a due-on-sale clause or with the mortgagee's written permission.

Buying a property *Subject-To* an existing mortgage occurs when the buyer takes over the loan obligation without the existing borrower's being released from the liability, and without formal permission of the lender. Caution should be taken when buying property subject-to the existing mortgage—especially when a due-on-sale clause is involved—because the lender may be able to call the loan due even if you're making your payments on time.

In other words, be cautious of *Due-on-Sale* and *Alienation* clauses written into loan documents. Without going into great detail, they both essentially mean the same thing, that is, if the title transfers to another party, the lender can call the total amount owed due and payable within 30 days. Or the lender has the right to ask for assumption fees and an increased rate of interest. FHA and VA loans originated prior to the late 1980s do not have due-on-sale clauses, which makes them very attractive especially if the interest rate is below the market interest rate; they are fully assumable without credit qualification. These types of FHA and VA mortgages are referred to as *non-qual assumables*.

Interest-Only Loans

This type of financing requires the payment of interest only during the term of the loan. At the end of the term, the entire sum of principal is due and payable in one final balloon payment. For example, the annual payment schedule for an interest-only loan for $40,000 at 10 percent interest for a term of five years is as follows:

1st year $40,000 $\times$ .10 = $ 4,000 interest

2nd year $40,000 $\times$ .10 = $ 4,000 interest

3rd year $40,000 $\times$ .10 = $ 4,000 interest

4th year $40,000 $\times$ .10 = $ 4,000 interest

5th year $40,000 $\times$ .10 = $ 4,000 interest

5th year $40,000 balloon payment due

Prior to the Great Depression of the 1930s, the interest-only, balloon loan was the most common payment method for real estate financing. Many borrowers took out these loans for short terms expecting to renew them term after term, thus deferring payment of the principal almost indefinitely.

But the economy failed during the Depression, and most borrowers were unable to "roll over" or perpetuate their interest-only loans. The results were devastating. Lenders began calling loans, requiring the borrowers to pay the entire principal amount owing, which they did not have. Thus, lenders began foreclosing on these loans throughout the country.

The Great Depression made almost everyone, especially the financial industry, aware of the inherent dangers in this type of financing. Although interest-only balloon mortgages still have some uses in special situations, a safer type of financing is the *amortized loan.*

Fully Amortized Loans

An alternative to the interest-only loan was the fully amortized loan, featuring equal payments over its term, which would consist of both principal and interest. In contrast to the interest-only loan, the fully amortized loan commonly has a term of 10 to 30 years or more and is completely paid off at the end of its term.

Initial payments on the amortized loan do consist mostly of interest, but as the loan matures, more of each payment is applied toward principal since interest on an amortized loan is calculated on the loan's outstanding principal balance. Therefore, after each payment is made, the principal balance owing is reduced, resulting in a smaller interest portion and a larger principal portion of the overall payment.

Partially Amortized Loans

The partially amortized loan is similar to the fully amortized loan, except that a partial balloon will fall due at the end of the term. The purpose of this type of loan is to allow the borrower a smaller payment on the loan and to partially pay off the principal owing, thus reducing his regular monthly payment. This type of loan is popular when the seller finances his down payment in the property with a purchase money second mortgage.

Adjustable Rate Loans

Adjustable rate mortgages (ARMs) originated in the late 1970s, for the purpose of protecting long-term mortgage lenders from radical changes in market interest rates. Traditionally, conventional lenders were lending out their funds at reasonable interest rates, and rightly so as their cost of acquiring that money seldom fluctuated much up or down. But along came the hyper-inflationary times of the late 1970s and the early 1980s, and the cost of money to lenders went up dramatically. At the same time these lenders had billions of dollars loaned out at interest rates substantially below what it cost them to acquire these funds. Thus, the arrival of the adjustable rate mortgage.

ARMs vary somewhat in form, but basically they are similar in function. The initial rate of interest that the loan originated at is allowed to fluctuate over the term of the loan. Usually, if the interest rate originates at 9 percent, it is allowed to increase up to 6 points to a limit of 15 percent, with a maximum increase of 2 percent during any 12-month period. Typically, the interest rate charged is tied to some index. In other words, if the index rate goes up, your ARM interest rate goes up, but not to exceed 2 points in one year, and not to exceed 6 points over the term of the loan.

Usually a borrower can originate an ARM at a lower interest rate than that of a conventional loan, mainly due to a lesser amount of inflation risk realized by the lender. However, the borrower must realize that the interest rate of the ARM has the potential to increase 6 points over the term of the loan. For instance, on a loan of $80,000 at 8 percent for 30 years the principal and interest payment would be $587.02. For the same loan and term at 14 percent (the 6 percent maximum increase allowed), the principal and interest payment would be $947.90, or a monthly difference of $360.88. Over the entire term of 30 years, that's the difference of over $129,000. As you can see, ARMs may represent a significant risk to the borrower.

Convertible and two-step ARMs are more recent innovations in real estate financing. A convertible ARM can be changed into a fixed-rate loan, with the lender setting certain limits at which the conversion can be made. Offerings of convertible ARMs consist of convertibility to a fixed rate during the first five years of the term of the loan at a cost of say $500 to $750. Essentially, a two-step ARM starts you out at a lower rate of interest and then automatically switches you into a fixed-rate mortgage after 3, 5, or 7 years at the then prevailing market level fixed interest rate plus 0.5 to 1.0 percent.

Graduated Loans

Also known as the Graduated Payment Mortgage (GPM), this plan offers smaller initial loan payments which become larger as the term goes on. This type of loan anticipates the borrower's future ability to repay the loan in expectation of later income growth to meet the GPMs schedule of increasing payments.

Land Contract (Contract of Sale)

A land contract, sometimes referred to as a contract for deed, contract of sale, or agreement of sale, is a contract between buyer and seller without the involvement of a financial institution. Under a land contract, a buyer agrees to purchase a property and pay principal and interest to the seller. Title to the property remains with the seller until conditions of the contract are fulfilled. The buyer retains possession of the property. However, if the buyer should default on the agreement (not pay as agreed), the property would revert to the seller.

Land contracts may be useful in "wrapping" existing low interest rate financing (see later section on wraparounds). Caution must be taken when structuring buyer and seller conditions in a land contract because the law covering this topic is vague, and the status of land contract sales varies from state to state. Therefore, it is advisable to consult with a trusted and competent attorney before involving yourself with this form of financing.

Purchase-Money Seconds

This is a type of financing in which the seller of the property takes back a loan in the property, instead of taking cash. For example, you buy a house for $80,000 with a $5,000 down payment, and you assume an existing $50,000 loan. The $25,000 balance remaining is carried back by the seller in the form of a purchase-money second mortgage payable under terms you negotiate with the seller. In this particular example, $30,000 represents the seller's equity in the property. You pay $5,000 down, and instead of $25,000 cash, the seller takes back a second mortgage of $25,000.

Terms on the $25,000 purchase-money second are negotiable and can take shape according to the needs of both the buyer and seller. Probably most advantageous for the buyer would be an interest-only note for a term of 10 years. The rate of interest is negotiable. The lower the rate of interest you can negotiate for yourself, the better off you will be financially. We have seen second mortgages retained by sellers as low as 0 percent and as high as 20 percent.

If you do negotiate for an interest-only second, keep in mind that under an interest-only mortgage nothing will be applied toward the principal owing and the entire principal will be due at the end of the term. Thus, because of inflation you will have the advantage of paying back the entire principal balance of the note at an extended future date with cheaper deflated dollars.

Although interest-only is the lowest payment form of note, a fully amortized note payable in equal monthly installments would pay off the entire amount owing by the end of the loan's term. This would inhibit your monthly cash flow because of the higher monthly payment; however the loan would be completely paid off at term's end.

There is a midrange area of negotiation between an interest-only note and a fully amortized note. You could negotiate for a partly amortized note wherein a portion of the principal amount would be paid off monthly; thus you would owe substantially less at the end of the term. Also, you could have a $25,000 balance owing amortized over 20 years and payable in 10 years. This method would keep monthly payments relatively low and would help to pay off a large portion of principal during the 10 years, with only a small balance owing.

Purchase-money seconds are an integral part of profitable real estate investing primarily because you can create inexpensive seller financing which, in most cases, can be assumed by the next buyer. You can actually earn more money by keeping your interest rates low and then reselling your properties at higher rates of interest.

Some years back, I (McLean) found a great property that, at first glance, appeared impossible to purchase with a small down payment, nor was it likely for the seller to carry back any financing. This beautiful property had an existing 8 percent first loan of $40,000, and the lender wanted $25,000 down. The list price was $119,000, and the listing agent doubted that the seller would be willing to carry back a second loan. Not to be denied, I made an offer of $92,000; I would pay $10,000 down and assume the existing first loan of $40,000, and the seller was to carry back a second loan at 9 percent for the balance owing of $42,000. Neither my agent nor the seller's agent believed this offer had a one-in-a-hundred chance of being accepted.

But to everyone's surprise the seller made a counteroffer at a price of $96,000 while accepting all the financing terms of my original offer. Therefore, the only change from my original offer was the price, from $92,000 to $96,000, which increased the amount of the second loan carried back from $42,000 to $46,000. I gladly accepted the counteroffer.

In the preceding example, I created $46,000 in new low-interest financing on a property that at first glance you'd have thought would never sell under such advantageous terms. Six months after I purchased this lovely moneymaker, I sold it for $115,000 on a long-term land contract, and I would net $350 per month on it for the next 20 years. The main reason for the property's profitability was the (then) low interest rates that were maintained after the sale. I collected 11.5 percent on the total balance owing.

As this experience suggests, you never really know whether a seller will carry back a note unless you at least attempt to create low-interest secondary financing by making a credible offer.

Cash-Out Seconds

A "cash-out" second loan is different from a purchase-money second loan because it is created from equity in property already owned. For instance, you own a property with $50,000 equity in it. You could take out a second mortgage against that equity to make home improvements, pay for a college education, or buy additional income property. Usually, institutional lenders fund this type of loan in amounts up to 80 to 90 percent of the equity in the property. However, for homeowners, many lenders now are giving 100 percent homeowner equity loans.

Cash-out seconds are often an expensive method of financing real estate and substantially reduce your equity in the property. We would recommend arranging a second loan of this type primarily when you can use the proceeds to purchase additional income property, and only when that property is an excellent bargain, wherein the investment will at least cover the cost of the new loan.

Note about Junior Mortgages.   While we are discussing second mortgages, it is important to clear up certain myths or misunderstandings about the safety of these loans. In the 1930s, the era of the Great Depression, many junior lien holders (second, third, etc., mortgage holders) were wiped out in a foreclosure when the borrower did not make loan payments. Back in those days when a first mortgage lender began foreclosure proceedings, the secondary and/or junior lien holders had to pay off the entire first mortgage balance to protect their second mortgage interest and to stop the foreclosure proceedings, otherwise the second mortgage interest would be wiped out in the foreclosure sale.

This is not the case today. Now if the borrower defaults on either a first or second mortgage (or third, fourth, etc.), only the missed payments and late fees, if any, are required to be paid by the secondary lender to protect his mortgage interest. Therefore, in the event of a pending foreclosure by a prior mortgage holder, no longer is the entire balance due in one sum to protect a secondary mortgage.

Equity Sharing

Another method available to help finance your purchase is equity sharing, also known as shared equity, equity participation, equity partnership, and shared appreciation. This concept originated out of the need to pair cash-short buyers with cash-rich investors. These two share ownership of the property, and both will gain later when the property is sold for a profit.

Here's how it works. Let's say you are short of cash to make a down payment on a home and your parents want to help. Your parents would agree to make the down payment in exchange for a one-half interest in the house. You agree to occupy the house, maintain it, and pay fair market rent to your parents for their interest in the property. You and your parents split the costs of principal and interest, property taxes, and insurance. Your half-owner parents, because they are rental property owners, can claim income-tax deductions of mortgage interest, property taxes, and depreciation. (If, on the other hand, the parents had made the down payment simply as a gift, they would receive no tax or appreciation benefits.) Your tax deductions will be the same as for all homeowners, that of mortgage interest and property taxes.

Taking title to a property under equity sharing is the same as purchasing a home on your own. Both parties go on the title according to state law, and both parties sign the mortgage note and take responsibility for its payment.

Equity-sharing transactions require one additional step to home ownership. A contract (written agreement) between co-owners is necessary to spell out exactly the important points of the agreement, such as ownership percentages, rent to be charged, buyout options, specifics on resale, and responsibility for repairs and maintenance. In addition, the contract should specify procedures in the event of death, default, disability, bankruptcy of a co-owner, or acts of God, such as floods, earthquakes, and tornadoes.

Equity sharing then can be beneficial to both the investor and the owner/occupant. The owner/occupant can eventually buy out the investor, sell the house, and use the proceeds for a down payment on another house. The investor has tax advantages from his ownership interest of a rental property and can share in the appreciation (for an excellent discussion of the shared equity concept, see David Sirken, *The Home Equity Sharing Manual*, 1995, New York: John Wiley & Sons).

Chattel Mortgage

Used much less frequently now than in years gone by, a real estate investor might use a chattel mortgage to finance, say, a new set of stoves, refrigerators, and window air conditioners for all the units in her fourplex. The term chattel simply refers to personal property as opposed to real estate.

Knowledge of chattel mortgages can be useful to you at the time you buy rental homes and apartment buildings. If the sale includes personal property such as ranges, refrigerators, or furniture, you will want to make sure any chattel mortgages that serve as liens against this personal property are disclosed to you. When such liens are present, the seller should either pay them off or give you a credit at closing for any unpaid balances (in some cases, these credits may offset part of the cash you need for your down payment).

Personal Loans

Many real estate investors raise part (or all) of the cash they put into a property as a down payment through personal loans that are "secured" only by an investor's creditworthiness. In days before credit card cash advances (which are the most popular type of personal loan), personal loans were called signature loans.

As you build your wealth through growing real estate equity, you'll find that many lenders will gladly grant you signature loans for $10,000, $25,000, or even $100,000, if your credit record and net worth can support repayment. You can then use the money from these signature (personal loans) to help you buy even more real estate.

Although many mortgage lenders have rules against using personal loans for down payments, many beginning and experienced investors routinely find ways over or around those rules. In addition, sellers who finance their own property sales will seldom care very much about where you're getting your down payment money. So, if you're short on cash, don't let that stop you from buying rental properties. Consider using some type of cash advance or signature loan to raise money for your down payment. But, if you do rely on this type of financing don't forget to weigh the risk factors we discussed earlier in the chapter.

Wraparound Mortgage

The wraparound loan is used when the seller of real property wants to maintain existing low-interest financing, so he "wraps" the existing loans with a new wraparound loan at a higher interest rate. The seller continues making payments on the existing low-interest loans while the buyer makes payments to the seller on the new wraparound loan. The seller would then earn a profit on the spread in interest rates. The wraparound works best during periods when interest rates shoot up. Figure 2.1 illustrates how an example might work.

In this Figure 2.1, the seller creates and carries a new loan of $110,000 at 11.5 percent. Payments on existing first and second loans total $850 per month. Payments on the new wraparound loan are $1,089 per month, therefore the seller earns a $249 per month profit. Usually, the buyer gains in this transaction because the interest rate charged by the seller still falls below the then prevailing market interest rate. (Note, though, that if you "wrap" a nonassumable mortgage, the seller's underlying mortgage lender may choose to exercise its "due-on-sale" clause. If that happened, you and the sellers would have to work out some other type of financing arrangement.

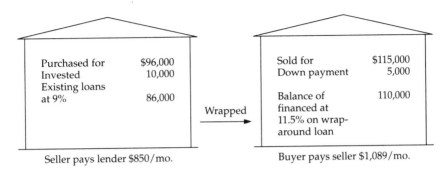

Purchased for	$96,000
Invested	10,000
Existing loans at 9%	86,000

Seller pays lender $850/mo.

Wrapped →

Sold for	$115,000
Down payment	5,000
Balance of financed at 11.5% on wrap-around loan	110,000

Buyer pays seller $1,089/mo.

Figure 2.1   Wraparound Loan Example

Summing Up Types of Financing

As you can now see from the preceding discussion, you can draw on many different types of financing when purchasing rental homes and apartments. In addition, as investors become more sophisticated, they frequently mix and match techniques.

For example, to purchase a fourplex, an investor might (1) assume the seller's adjustable rate mortgage; (2) get the seller to carry back an interest only second mortgage for part of the difference between the property's sales price and the outstanding balance on the existing ARM; (3) borrow part of the down payment from his father; and (4) come up with the remaining money in cash:

Mix and Match Example

Purchase Price	$200,000	
ARM Balance		$137,000
Seller Second		40,000
Personal Loan		15,000
Cash from Investor		8,000
Total Proceeds		$200,000

We are not encouraging you to get so creative in your financing that you run a serious risk of default. But we do want you to realize that those investors who creatively pursue their financing solutions are often able to make deals work that at first seem "impossible." Don't pass up a good buy without first exploring all your financing possibilities.

WHAT GENERAL UNDERWRITING STANDARDS DO LENDERS APPLY?

Before you can use any type of new financing from an institutional mortgage lender (bank, S&L, credit union, mortgage banker, etc.), you'll have to complete a mortgage loan application. To evaluate this application, most lenders will consider a variety of mortgage underwriting guidelines. The more you can learn about these guidelines, the greater the chance that you'll be able to locate a lender who will approve the loan you want. Here are the eight standards that lenders typically apply:

1. Owner occupancy.
2. Collateral (property characteristics).
3. Loan-to-value ratio.
4. Amount and source of down payment and reserves.
5. Capacity (monthly income).
6. Credit history.
7. Personal characteristics.
8. Compensating factors.

Owner Occupancy

In one sense, owner occupancy is the most important underwriting standard of all. That's because most (but not all) easier qualifying, low down payment finance plans apply only to owner-occupied properties. In addition, many lenders finance owner-occupied properties with a slightly lower interest rate than those properties occupied exclusively by tenants.

What this means is that if you plan to buy, say, a two-, three-, or four-unit investment property, to obtain financing on the most favorable terms, you should plan to live in one of the units. If after 6 to 12 months or so, you decide living with your tenants is not for you, then you can move out and put a tenant into the unit you've vacated.

Similarly, if you plan to invest in a single-family house, condominium, co-op, or townhouse, to get the best financing, you might want to at first rent out your present home and temporarily move into the investment property. It's always easier to finance the property in which you intend to live—but keep in mind you don't have to live there forever.

Collateral (Property Characteristics)

Every financial institution sets standards for the properties that they will accept as collateral for their mortgage loans. Some lenders won't finance properties larger than four units. Some won't finance properties in poor condition or those located in run-down neighborhoods. Many lenders also want to make sure that a property is serviced by all appropriate utilities (e.g., some lenders avoid properties that lack sewer lines). Paved streets, conformance with zoning and building regulations, and proximity to schools, public transportation, shopping, and job centers may also be considered.

Because of these property underwriting standards, before you look at properties and write up an offer to buy, verify that the property meets the criteria of the lender and loan program that you intend to use. Otherwise, you will not only waste time, but you may waste money in loan application, appraisal, and other miscellaneous fees. (Often these fees are nonrefundable.)

Loan-to-Value Ratios (L-T-V)

Earlier when we discussed leverage, we introduced the concept of loan-to-value ratios. In addition to serving as a measure of leverage, though, mortgage lenders specify loan-to-value ratios as an underwriting standard.

Since lenders lost so much money in real estate loans in the late 1980s and early 1990s, they now shy away from investment property (non-owner-occupied) loans with high (above 80 percent) loan-to-value ratios, and many lenders insist on 70 percent maximums. For example, if you wanted to buy a $200,000 fourplex, many lenders would limit their first mortgage amount to no more than $140,000 to $160,000.

However, that 70 percent loan-to-value ratio doesn't necessarily mean that you must put 30 percent down. Many lenders will okay a seller carryback of another 10 to 20 percent of the purchase price. So, even with a 70 percent L-T-V, you may be able to buy with just 10 to 20 percent cash down (and possibly less).

Amount and Source of Down Payment and Reserves

Consider in the preceding example that the lender sets a 70 percent L-T-V for its first mortgage. But you've found a cooperative seller who will carry back a second mortgage for the entire remainder of the purchase price. Will the financial institution approve your loan application? Maybe, maybe not.

Regardless of L-T-V, many lenders like to see their borrowers put at least some of their own cash into their properties at the time they buy them. Moreover, they'll probably ask you where you're getting the cash. The best source is your savings account or stock portfolio. In contrast, most lenders would not want to hear that you're taking a $10,000 cash advance against your Visa Gold Card.

Similarly, most lenders will want to know how much cash (or other liquid assets) you will have on hand after you close your loan. Ideally, they would like you to have at least enough cash in reserve to cover two or three months of mortgage payments.

Capacity (Monthly Income)

As another underwriting guideline, mortgage lenders will evaluate your monthly income from employment and other sources as well as the expected income (less expenses) from the property you're financing. For owner-occupied properties, a lender may place the most emphasis on "qualifying ratios." A qualifying ratio is simply the percentage of your income that the lender sets as the amount you can "safely" allocate to making your mortgage payments (principal, interest, property taxes, and insurance). For example, if a lender sets a 28 percent housing cost qualifying ratio and you gross $4,000 a month, the lender may limit you to a mortgage payment (PITI) of $1,120 a month.

In terms of property rental income and expenses, lenders may apply a debt coverage ratio (DCR). A debt coverage ratio shows the lender that the property can be expected to produce enough income to cover expenses and debt service (principal and interest). here's a simple example for a fourplex whose units rent for $750 a month:

Gross annual income (4 × $750 × 12)	$36,000
less	
Vacancy	2,160
Operating expenses and upkeep	7,200
Property taxes and insurance	2,360
leaves	
Net operating income (NOI)	$24,280

If a lender wants to see a 25 percent safety margin of income over debt service, you would calculate your maximum allowable mortgage payment by dividing the property's annual NOI by a debt coverage ratio of 1.25:

$$\frac{NOI}{DCR} = \text{Annual mortgage payment}$$

$$\frac{\$24,280}{1.25} = \$19,424$$

To check, we reverse the calculations:

$$\frac{NOI}{\text{Debt service}} = \text{Debt coverage ratio}$$

$$\frac{\$24,280}{\$19,424} = 1.25$$

From these calculations, you can see that with a 1.25 debt coverage ratio, the property will produce enough income to support a monthly mortgage payment of $1,619 ($19,424 annual mortgage payment/12). To figure how much loan a mortgage payment of $1,619 a month will pay off (amortize) over a 30-year term, refer to Table 2.1.

At mortgage interest rates of say 7.5, 9, or 10.5 percent, the lender would consider loaning you up to $231,617, $201,118, or $176,940, respectively. Here are the numbers:

7.5% Mortgage Interest Rate

$$\frac{\$1,619}{\$6.99} = \$231,617 \text{ loan amount}$$

9% Mortgage Interest Rate

$$\frac{\$1,619}{\$8.05} = \$201,118 \text{ loan amount}$$

10.5% Mortgage Interest Rate

$$\frac{\$1,619}{\$9.15} = \$176,940 \text{ loan amount}$$

As these figures show, given a monthly mortgage payment amount, lower interest rates dramatically boost your borrowing power. But for many lenders, it's the debt coverage ratio that will at least partially determine the amount of the qualifying mortgage payment that will figure into the basic calculation of your "maximum" mortgage loan for any given property.

Table 2.1   Monthly Payment Required per $1,000 of Original
Mortgage Balance*

Interest (%)	Monthly Payment	Interest (%)	Monthly Payment
2.5	$3.95	7.5	$ 6.99
3.0	4.21	8.0	7.34
3.5	4.49	8.5	7.69
4.0	4.77	9.0	8.05
4.5	5.07	9.5	8.41
5.0	5.37	10.0	8.77
5.5	5.67	10.5	9.15
6.0	5.99	11.0	9.52
6.5	6.32	11.5	9.90
7.0	6.65	12.0	10.29

* Term = 30 years.

Credit History

Do you need good credit to buy rental homes and apartments? No. But
good credit certainly expands your possibilities. Without good credit,
you'll primarily be limited to buying properties with seller financing
or nonqualifying assumable mortgages. (These techniques are described later in this chapter.) With an excellent credit history, though,
lenders will roll out the red carpet for you. You're a very desirable customer. So, you should do all that you can to strengthen your credit
record and build up your reputation for meeting all of your credit obligations on or before their due dates.

We do want to point out, however, that "good credit" today, doesn't
mean what it used to mean. Some mortgage lenders in today's highly
competitive mortgage market will accept borrowers who have experienced foreclosure, repossession, and bankruptcy. The general rule,
though, is that to qualify with these lenders: (1) you must have clean
(preferably spotless) credit for the past 18 to 24 months; (2) you must be
able to attribute you adverse credit to divorce, unemployment, accident,
illness, or other calamity; and (3) you must show that you're now firmly
in control of your present and future financial well-being.

It's not true that just because you've faced serious credit problems
in the past that you must wait 5, 7, or 10, years before you can qualify
for a new mortgage. And this statement is especially true if you're
planning to live in the property you buy. Remember, lenders nearly always give their easiest and best terms to owner occupants.

Personal Characteristics

Although lenders are not permitted to consider your age, race, religion, sex, marital status, or disability when they evaluate your loan application, they can and do look to other personal characteristics such as:

- Education level.
- Career advancement potential.
- Job stability.
- Stability in the community.
- Experience in property ownership.
- Saving, spending, and borrowing habits.
- Dependability.
- Dress and mannerisms.

We don't mean to say that a mortgage lender will turn you down for a loan because you've dropped out of high school, dyed your hair purple, wear a silver nose ring, change jobs every 6 months, or don't have a telephone in your own name. On the other hand, even though officers and loan underwriters may use computers to help them score their mortgage applications, subtle (and not so subtle) influences still count.

Owning and managing income property is serious business. And lenders want to make sure that they can trust you to take these responsibilities seriously. So do everything you can to convince the lender that you are a solid and dependable worker, citizen, and borrower. As the legendary banker J. P. Morgan once told a U. S. Congressional Committee, "Money cannot buy credit. Because a man I do not trust could not get credit from me on all the bonds of Christendom." Yes, J. P. Morgan affirms, character counts.

Compensating Factors

As you evaluate yourself and your property in terms of the preceding underwriting guidelines, remember, these are *guidelines*. The great majority of lenders do not mechanically accept or reject their mortgage loan applications. Instead, they weigh and consider.

This means that by emphasizing your positive and playing down or explaining away negatives you can subjectively influence the lender to approve your loan. If your debt coverage ratio is low, show the lender how you plan to improve the property and increase rents. If you've got blemished credit, offset it with a higher down payment.

If you've frequently changed jobs, point out the raises and promotions you've received. If you lack experience in property ownership or property management, tell the lenders how you've educated yourself by reading real estate books and how you've developed a sensible management plan (see Chapter 9).

Use employer letters, landlord references, prepared budgets, or any other documentation or evidence that you can come up with to justify your loan request. Anything to persuade the lender that you are willing and able to pay back the money you borrow as agreed may help. In close (and not-so-close) calls, compensating factors can make the deciding difference in your favor.

WHAT TYPES OF LOANS MAKE FINANCING EASIER?

If you've got plenty of monthly income, cash, and credit you probably can finance your rental homes through newly originated *conventional* mortgages issued by banks, S&Ls, credit unions, mortgage bankers, or other financial institutions. A conventional mortgage usually refers to real estate financing that is made without any special government program. Conventional loans generally apply the toughest underwriting standards to borrowers.

On the other hand, if you can't (or don't want to) try to qualify for a conventional loan, you've got a number of other easier qualifying possibilities to consider. These include:

1. FHA 203(b) loans.
2. VA loans.
3. PMI loans.
4. FHA 203(k) loans.
5. Assumable mortgages.
6. Seller financing.

Although the first three loan programs in the list are limited to owner-occupied rental properties, the last three may be used by owner occupants or strictly investor owned, tenant-occupied houses and apartments.

FHA 203(b)

For investors without much cash, the Federal Housing Administration's (FHA) 203(b) mortgage has proved very popular. Besides single-family houses, condominiums, manufactured (mobile) homes, and townhouses, you can use the FHA 203(b) program to finance owner-occupied two- to four-unit apartment buildings. The only major drawback to this type of finance plan is that the maximum loan limits may not go as high as you might like.

Maximum Loan Limits*

	Lower Cost Cities	Higher Cost Cities
1 unit	$ 77,197	$152,362
2 units	114,000	194,100
3 units	138,000	234,600
4 units	160,500	291,600

To determine exactly how much you might be able to borrow under this program in your city, talk with a realtor or mortgage lender (a Direct Endorsement lender) who is deeply experienced in the ins and outs of FHA financing. In terms of required down payment, FHA uses the following formula:

3% × the first $25,000 of your purchase price: plus,

5% × the next $100,000 of your purchase price; plus,

10% × any amount over $125,000

For example, a property priced at $135,000 would require a down payment of $6,750. As several added benefits for cash-short buyers, FHA permits borrowers to finance most of their closing costs right into their mortgage loan, and if you sweet-talk your parents or other close relative into "gifting" you the money for a down payment, FHA won't require you to put any of your own cash into the purchase.

When financing with an FHA loan, you may select from a variety of fixed-rate, adjustable-rate, and graduated payment plans. FHA also tells its authorized mortgage lenders to use liberal (relatively easy) underwriting guidelines. For owners who are willing to live in their

---

*The limits are increased periodically by Congress.

rental properties (as least for some minimum period), FHA home finance plans are definitely worth looking into.

Department of Veterans Affairs (VA)

Unless you're buying a VA foreclosure (see Chapter 7), you must have worn our country's uniform either on active duty or while serving in the reserves in order to apply for newly originated VA home financing. But if you do meet these service requirements, you should complete VA Form 26-1880. This form is available from most mortgage lenders who make VA loans and is a request for a Certificate of Eligibility. Once your Certificate of Eligibility is issued and you locate a property you want to buy, you can begin the VA loan application process.

Like FHA, investors may use a VA mortgage to finance any type of owner-occupied single-family home or two- to four-unit rental apartment building. Also, like FHA, VA lenders use relatively easy qualifying standards. As an added advantage, however, for properties priced up to $184,000, borrowers need not make a down payment.

Should you want to buy a property priced higher than $184,000, many lenders permit a down payment of 25 percent of the price in excess of $184,000. For example, if you find a great fourplex priced at $250,000, you should be able to buy that property with a VA loan with just $16,500 ($66,000 × 25%) down, or in this case, 6.6 percent of your purchase price. In addition to fixed-rate mortgages, ARMs and GPMs have been available as VA loans in recent years. For eligible veterans, the VA loan is one of the best ways to get started in real estate investing. (For current loan limit regulations, check with a VA lender.)

Private Mortgage Insurance (PMI)

Another source of low down payment financing for one- to four-unit, owner-occupied properties are loans backed by private mortgage insurance. For single-family homes and condominiums, 3 percent down (97 percent L-T-V) loans are possible. For two- to four-unit properties, you can probably find loans that require just 5 percent to 10 percent down (95 percent to 90 percent L-T-Vs). Loan limits range primarily between $200,000 and $400,000, but can sometimes go as high as $500,000 to $600,000.

The loan limits, down payments, and underwriting standards that apply to PMI loans are difficult to state precisely because they're based on private contractual agreements between specific mortgage lenders and private mortgage insurance companies. In addition, even these contractual agreements allow for some lender flexibility and gray areas. Plus, for some borrowers, lenders will negotiate PMI loan terms on a case-by-case basis with a private mortgage insurer.

The advantages of PMI over FHA are that PMI loans may offer higher loan limits and lower mortgage insurance premiums. The disadvantages are that PMI loans typically apply stricter qualifying standards, and to locate low-down, high limit loans for three- and four-unit properties, you'll have fewer potential lenders to choose from. The reason is that the main players in the secondary mortgage market (Fannie Mae and Freddie Mac) won't buy three- or four-unit loans with L-T-Vs above 80 percent—even with PMI. Nevertheless, these high-dollar, low-down loans can be found if you're willing to look for them.

FHA 203(k)

In contrast to the three loan programs just discussed [FHA 203(b), VA, and PMI], the FHA 203(k) finance plan is directed at either *investors* or owner occupants. For owner occupants, the plan is similar to FHA 203(b) in terms of easier qualifying standard, loan limits, high loan-to-value ratios (low down payments), and types of properties (1–4 units). However, the major difference is that FHA 203(k) is designed to help you acquire and renovate "fix-up" properties with just one loan.

For example, say you find an $112,500 duplex that if fixed up would be valued at $160,000. To do the necessary work, though, will require $27,000. With FHA 203(k), that's no problem. With this loan, you can borrow the full $139,500 ($112,500 + $27,000) you'll need to buy and upgrade the property. Your cash down payment would be around $7,000, and your monthly payments won't start until you move into the property.

For investors, FHA 203(k) works basically the same as it does for owner occupants, except that investors must put 15 percent down. In the preceding example, the investor's down payment would total $20,925. If the investor wanted to, though, once the fix-up was completed, he or she could immediately sell the property to a first-time buyer for nothing down at the full appraised value of $160,000. The "first-time" buyer could obtain a $150,750 FHA insured first mortgage and give the investor a second mortgage of $9,250 ($150,750 + $9,250 = $160,000).

Although in the past, the FHA 203(k) plan has been plagued by red tape and bureaucratic delays, during 1995 FHA streamlined the program. Now, many mortgage lenders are approaching the program with newfound enthusiasm. For more details about 203(k) and a list of 203(k) lenders in your area, call FHA at (202) 708-2720.

Assumable Mortgages

As we discussed earlier, most mortgages on one- to four-family properties include a due-on-sale clause. When you buy a property, more than likely the seller will have to pay off any existing loans against the property and you'll have to arrange new financing. There are, however, three notable exceptions to this general rule. FHA loans, VA loans, and many conventional ARMs all permit mortgage assumptions. Whereas most conventional lenders will require you to pass some qualifying standards before you assume their ARMs, FHA and VA assumable loans come in both varieties: (1) nonqualifying (NQ, non-qual, simple) assumptions, and (2) qualifying assumptions.

With either a nonqualifying or a qualifying assumption, you generally pay the sellers their equity (in cash, a second mortgage, a personal note, or some agreed combination) and take over the seller's mortgage payments. This means that the specific amount and terms of your down payment is subject to negotiation between you and the sellers. Plus, with a nonqualifying assumable, you don't even need to let the lender check your credit, verify your employment, or ask whether you plan to live in the property. A nonqualifying assumption is truly a "no questions asked" assumption.

Non-qual assumptions are becoming more difficult to find. Before the late 1980s, all FHA and VA loans were NQ assumables. However, after the late 1980s (1989 for FHA, 1988 for VA), government policy changed. FHA and VA loans originated after those dates now require lender approval for assumptions. Nevertheless, hundreds of thousands of the older non-qual loans are still out there and do frequently come onto the market. So if you want to avoid lender qualifying, keep your eyes open for properties with FHA or VA non-qual assumable mortgages.

Seller Financing

The ultimate way to avoid lender qualifying is to persuade the sellers to finance your purchase. Although only a minority of sellers may publicize their willingness to carry back all (or part) of your financing, many more will do so when asked. What people say they will do in the abstract is one thing. But what they will actually do when they're holding a signed offer to buy in their hands is quite another.

Besides avoiding lender scrutiny, seller financing frequently offers you the following benefits:

1. Low down payment/deferred down payment.
2. Below market interest rate.
3. Lower closing (settlement) costs.
4. No loan application or originating fees.
5. Relatively quick completion of financing.
6. Easier (or no) qualifying standards.
7. Complete flexibility (no rules or regulations to follow; everything's negotiable including assumability for your future buyer).
8. No occupance, no appraisal, or property condition underwriting standards apply (for your own protection, you may want to get the property professionally appraised and inspected for latent defects, termites, or environmental problems).

Whether you want to buy an investment home to live in or a property to rent out exclusively to tenants, a careful search of properties for sale will always turn up some sellers who will help you finance your goal. Sellers need to get their properties sold. And there is no better way for them to do this than to accept seller financing. Get out and make offers. You'll be pleasantly surprised at the favorable terms you can negotiate.

WHERE CAN YOU FIND FINANCING?

In addition to sellers, we can discuss primary sources of financing for small rental properties in three categories: (1) financial institutions, (2) mortgage bankers, and (3) mortgage brokers.

Financial Institutions

The major types of depository financial institutions that make mortgage loans include banks, savings and loan associations, and credit unions. In total, these financial institutions consist of more than 10,000 different lenders. To say that the mortgage market is highly competitive is hardly an understatement. Moreover, they're competitive not just in interest rates and fees, but also in underwriting standards, loan limits, types of properties, down payments, and other important factors.

Furthermore, with a rapidly expanding information highway, you won't have to visit (or even telephone) lenders to comparison shop. You'll be able to review loan offerings right from your home or the office of a real estate broker or mortgage broker (see following sections).

We should point out one central distinction, though, among the types of loans made by financial institutions. This is the distinction between conforming loans and portfolio loans. Loans that meet the underwriting guidelines of the big-time secondary market firms, Freddie Mac (Federal Home Loan Mortgage Corporation) and Fannie Mae (Federal National Mortgage Association), are called conforming loans. Although lenders who make conforming loans exercise some flexibility in qualifying borrowers and properties, for the most part their underwriting standards are decided for them.

On the other hand, portfolio lenders hold their real estate mortgages in house, rather than sell them into the secondary market. As a result, each individual portfolio lender is relatively free to set its own underwriting and qualifying criteria. So, if you can't get a conforming loan to meet your financing needs, shop the mortgage market for a portfolio lender. With greater product flexibility, a portfolio lender may offer you just the right financing to work out the deal you want.

Mortgage Bankers

Mortgage bankers are nondepository mortgage companies that typically make loans from their own funds. They then sell these loans to Fannie Mae, Freddie Mac, and other secondary market firms. Like many depository financial institutions mortgage bankers typically offer a broad range of conventional, FHA, and VA loan products. However, since mortgage bankers typically sell their loans rather than hold them in their own mortgage portfolio, they are conforming lenders.

Mortgage Brokers

Unlike depository financial institutions and mortgage bankers, mortgage brokerage firms do not actually fund mortgage loans. Instead, they "broker" loans (find borrowers and process loan applications) of a broad variety of lenders, which may include S&Ls, banks, credit unions, life insurance companies, pension funds, and even mortgage bankers.

In recent years, mortgage brokers throughout the United States have processed as much as 50 percent of the mortgage business. Three advantages have propelled their rapid growth:

1. A mortgage broker can discuss your needs, take your loan application, and then try to match your needs to the right lender. Since mortgage brokers may do business with anywhere from a dozen to more than 100 different lenders, you stand a better chance of getting your loan approved on the terms you prefer.

2. If it should turn out, though, that the first lender contacted by the broker doesn't approve your loan, the broker can try somewhere else. Plus, since the broker has already put together your loan file documents and verifications, you shouldn't have to complete that process again.

3. Mortgage brokers seldom work on salary. To earn a living, they must get their borrowers approved. In other words, mortgage loan brokers essentially work as mortgage entrepreneurs. They can earn enough to make their own mortgage payments only when they close loans. No one will work harder on your behalf than an ambitious, creative, and competent mortgage broker.

Is there a major downside to using a mortgage broker? Possibly. Some brokers overpromise and underdeliver. Some brokers use age-old bait-and-switch tactics. Some charge excessive fees. And some are here today and gone tomorrow. So, in addition to ambition, creativity, and competence, you want to select a trustworthy broker who is career oriented—not someone who is simply out for the fast buck.

Before you commit to a broker (or for that matter, any mortgage lender), check references. Make sure he or she has a track record of dependable service.

SUMMARY

Most Americans recognize the benefits of investing in real estate, but far too many of these people don't understand the ins and outs of real estate financing. To help you overcome this potential obstacle, we have answered five basic questions in this chapter: (1) How much should you borrow? (2) What types of financing are available? (3) What underwriting standards apply? (4) What kinds of loan programs make financing easier? and (5) Where can you borrow the money you need?

In thinking about financing, it's important to recognize how to magnify your real estate returns through leverage, but also to make sure you've allowed for potential risks. Buying properties with little or no down payment can give you a good start toward building wealth in real estate only if you have sufficient reserves (cash, income from employment, other assets, additional borrowing power) to see you through periods of vacancies and unexpected expenses.

Unless you have solid evidence of strong economic fundamentals, never assume that abnormally high rates of property appreciation will continue indefinitely. If you buy a property that produces negative cash flows, you should construct a plan to reduce (or preferably eliminate) those negatives through property improvements and more effective management. Don't merely assume, "Inflation will bail me out."

On the other hand, though, we don't mean to imply that you should avoid all risks. No one can get ahead in life by keeping their money in CDs or by turning down investment proposals because "the future's too uncertain." Over the long run, even relatively low rates of inflation will push up the values of your properties by multiples of two, three, four (or more). Nothing is more certain than that well-selected real estate will cost much more 10, 20, or 30 years from now than it does today.

So use the financing tools and techniques in this chapter to help you structure a real estate financing package that not only will get you started in investing, but also is sensible enough to weather any downturns that may temporarily cloud your forecasts. The past teaches two lessons about real estate: (1) Those investors who believe they can get rich quick without knowledge, effort, or prudence soon experience the unfortunate results of their mistaken notions; and (2) those investors who develop a sound long-term plan to buy, finance, improve, manage (and possibly sell off their real estate) tend to build wealth. Our goal for this book is to help you join this latter group of successful investors.

3 APPRAISAL: A SHORT COURSE IN VALUING PROPERTIES

As you've just learned from Chapter 2, to buy real estate you must understand real estate financing. But to buy real estate *profitably,* you must also understand real estate valuation.

Too many real estate investors, to their regret, lost sight of this critical point during the 1980s. In fact, even today, most popular how-to books on real estate investing still give short shrift to valuing properties. Why this fatal shortcoming? It's because in days gone by, authors and investors believed "inflation cures all mistakes." For example, David Schumacher says in his otherwise excellent book:

> The amount I paid for this property is inconsequential because of the degree to which the property has appreciated in value . . . In my opinion, it is ridiculous to quibble over $5,000 or even $50,000 in price if you are buying for the long term. . . . In 1963, I bought a four-unit apartment building for $35,000. Suppose I had paid $100,000 for it. It still wouldn't have made any difference because it's worth $1.2 million today.

Other top-selling real estate books have advised would-be investors to use the tactic of telling sellers, "You name the price, I'll name the terms." In other words, if the property owner would commit to sell on easy terms (usually little or nothing down), the buyer would agree to the seller's price. "Who cares what you pay today?" the promoters said, "What's important is all that money you're going to make when you sell."

MAKE MONEY WHEN YOU BUY, NOT JUST WHEN YOU SELL

Well, yes, long-term appreciation will boost a property's value. But if you overpay, you may have to wait four or five years (or more) for the market to catch up. During that period you could have been building wealth. In addition, the higher the price you pay (especially with high L-T-V financing), the larger your mortgage payments and the lower your net annual cash flow.

Whenever possible, make money when you buy a property, not just when you sell. We believe that you reduce your risk and increase your chance for good returns when you buy properties at or (preferably) below their market values.

WHAT IS MARKET VALUE?

To the naive, terms such as "appraisal value," "sales price," and "market value" all mean the same thing. But they are actually different concepts. Appraised value is a generic concept that could refer to an insurance appraisal, a property tax appraisal, an estate tax appraisal, *or* a market value appraisal. Sales price refers to the nominal price at which a property has sold. That price could be higher, lower, or equal to the market value. Thus when professionals speak about "market value," they are referring only to a special type of appraisal and sales price.

Generally, to meet the criteria of market value, a property must be sold under the following five conditions:

1. Buyer and seller are typically motivated. Neither is acting under duress.

2. Both buyer and seller are well-informed about the market and are acting in their own best interest.

3. The marketing period and property promotion permit reasonable exposure of the property to potential buyers.

4. There are no special terms of financing other than those typically available in similar sales.

5. No unusual sales concession is made by either the seller or the buyer.

Let's say that two homes recently sold in a neighborhood where you're interested in buying: 37 Oak sold at a price of $138,000, and 164 Maple sold at a price of $155,000. Both homes were in good condition, three-bedroom, two-bath structures of around 2,100 square feet. You locate a very similar house at 158 Oak that's priced at $134,690. Is that a good (below market value) price? Maybe, maybe not. Before you draw any firm conclusions, you would have to investigate the terms and conditions of those other two sales:

1. What if the sellers of 164 Maple had carried back a nothing down, 6 percent, 30-year mortgage for their buyers?

2. What if the buyers of 37 Oak had just flown into Peoria from San Francisco and had bought the first house they saw because, "It was such a steal. You couldn't find anything like it in San Francisco for less than $400,000."

3. What if the sellers of 37 Oak had agreed to pay all of their buyer's closing costs and leave their authentic Chippendale buffet because it was too large to move to their new retirement condominium in Florida?

Sales Price Doesn't Necessarily Equal Market Value

When you're shopping properties, it's not enough to know the prices at which other similar homes have sold. You also must learn whether the buyers or sellers acted without full market knowledge, gave any unusually favorable (or onerous) terms of financing, had to sell (or buy) in a hurry, or made any other concessions that might have pushed the sales price up or pulled it down. Should you find that the sales of any comparable properties did not meet the criteria of a "market value" transaction, you would want to duly weigh that information before you decided on a price for any properties that you are considering.

Lenders Only Loan against Market Value

When you apply for a mortgage loan, you may tell the lender that your purchase price is $200,000 and you would like a loan of $180,000 (a 90 percent L-T-V). However, the lender will not assume that the price you've offered accurately reflects the property's market value.

First, the lender will ask you about special financing terms (e.g., a $20,000 seller second) and sales concessions (e.g., the sellers plan to buy down your interest rate for three years and pay all closing costs). If your transaction violates market value norms, the lender won't loan you 90 percent of your $200,000 purchase price—even if it routinely does make 90 percent L-T-V loans. The lender may say that the special financing terms or sales concessions are actually worth $10,000. Therefore, it will base your 90 percent L-T-V on $190,000, not your $200,000 purchase price.

Second, to further verify that your sales price of $200,000 represents market value, the lender will order an appraisal. If the appraiser comes back with a figure that's less than $200,000, the lender will use the lesser amount to calculate a 90 percent L-T-V loan. However, you don't have to accept a low appraisal. You can get a copy for critique, or you can ask the lender to order a new appraisal with another appraiser. The lender primarily wants a file document (appraisal) to justify its lending decision. If you provide an acceptable (revised or remade) appraisal of a satisfactory amount, you'll get the loan you want.

On the other hand, just because an appraiser comes up with a market value estimate that equals or exceeds your purchase price, don't assume the appraisal is accurate. You must accept responsibility for your offering price. Lenders frequently tell their appraisers what kind of number they need to make a deal work as planned. As a result, appraisers know that if they "low ball" too many loan appraisals, lenders will stop calling them.

Similarly, if you're a good customer of the bank (or if the bank would like you to become a good customer), the loan officer may share this information with the appraiser. We know of many instances where appraisers have acquiesced to "subtle" hints from a bank executive and brought in appraisals at the "high end" of the market value range.

To invest successfully in real estate, you'll have to work with appraisers, and you may want to solicit their opinions, but never accept those opinions as gospel. Consequently, you can best protect yourself against erroneous appraisals (your own, as well as others) by understanding the three approaches typically used to estimate market values.

THE THREE APPROACHES TO VALUE

In general, real estate investors, mortgage lenders, and real estate appraisers derive their estimates of market value by looking at an existing subject property from three different perspectives:

1. *Cost approach.* Using the cost approach, investors calculate how much it would cost to build a subject property at today's prices, subtract for various items of depreciation, and add to that figure the current value of the lot (site).

2. *Comparable sales approach.* Using the comparable sales approach, investors compare a subject property with other similar (comp) properties that have recently sold. Then, by adjusting prices for the positive and negative features of each of the comps as compared to the subject property, they can get a pretty good idea of a subject property's market value.

3. *Income approach.* Using the income approach, investors estimate the rents a property can be expected to produce and then convert those rents (income stream) into a capital (market) value amount.

By evaluating a property from several different perspectives, you can correlate each approach with the others to give you a higher degree of confidence concerning a property's value. However, when your value estimates deviate from each other by substantial margins, you know that (1) you've either made a mistake, (2) the data you're working with is inaccurate, or (3) the market is acting "crazy" and is about to change in one direction or another.

As an aid to using and interpreting these three approaches, Figure 3.1 shows a typical appraisal form for a single-family home. If you will refer to this form when reading the following sections, you'll get a better idea of what we are talking about. In addition, you might consider making photocopies of this form (or picking up originals at a local appraisal office) and use them to record property and market information as you shop for your investments.

PROPERTY DESCRIPTION

Before you can accurately estimate the value of any property, you must first be able to describe the features of the property and its neighborhood in great detail. Not surprisingly, perhaps, novice investors frequently err in their valuations because they make their decisions on superficial inspections rather than detailed analysis. By giving attention to each of the neighborhood and property features shown on this form, you'll reduce the chance of missing something important.

UNIFORM RESIDENTIAL APPRAISAL REPORT

Property Description   File No.   SAMPLE

SUBJECT

Property Address	City State Zip Code
Legal Description	County
Assessor's Parcel No.	Tax Year R.E. Taxes $ Special Assessments $
Borrower	Current Owner Occupant ☐ Owner ☐ Tenant ☐ Vacant
Property rights appraised ☐ Fee Simple ☐ Leasehold	Project Type ☐ PUD ☐ Condominium (HUD/VA only) HOA$ /Mo.
Neighborhood/Project Name	Map Reference Census Tract
Sale Price $ Date of Sale	Description and $ amount of loan charges/concessions to be paid by seller
Lender/Client	Address
Appraiser	Address

NEIGHBORHOOD

Location	☐ Urban ☐ Suburban ☐ Rural	Predominant occupancy	Single family housing / Present land use % / Land use change
Built Up	☐ Over 75% ☐ 25-75% ☐ Under 25%		PRICE $(000) / AGE (yrs)
Growth Rate	☐ Rapid ☐ Stable ☐ Slow	☐ Owner	One family ___ / ☐ Not likely ☐ Likely
Property Values	☐ Increasing ☐ Stable ☐ Declining	☐ Tenant	Low ___ / 2-4 family ___ / ☐ In process
Demand/supply	☐ Shortage ☐ In balance ☐ Over Supply	☐ Vacant (0-5%)	High ___ / Multi-family ___ / To:
Marketing Time	☐ Under 3 mos. ☐ 3-6 mos. ☐ Over 6 mos.	☐ Vacant (over 5%)	Predominant ___ / Commercial ___

Note: Race and the racial composition of the neighborhood are not appraisal factors.

Neighborhood boundaries and characteristics: _____

Factors that affect the marketability of the properties in the neighborhood (proximity to employment and amenities, employment stability, appeal to market, etc.): _____

Market Conditions in the subject neighborhood (including support for the above conclusions related to the trend of property values, demand/supply, and marketing time — such as data on competitive properties for sale in the neighborhood, description of the prevalence of sales and financing concessions, etc.): _____

PUD

Project information for PUDs (If applicable) -- Is the developer/builder in control of the Home Owners' Association (HOA)? ☐ Yes ☐ No

Approximate total number of units in the subject project _____. Approximate total number of units for sale in the subject project _____

Describe common elements and recreational facilities:

SITE

Dimensions	Topography
Site Area Corner Lot ☐ Yes ☐ No	Size
Specific zoning classification and description	Shape
Zoning compliance ☐ Legal ☐ Legal nonconforming (Grandfathered use) ☐ Illegal ☐ No zoning	Drainage
Highest & best use as improved: ☐ Present use ☐ Other use (explain)	View

Utilities	Public	Other	Off-site Improvements Type	Public	Private	
Electricity	☐		Street	☐	☐	Landscaping
Gas	☐		Curb/gutter	☐	☐	Driveway Surface
Water	☐		Sidewalk	☐	☐	Apparent Easements
Sanitary sewer	☐		Street lights	☐	☐	FEMA Special Flood Hazard Area ☐ Yes ☐ No
Storm sewer	☐		Alley	☐	☐	FEMA Zone Map Date
						FEMA Map No.

Comments (apparent adverse easements, encroachments, special assessments, slide areas, illegal or legal nonconforming zoning use, etc.):

DESCRIPTION OF IMPROVEMENTS

GENERAL DESCRIPTION	EXTERIOR DESCRIPTION	FOUNDATION	BASEMENT	INSULATION
No. of Units ___	Foundation ___	Slab ___	Area Sq.Ft. ___	Roof ___ ☐
No. of Stories ___	Exterior Walls ___	Crawl Space ___	% Finished ___	Ceiling ___ ☐
Type (Det./Att.) ___	Roof Surface ___	Basement ___	Ceiling ___	Walls ___ ☐
Design (Style) ___	Gutters & Dwnspts. ___	Sump Pump ___	Walls ___	Floor ___ ☐
Existing/Proposed ___	Window Type ___	Dampness ___	Floor ___	None ___ ☐
Age (Yrs.) ___	Storm/Screens ___	Settlement ___	Outside Entry ___	Unknown ___ ☐
Effective Age (Yrs.) ___	Manufactured House	Infestation ___		

ROOMS	Foyer	Living	Dining	Kitchen	Den	Family Rm.	Rec. Rm.	Bedrooms	# Baths	Laundry	Other	Area Sq. Ft.
Basement												
Level 1												
Level 2												

Finished area above grade contains: Rooms;   Bedroom(s);   Bath(s)   Square Feet of Gross Living Area

IMPROVEMENTS

INTERIOR	Materials/Condition	HEATING	KITCHEN EQUIP.	ATTIC	AMENITIES	CAR STORAGE:
Floors		Type	Refrigerator ☐	None ☐	Fireplace(s) #	None ☐
Walls		Fuel	Range/Oven ☐	Stairs ☐	Patio	Garage ___ # of cars
Trim/Finish		Condition	Disposal ☐	Drop Stair ☐	Deck	Attached ___
Bath Floor		COOLING	Dishwasher ☐	Scuttle ☐	Porch	Detached ___
Bath Wainscot		Central	Fan/Hood ☐	Floor ☐	Fence	Built-In ___
Doors		Other	Microwave ☐	Heated ☐	Pool	Carport ___
		Condition	Washer/Dryer ☐	Finished ☐		Driveway ___

Additional features (special energy efficient items, etc.): _____

COMMENTS

Condition of the improvements, depreciation (physical, functional, and external), repairs needed, quality of construction, remodeling/additions, etc.: _____

Adverse environmental conditions (such as, but not limited to, hazardous wastes, toxic substances, etc.) present in the improvements, on the site, or in the immediate vicinity of the subject property: _____

Figure 3.1 Appraisal Report

COST APPROACH

ESTIMATED SITE VALUE . . . . = $ _____

ESTIMATED REPRODUCTION COST-NEW-OF IMPROVEMENTS:

Dwelling _____ Sq.Ft. @ $ _____ = $ _____

_____ Sq.Ft. @ $ _____ = _____

  = _____

Garage/Carport _____ Sq.Ft. @ $ _____ = _____

Total Estimated Cost New . . . . = $ _____

Less   Physical | Functional | External

Depreciation _____ = $ _____

Depreciated Value of Improvements . . . . = $ _____

"As-is" Value of Site Improvements . . . . = $ _____

INDICATED VALUE BY COST APPROACH . . . . = $ _____

Comments on Cost Approach (such as, source of cost estimate, site value, square foot calculation and, for HUD, VA and FmHA, the estimated remaining economic life of the property):

ITEM	SUBJECT	COMPARABLE NO. 1		COMPARABLE NO. 2		COMPARABLE NO. 3	
Address							
Proximity to Subject							
Sales Price							
Price/Gross Liv. Area	☑	☑		☑		☑	
Data and/or Verification Sources							
VALUE ADJUSTMENTS	DESCRIPTION	DESCRIPTION	+ (-) $ Adjustment	DESCRIPTION	+ (-) $ Adjustment	DESCRIPTION	+ (-) $ Adjustment
Sales or Financing Concessions							
Date of Sale/Time							
Location							
Leasehold/Fee							
Site							
View							
Design and Appeal							
Quality of Construction							
Age							
Condition							
Above Grade	Total Bdrms Baths	Total Bdrms Baths		Total Bdrms Baths		Total Bdrms Baths	
Room Count							
Gross Living Area	Sq. Ft.	Sq. Ft.		Sq. Ft.		Sq. Ft.	
Basement & Finished Rooms Below Grade							
Functional Utility							
Heating/Cooling							
Energy Efficient Items							
Garage/Carport							
Porch, Patio, Deck, Fireplace(s), etc.							
Fence, Pool, etc.							
Net Adj. (total)		☐ + ☐ – $		☐ + ☐ – $		☐ + ☐ – $	
Adjusted Sales Price of Comparable		$		$		$	

(Left margin vertical label: SALES COMPARISON ANALYSIS)

Comments on Sales Comparison (including the subject property's compatibility to the neighborhood, etc.): _____

ITEM	SUBJECT	COMPARABLE NO. 1	COMPARABLE NO. 2	COMPARABLE NO. 3
Date, Price, and Data Source for prior sales within year of appraisal				

Analysis of any current agreement of sale, option, or listing of the subject property and analysis of any prior sales of subject and comparables within one year of the date of appraisal: _____

INDICATED VALUE BY SALES COMPARISON APPROACH . . . . $_____

INDICATED VALUE BY INCOME APPROACH (If Applicable) Estimated Market Rent $ _____ /Mo. x Gross Rent Multiplier _____ = $ _____

This appraisal is made ☐ "as is" ☐ subject to repairs, alterations, inspections, or conditions listed below ☐ subject to completion per plans and specifications.

Conditions of Appraisal: _____

Final Reconciliation: _____

RECONCILIATION

The purpose of this appraisal is to estimate the market value of the real property that is the subject of this report, based on the above conditions and the certification, contingent and limiting conditions, and market value definition that are stated in the attached Freddie Mac Form 439/Fannie Mae Form 1004B (Revised _____).

I (WE) ESTIMATE THE MARKET VALUE, AS DEFINED, OF THE REAL PROPERTY THAT IS THE SUBJECT OF THIS REPORT, AS OF _____ (WHICH IS THE DATE OF INSPECTION AND THE EFFECTIVE DATE OF THIS REPORT) TO BE $ _____

APPRAISER	SUPERVISORY APPRAISER (ONLY IF REQUIRED):	Inspect Property
Signature	Signature	☐ Did ☐ Did Not
Name	Name	
Date Report Signed	Date Report Signed	
State Certification # _____ State	State Certification # _____	State
Or State License # _____ State	Or State License # _____	State

Figure 3.1 *(Continued)*

Owner/Borrower		Property Address	
Lender/Client			

DEFINITION OF MARKET VALUE: The most probable price which a property should bring in a competitive and open market under all conditions requisite to a fair sale, the buyer and seller, each acting prudently, knowledgeably and assuming the price is not affected by undue stimulus. Implicit in this definition is the consummation of a sale as of a specified date and the passing of title from seller to buyer under conditions whereby: (1) buyer and seller are typically motivated; (2) both parties are well informed or well advised, and each acting in what he considers his own best interest (3) a reasonable time is allowed for exposure in the open market; (4) payment is made in terms of cash in U. S. dollars or in terms of financial arrangements comparable thereto; and (5) the price represents the normal consideration for the property sold unaffected by special or creative financing or sales concessions* granted by anyone associated with the sale.

*Adjustment to the comparables must be made for special or creative financing or sale concessions. No adjustments are necessary for those costs which are normally paid by sellers as a result of tradition or law in a market area; these costs are readily identifiable since the seller pays these costs in virtually all sales transactions. Special or creative financing adjustments can be made to the comparable property by comparisons to financing terms offered by a third party institutional lender that is not already involved in the property or transaction. Any adjustment should not be calculated on a mechanical dollar for dollar cost of the financing or concession but the dollar amount of any adjustment should approximate the market's reaction to the financing or concessions based on the appraiser's judgment.

STATEMENT OF LIMITING CONDITIONS AND APPRAISER'S CERTIFICATION

CONTINGENT AND LIMITING CONDITIONS: The appraiser's certification that appears in the appraisal report is subject to the following conditions:

1. The appraiser will not be responsible for matters of a legal nature that affect either the property being appraised or the title to it. The appraiser assumes that the title is good and marketable and, therefore, will not render any opinions about the title. The property is appraised on the basis of it being under responsible ownership.

2. The appraiser has provided a sketch in the appraisal report to show approximate dimensions of the improvements and the sketch is included only to assist the reader of the report in visualizing the property and understanding the appraiser's determination of its size.

3. The appraiser has examined the available flood maps that are provided by the Federal Emergency Management Agency (or other data sources) and has noted in the appraisal report whether the subject site is located in an identified Special Flood Hazard Area. Because the appraiser is not a surveyor, he or she makes no guarantees, express or implied, regarding this determination

4. The appraiser will not give testimony or appear in court because he or she made an appraisal of the property in question, unless specific arrangements to do so have been made beforehand.

5. The appraiser has estimated the value of the land in the cost approach at its highest and best use and the improvements at their contributory value. These separate valuations of the land and improvements must not be used in conjunction with any other appraisal and are invalid if they are so used.

6. The appraiser has noted in the appraisal report any adverse conditions (such as, needed repairs, depreciation, the presence of hazardous wastes, toxic substances, etc.) observed during the inspection of the subject property or that he or she became aware of during the normal research involved in performing the appraisal. Unless otherwise stated in the appraisal report, the appraiser has no knowledge of any hidden or unapparent conditions of the property or adverse environmental conditions (including the presence of hazardous wastes, toxic substances, etc.) that would make the property more or less valuable, and has assumed that there are no such conditions and makes no guarantees or warranties, express or implied, regarding the condition of the property. The appraiser will not be responsible for any such conditions that do exist or for any engineering or testing that might be required to discover whether such conditions exist. Because the appraiser is not an expert in the field of environmental hazards, the appraisal report must not be considered as environmental assessment of the property.

7. The appraiser obtained the information, estimates, and opinions that were expressed in the appraisal report from sources that he or she considers to be reliable and believes them to be true and correct. The appraiser does not assume responsibility for the accuracy of such items that were furnished by other parties.

8. The appraiser will not disclose the contents of the appraisal report except as provided for in the Uniform Standards of Professional Appraisal Practice.

9. The appraiser has based his or her appraisal report and valuation conclusion for an appraisal that is subject to satisfactory completion, repairs, or alterations on the assumption that completion of the improvements will be performed in a workmanlike manner.

10. The appraiser must provide his or her prior written consent before the lender/client specified in the appraisal report can distribute the appraisal report (including conclusions about the property value, the appraiser's identity and professional designations, and references to any professional appraisal organizations or the firm with which the appraiser is associated) to anyone other than the borrower; the mortgagee or its successors and assigns; the mortgage insurer; consultants; professional appraisal organizations; any state or federally approved financial institution; or any department, agency, or instrumentality of the United States or any state or the District of Columbia; except that the lender/client may distribute the property description section of the report only to data collection or reporting service(s) without having to obtain the appraiser's prior written consent. The appraiser's written consent and approval must also be obtained before the appraisal can be conveyed by anyone to the public through advertising, public relations, news, sales, or other media.

Figure 3.1 *(Continued)*

Subject Property Identification

Although the subject property identification is fairly self-explanatory, on occasion some of these data may need further investigation. For example, the address of one of my previous homes was 73 Roble Road, Berkeley, California 94705. However, the home was not actually located in Berkeley, it was located in Oakland. The house sat back from Roble Road (which is in Berkeley) about 100 feet—just far enough to put it within the city limits of Oakland. As a result, the city laws governing the property (zoning, building regulations, permitting, rent controls, school district, etc.) were those of Oakland, not Berkeley.

Similarly, Park Cities (University Park and Highland Park) are high-income independent municipalities located within the geographic boundaries of Dallas, Texas. Among other amenities, Park Cities are noted for their high-quality schools. Yet if you lived in Park Cities on the west side of the North Dallas Tollway, your children would be required to attend the lesser regarded schools of the Dallas Independent School District.

Street and city address don't always tell you what you need to know about a property. Strange as it may seem, sometimes a property may not be located where you think it is.

Neighborhood

As you can see from the appraisal form, to investigate a neighborhood you should note the types of neighborhood properties, the percentage that are owner occupied, vacancy rates among rentals, predominant housing price (and rental) ranges, the availability and quality of government services, and convenience to shopping districts, schools, employment centers, parks and recreational amenities, and its general desirability to the market.

Most important, note the changes in the neighborhood that you see occurring over the next three to five years. Is the neighborhood stable or moving to higher rates of owner occupancy? Are people fixing up their properties? Do neighborhood merchants and residents take pride in their homes and the surrounding area? Is a neighborhood (or homeowners) association working to improve the area? If not, could such an association be organized and motivated to make the neighborhood a better place to live, shop, work, and play?

Whenever you invest in a property, you're not just buying the present. You're buying into the future. So the real question you want to answer shouldn't focus exclusively on the here and now. Close your eyes and envision how the neighborhood will (or could be made to) look five years from now.

Site Characteristics

Many beginning real estate investors fail to recognize how important the size and features of a site may be to a total property's current and future value. Depending on the neighborhood, site value could account for less than 10 percent to more than 90 percent of a property's selling price. Smart investors pay as much attention to the site as they do to the structure.

In addition to site size and features (see appraisal), you will want to check the types of government regulations that apply to the site. As a minimum, determine whether the property complies with all zoning, occupancy, environmental, and building regulations. Many two- to four-unit (and larger) properties have been modified (rehabbed, cut up, added on to, repaired, rewired, reroofed, etc.) in ways that do not comply with current laws and regulations. Furthermore, laws change. Even if in the past the property did comply, it may violate today's legal standards.

Consequently, property features or uses may be considered as (1) legal and conforming; (2) legal and nonconforming; and (3) illegal. When a property meets all of today's legal standards, it's called legal and conforming. If it met past standards which don't meet current law, but have been "grandfathered," the property is said to be legal and non-conforming. And if the property includes features or uses that violate standards which have not been grandfathered as permissible, those features or uses are illegal.

We are not saying that you should never buy a property that fails to meet current law. But, if you do, buy with your eyes open. Adjust your offering price downward to reflect the risk that you may be forced to bring the property up to code. Just as important, any health, safety, or environmental violations may expose your tenants to injury. Apart from the moral implications, violations of these codes have been known to result in legal nonpayment of rent, large lawsuits for damages, and on occasion even criminal liability. So, verify code compliance before you decide how much you're willing to pay for a property. Violations can cost you big dollars.

Improvements

After thoroughly investigating site size, features, and improvements (e.g., parking lots, driveways, fencing, landscaping, utilities, sewage disposal), you will want to fully describe the size, condition, quality, and appeal of the house or apartment units located on the site.

As you will see when we explain the different approaches to valuation, building size ranks as one of the most important determinants of value. Measuring size (room count, square footage), however, is not always easy or straightforward.

Once you begin to look at properties, you'll find converted basements, garages, and attics; you'll find heated/cooled and unheated/uncooled living areas; you'll find "bedrooms" without closets and "dining areas" without space for a family-sized table and chairs, let alone a buffet or china cabinet; you'll find rooms with 6-foot ceilings or lower, and rooms with 12-foot ceilings or higher; you'll find some storage areas that are easily accessible and others that can only be reached while crawling on your hands and knees, or perhaps, standing on a ladder.

In other words, you'll find that all rooms and living areas are not created equally. Therefore, you can't simply note that a house is a three-bedroom, two-bath, ranch with 2,100 square feet of space. You must also note the relative quality and livability of the rooms and storage areas within the house.

In addition, not everyone measures square footage in the same way. In a recent experiment, a builder asked five appraisers to measure one of his new homes. In sales promotion literature, the builder listed the home as 3,103 square feet. The closest appraiser came up with a square footage count of 3,047 square feet. Other appraisers came up with measures that ranged between 2,704 square feet and 3,312 square feet. Such differences can occur not just because of mistakes, but also because there are no "square footage police" who prescribe or enforce measurement methods.

So, when someone describes a property to you in terms of room count and/or square footage, don't casually accept that information. Question the source and methodology. Qualify the answer with your own judgment; and when accuracy counts, measure the property yourself.

THE COST APPROACH

The cost approach to value is based on the idea that an investor can choose to build a new property or buy an existing one. Thus, cost sets an upper limit to the price someone would be willing to pay. If you could build a new house for $140,000 (including the cost of a lot), then you wouldn't be willing to pay $150,000 for a similar home located just down the street that's already built. In fact, you shouldn't even pay

$140,000 for that house down the street because it's no longer new and has probably experienced some depreciation.

Calculate Cost to Build New

You can easily follow the logic of the cost approach by referring to the appraisal form. First, calculate how much it would cost to build the property using the dollars per square foot construction costs that would apply in your area for the type of property you're valuing.

Since reproduction cost relates directly to the size and quality of the building, you can see why an accurate property description sets a prerequisite for accurate valuation. Further notice that the cost of any extras (crystal chandelier, high grade wall-to-wall carpeting, upgraded appliances and plumbing fixtures, sauna, hot tub, swimming pool, garage, carport, patios, porches, etc.) that normally would not be considered as part of a property's basic construction costs must be added in separately.

Subtract Depreciation

After you calculate how much it would cost to rebuild a subject property at today's construction costs, you next subtract an amount for depreciation. Typically, as a property ages it becomes less desirable than a new property because of both physical and functional depreciation. Physical depreciation refers to wear and tear. As a property is exposed to time, weather, people, use and abuse, it deteriorates. Frayed carpets, faded paint, cracked plaster, rusty plumbing, and leaky roofs bring down a property's value compared with new construction. Exactly how much is a judgment call. But to fill in a number, you can estimate, say, 10 percent or 20 percent; if the property is really rundown, even 50 percent depreciation or greater might be warranted. Or, instead of applying a percentage deprecation figure, you could actually itemize the costs of the repairs and renovations that would put the property in top condition.

Usually though, itemized repairs don't work as well as percentage estimates, because for example, there is no financially feasible way to upgrade an 8-year-old roof, 4-year-old carpeting, or a 9-year-old furnace to like-new condition. In either case, though, your goal is the same. You must estimate how much the subject property has physically depreciated vis-à-vis a newly constructed property of the exact same size, quality, and features.

Likewise, you must estimate a figure for functional depreciation. Whereas physical depreciation refers to wear and tear through use and abuse, functional depreciation refers to the loss of value resulting because of such things as outdated dark wood paneling, poor floor plan, low-amperage electrical systems, or even out-of-favor color schemes or architectural design. Note that a property could show very little wear and tear (physical depreciation), yet still suffer substantial functional depreciation because the features of the property no longer appeal to a majority of potential buyers or renters.

External (locational) depreciation occurs when a structure is no longer the highest and best use for a site. For example, say you locate a wonderfully well-kept little house located in an area that's now predominantly commercial. In fact, zoning of the site has been changed. More than likely, the house would add little or nothing to the site's value. When someone buys the "house," they will probably tear it down to make way for a new retail store or office building.

For properties such as this, even though the house is in near-perfect condition, external (locational) depreciation would render it obsolete. Thus, external depreciation would approach 100 percent. With or without the house, the site would sell at approximately the same price.

Site Value

Since under ordinary circumstances, land isn't manufactured, you can't calculate its cost in the same way that you can calculate the cost to construct a house or apartment building. Consequently, to estimate site value, ideally you try to find similar (vacant) lots that have recently sold, or lots that have sold with "teardowns" on them, as in the preceding example. In evaluating similar sites, though, make sure you closely compare all features such as size, frontage, topography, government regulations, subdivision rules, and other features that would affect the values of the respective sites.

Estimate Market Value (Cost Approach)

As you can see on the appraisal form, once you've calculated a property's reproduction cost as if newly built, subtracted out depreciation, and added in site value, you have arrived at the estimated market value of the subject property via the cost approach. Because of the inherent difficulties of measuring construction costs, depreciation, and site value, the cost approach won't give you the perfect answer to a market value problem. But it will give you a ballpark figure to use as a check against the comparative sales approach and income approach. Here's a simple example of the cost approach: Property description: 6-year-old, single-family house of 2,200 square feet with a two-car 500-square-foot garage, deck, pool, sprinkler system, and upgraded carpets, appliances, and kitchen cabinets situated on a $40,000 lot.

Dwelling (2,200 × $72 psf base cost of new construction)	$158,400
Upgrades	9,000
Deck, pool, sprinklers	14,500
Garage (500 × $22)	11,000
Total	$192,900
less	
Physical depreciation @ 10%	19,290
Functional depreciation @ 5%	9,625
Total depreciated value	$163,985
plus	
Site improvements (sidewalks, driveway, landscaping)	12,500
Lot value	40,000
equals	
Indicated market value cost approach	$216,485

To further interpret the cost method of valuation, recognize that when this approach produces a value figure that substantially exceeds the value estimates derived by the comp sales and income approaches, that fact usually signals imminent value increases for existing properties. The reason for this logic is that sensible builders will not build new construction unless they can create properties that can be sold (or rented) at a price high enough to cover costs. Consequently, the supply of newly built properties falls until growing demand pushes up the market prices of existing properties. Once the prices of older properties approach the cost to build new, builders then can increase their construction of new homes and apartments. The real estate cycle begins another phase.

THE COMPARABLE SALES APPROACH

Generally for houses, condominiums, coops, townhouses, and small rental apartment buildings, the comparable sales approach produces the most accurate estimate of market value. If you want to know the price at which any specific property should sell, find out the recent selling prices of other similar properties.

Select Comparable Properties

The key then to the comparable sales approach is to select recently sold properties that closely match a subject property. Ideally, the "comp sales" should be located in the same neighborhood or development and conform in size, age, features, condition, quality of construction, room count, and floor plan. Of course, finding perfect matches is usually difficult (if not impossible) because every property has at least a few unique characteristics.

To the extent, though, that the comp sales are reasonable close matches for a subject property, you can calculate a preliminary value estimate by using price per square foot of gross living area comparisons.

For example, say you locate three comp sales of 1,680 square feet, 1,840 square feet, and 1,730 square feet. These homes sold recently for the respective prices of $112,560, $106,720, and $105,530. To figure the selling price per square foot of living area for these homes, you simply divide the total square footage into each respective sales price:

Comp 1
$$\frac{\$112,560}{1,730} = \$67$$

Comp 2
$$\frac{\$106,720}{1,840} = \$58$$

Comp 3
$$\frac{\$105,530}{1,730} = \$61$$

If the subject property has 1,796 square feet of living area it should be worth something in the range of say $60 to $65 per square foot, or $107,760 to $116,740.

Approximate Value Range—Subject Property

$60 × 1,796 = $107,760

$65 × 1,796 = $116,740

In practice, however, you would not want to end your comp sales approach with this preliminary figure. To gain more confidence in your value estimate you would match up the comparables properties to the subject property on a feature-by-feature basis.

Adjusting for Differences

After you, your real estate agent, or an appraiser selects appropriate comparables, their sales prices are adjusted up or down to compensate for their features that may be inferior or superior to the subject property. Here's a brief example of this adjustment process:

Adjustment Process (Selected Features)

	Comp 1	Comp 2	Comp 3
Sales price	$112,560	$106,720	$105,530
Features			
Sales concessions	0	− 5,000	0
Financing concessions	− 7,500	0	0
Date of sale	0	+ 5,000	0
Location	0	0	− 10,000
Floor plan	0	+ 2,500	0
Garage	+ 5,500	0	+ 8,500
Pool, patio, deck	− 4,500	− 6,500	0
Indicated value of subject	$106,060	$102,220	$104,030

Remember, a detailed adjustment process helps you more carefully answer the question: Based on the selling prices of similar houses, what is the market value of the subject property? Although our preliminary price per square foot estimate of market value showed the subject to be worth between $107,760 and $116,740, after adjustments it appears a price range of $102,000 to $106,000 would be more in line with the market.

Explaining the Adjustments

Whenever you make an adjustment, you are trying to equalize a subject property and its comparable with respect to a selected feature. You're asking, "At what price would the comparable have sold if it had been exactly like the subject property?" For example, consider the $7,500 adjustment for Comp 1 for financing concessions.

In this sale, the sellers carried back a 90 percent L-T-V mortgage on the property at an interest rate of 7 percent. At the time, market financing usually required a 75 percent L-T-V and an 8.5 percent interest rate for investor financing on this type of property. So without this favorable owner financing, Comp 1 would probably have sold for $7,500 less than its actual sales price of $112,560. Since market value assumes financing on terms typically available in the market, the extra value of this OWC (owner will carry) financing had to be subtracted from Comp 1's nominal sales price. Here are the explanations for several other adjustments.

1. *Comp 1 garage at $5,500:* The subject property has an oversized double-car garage but Comp 1 only has a single-car garage. With a better garage like the subject's, Comp 1 would have brought a higher sales price.

2. *Comp 1 pool, patio, and deck at − $4,500:* Comp 1 is superior to the subject property on this feature because the subject lacks a deck and tile patio. Without this feature, Comp 1 would have sold $4,500 less.

3. *Comp 2 sales concession at − $5,000:* The $106,720 sales price in this transaction included the seller's custom-made drapes, a washer and dryer, and a Sears storage shed. Since these items aren't customary in this market, the sales price had to be adjusted downward to equalize this feature with the subject property whose sale will not include these items.

4. *Comp 2 floor plan at $2,500:* Unlike the subject property, this house lacked convenient access from the garage to the kitchen. The garage was built under the house and residents had to carry groceries up an outside stairway to enter the kitchen. With more conventional access, the selling price of Comp 2 would probably have increased by $2,500.

5. *Comp 3 location at − $10,000:* This house was located on a cul-de-sac and its rear yard backed into an environmentally protected wooded area. In contrast, the subject property is sited on a typical subdivision street and its rear yard abuts that of a neighbor. Hence on this feature, the market would consider the subject property $10,000 inferior to Comp 3.

At this point you may be asking "How do you come up with the specific dollar amounts for each of the adjustments?" To that question, there's no easy answer. Generally, it comes from the knowledge you will gain from observing many different property transactions over a period of years. Until that time, though, you can rely to a certain extent on the knowledge of professionally competent realty agents and appraisers.

Nevertheless, even if you're relatively inexperienced you should always temper the opinions of others with your own judgments. Ask questions. Explore their reasoning. Verify their facts. In addition, as you look at properties, train yourself to keep your eyes open and identify all the differences that make a difference. Before you can attach numbers to each property's unique features, you first have to notice those differences.

THE INCOME APPROACH (GRM)

Near the bottom of the second page of the appraisal form, you can see a line labeled, *Indicated Value by Income Approach* (If Applicable). As shown here, the income approach refers to a method called the Gross Rent Multiplier (GRM).

To calculate market value using the GRM, you need to know the monthly rents and sales prices of similar houses or apartment buildings. For example, say you learn of the following sales of rental houses: (1) 214 Jackson was rented at $950 a month and sold for $114,000; (2) 312 Lincoln was rented at $875 a month and sold for $120,000; and (3) 107 Adams was rented at $1,050 a month and sold for $128,100. With this information, we can calculate a range of GRMs for this neighborhood:

$$\text{GRM} = \frac{\text{Sales price}}{\text{Monthly rent}}$$

Property	Sales Price		Monthly Rent		GRM
214 Jackson	$114,000	÷	$ 950	=	120
312 Lincoln	120,000	÷	875	=	137
107 Adams	128,100	÷	1,050	=	122

Now, if the property you are valuing would rent for $925 a month, you could calculate a value range using the GRMs indicated by other neighborhood rental houses:

GRM		Monthly Rent		Value
120	×	$925	=	$111,000
137	×	925	=	126,725
122	×	925	=	112,850

Because the GRM method does not adjust for sales or financing concessions, different features, location, property condition, or property operating expenses, its value estimates may be subject to considerable error. Yet, as a ballpark indicator, many real estate investors do routinely use it. As with the comp sales approach, the key to accurate GRM estimates is in selecting similar properties in the same neighborhood.

Multiple Unit Income Properties (GRM)

For multiple unit income properties, the gross rent multiplier is usually based on annual rent collections rather than monthly rents. For example:

Property	Sales Price		Total Annual Rents		GRM
2112 Pope (4-plex)	$280,000	÷	$35,897	=	7.8
1806 Laurel (6-plex)	412,000	÷	56,438	=	7.3
1409 Abbor (6-plex)	367,000	÷	53,188	=	6.9

The GRMs shown in these two examples *do not necessarily* correspond to the GRMs that would apply in your city. *Even within the same city,* different neighborhoods may show wide differences in GRMs. In the San Diego area, GRMs for single-family homes in La Jolla could range upward of 200; in nearby Clairmont, you can find GRMs in the 125 to 150 range; and in National City, GRMs may drop below 100. Also, even within the same neighborhood, GRMs for single-family houses often will run significantly higher than those of condominiums (or individual units within apartment buildings). Therefore, as with all appraisal methods, seek out good local market information before you apply GRMs.

INCOME CAPITALIZATION

Another income valuation approach that's generally used for multiple-unit income properties (but may be used to value smaller properties also) is called direct capitalization. To calculate market value with the direct capitalization method, you would use the following equation:

$$V = \frac{NOI}{R}$$

Where V represents the value to be estimated; NOI represents the net operating income of the property; and R represents the overall rate of return on capital that buyers of income properties typically require.

Net Operating Income

In real estate, net operating income is defined as annual gross potential rental income from a property less vacancy and collection losses, operating expenses, replacement reserves, property taxes, and property and liability insurance. Here's how a net income statement might look for an eight-unit apartment building where each apartment has a current market rent level of $725 a month:

Net Income Statement

1. Gross potential rents ($725 × 8 × 12)		$69,600
2. Income from parking and storage areas		6,750
3. Vacancy and collection losses @ 7%		−5,345
4. Effective gross income		$71,005
Less operating and fixed expenses		
5. Trash pick-up	$ 1,440	
6. Utilities	600	
7. Licenses and permit fees	275	
8. Advertising and promotion	1,200	
9. Management fees @ 6%	4,260	
10. Maintenance and repairs	4,000	
11. Yard care	650	
12. Miscellaneous	3,000	
13. Property taxes	4,270	
14. Property and liability insurance	1,690	
15. Reserves for replacement	2,500	
Total operating and fixed expenses	$23,885	
16. Net operating income (NOI)		$47,120

The following list explains each of the entries on the net income statement:

1. *Gross potential rents.* This is the total amount of rents that could be collected at current market rent levels and 100 percent occupancy.

2. *Income from parking and storage areas.* This property has a 16-car parking lot. Due to an extreme shortage of on-street and off-street parking in the neighborhood, the owner rents out the parking spaces separate from the apartment units. Also, the

owner has built storage bins in the basement of the building which are available for rental to tenants.

3. *Vacancy and collection losses.* Market vacancy rates in the area typically have ranged between 5 and 10 percent. Currently, all units in this building are rented, but even the best managed apartments experience some vacancies when apartments turn over. Also, to stay on the conservative side, some allowance is made for tenants who move out with rents owed beyond the amounts of their security deposits.

4. *Effective gross income.* This term refers to the actual amount of cash that the owner receives net of vacancy and collection, but before operating and fixed expenses.

5. *Trash pick-up.* Self-explanatory.

6. *Utilities.* In this property, tenants pay all their own utilities, but the property owner pays for lighting in the hallways, basement, and parking area.

7. *Licenses and permit fees.* Apartment building owners sometimes must pay business licenses or other fees. In this case, the owner pays a yearly fee to operate a "public" parking lot.

8. *Advertising and promotion.* These units generally rent via word of mouth and a "For Rent" sign that's posted on the property when vacancies are anticipated. However, as a conservative precaution, an advertising and promotion expense of $150 per year per unit is allocated to the operating budget.

9. *Management fees.* The owner of these apartments manages the property. Nevertheless, he should "pay" himself the same amount he would otherwise have to pay a property management firm. Returns for labor should be kept separate from returns for investment.

10. *Maintenance and repairs.* Similarly, the owner or his wife typically performs much of the cleaning, painting, and small repairs around this property. But these labors, too, deserve payment from the property's rent collections.

11. *Yard care.* The owner pays this amount to one of the tenants to keep the grass cut, rake leaves, and shovel snow off the walks the few times a year it may snow.

12. *Miscellaneous.* This expense covers legal fees, supplies, snow removal from the parking lot, periodical municipal assessments,

auto mileage to and from the property, and other items not accounted for elsewhere in the income statement.

13. *Property taxes.* City, county, and state taxes annually assessed against the property.

14. *Property and liability insurance.* This insurance reimburses for property damages resulting from perils such as fire, hail, windstorm, sinkholes, or hurricane. It also pays to defend against and compensate for lawsuits alleging owner negligence (e.g., slip-and-fall cases).

15. *Reserves for replacement.* Certain items such as roof, parking lot surface, plumbing, appliances, and carpeting last for a number of years and then must be replaced with a lump-sum expense. For income statement purposes, though, such lump sums should be smoothed out with annual allocations for replacement reserves.

16. *Net operating income (NOI).* Once you have itemized and totaled all operating expenses, subtract this amount from effective gross income and the resulting figure equals net operating income.

When you calculate NOI, you must make sure you have included all relevant expenses and have accurately estimated the amount of these expenses for the coming year. You must never accept a seller's income statement as accurate.

Whenever possible, ask to see the seller's Schedule E that pertains to the subject property and is reported to the IRS. The truth will probably sit somewhere in between the owner prepared income statement for sales purposes (where income is likely to be overstated and expenses understated) and a tax return (where income may be understated and expenses overstated). Also, even if the seller is perfectly truthful in reporting *last* year's income and expenses, you still must determine how those figures might change in the coming year(s). You're buying the future, not the past.

Are property tax assessments headed up? Are vacancy rates (or rent concessions) increasing? Have the utility companies scheduled any rate increases? Has the seller deferred maintenance on the property? Has the seller self-managed or self-maintained the property and omitted these noncash expenditures from the expense ledger? When it comes to calculating NOI, accept nothing on faith. Verify the reasonableness of every number.

Estimating Capitalization Rates (R)

After calculating NOI, you next need to decide what capitalization rate (R) you should use to convert the property's expected income stream into a capital value (lump-sum dollar amount).

In other words, when you buy a rental property you're actually paying now for the right to receive rents over the next 20, 30, or 40 years (or for however long you plan to own the property). So the question is, how much are those future rents worth in today's dollars (i.e., the property's market value)? If you believe the appropriate capitalization rate is 10 percent, then the market (capital) value of the eight-unit apartment building in this example equals $471,210:

$$\frac{47,121 \ (\text{NOI})}{.10 \ \ (\text{R})} = \$\,471,210 \ (\text{V})$$

But where does that 10 percent "cap rate" come from? You estimate it from the apparent cap rates that other investors have used to buy similar properties. For example, say an appraiser or real estate agent gives you NOI and sales price data on four other properties that have sold recently. From that data, you can estimate a market cap rate for those properties (provided those sales meet all the conditions of a market value transaction).

Market Data

Property	Sales Price	NOI	R
Hampton Apts. (8 units)	$452,900	$43,211	9.54%
Woodruff Apts. (6 units)	360,000	35,900	9.97
Adams Manor (12 units)	660,000	63,200	10.44
Newport Apts. (9 units)	549,000	53,700	9.78
Subject (8 units) (est.)	471,210	47,121	10.0

As you can see from the preceding market data, to buy small income properties similar to the subject property, investors have been using cap rates between 9.54 (.0954) and 10.44 (.1044) percent. So, it appears that a 10 (.10) percent cap rate for the subject property is about what the market indicates.

In real life you may not be able to locate enough similar properties with such a narrow range of cap rates. Instead, you might find that some properties have sold with cap rates of 7 or 8 percent (or lower) and others have sold with cap rates of 12 or 14 percent (or higher). Why such large differences?

Because investors aren't just buying a *quantity* of future rental income. They are also buying relative degrees of *quality*. In addition, they are paying for expected appreciation potential. Therefore, the lower the quality of the income stream, and the lower the expected rate of appreciation, the higher the appropriate capitalization rate.

To illustrate, let's say you're comparing two 4-plexes. One is a relatively new property located in a well-kept neighborhood in the direct vicinity of a city's growth corridor. The other is located in a deteriorating part of town where some factories and other employers have either moved out, closed, or laid off workers. Crime rates, too, are on the increase.

Comparing Cap Rates

Now, if the respective yearly NOIs for these two 4-plexes are $24,960 and $12,480, how much would investors be willing to pay for each property? If the investors applied a 10 percent cap rate to each property's income, they would value the properties as follows:

$$\frac{\$24,960 \ \ (NOI)}{.10 \ \ (R)} = \$ 249,600 \ (V)$$

$$\frac{\$12,480 \ \ (NOI)}{.10 \ \ (R)} = \$124,800 \ (V)$$

But more than likely, investors would not apply the same cap rate to these very different properties because the quality of their income streams differ. The "better" located property not only produces more rents, but also offers less risk and greater appreciation potential. So, we might actually see the NOIs of these two 4-plexes capitalized at rates of say, 8 percent and 14 percent, respectively:

$$\frac{\$24,960 \ \ (NOI)}{.08 \ \ (R)} = \$ 312,000 \ (V)$$

$$\frac{\$12,480 \ \ (NOI)}{.14 \ \ (R)} = \$ 89,143 \ (V)$$

Since most investors would rather own a property in a growth area, as opposed to a declining area, they are usually willing to pay significantly more for each dollar of income produced by such a property.

The Paradox of Risk and Appreciation Potential

Odd as it may seem, though, the high-priced "low-risk, high apprecia-tion potential" property may actually produce more risk and less appre-ciation potential than its low-priced cousin in another part of town. An analogy from the stock market will illustrate this paradox: In 1989, Sears was hitting hard times. It's sales growth was stagnant. It was losing its loyal base of customers. And its merchandise was losing its high quality, fair-priced reputation. On the other hand, Wal-Mart was on a roll. Year after year, it was chalking up sales growth of 15 percent a year. In retail-ing, Sears was a "has been" and Wal-Mart was the wave of the future.

The stock market reflected this outlook. Sears stock sold for a price earnings (P/E) ratio of 8. Wal-Mart stock sold for a price earnings (P/E) of 30. Translating these P/E ratios into capitalization rates, we could say that the R for Sears was 12.5 percent (1 $\div$ 8); and the R for Wal-Mart was 3.33 percent (1 $\div$ 30). Obviously, stock market investors believed that because of Wal-Mart's "lower-risk" and "higher-growth" potential, its stock (per $1 of company earnings) was worth far more than stock in Sears. But the market was proved wrong.

Within several years, the price of Sears stock had doubled and the price of Wal-Mart stock had faltered. Why? Because investors had overoptimistically bid up the price of Wal-Mart stock and had valued the Sears stock too pessimistically.

Always Compare Relative Prices

If you could buy either a high-growth company's stock at a P/E of 10 or a low-growth company's stock at a P/E of 10, by all means invest in the high-growth company. Similarly, if you could either buy a low-risk, high-appreciation potential property with a cap rate of 10 per-cent, or a higher risk, lower appreciation property with a cap rate of 10 percent, by all means buy the "low-risk, high-appreciation property." However, that's not how the world works.

In the real world investors bid up prices for high-quality growth area properties and "bid down" the prices of high-risk properties in less desirable neighborhoods. So, to figure out which type of property actually offers the most profit potential, you must compare their rela-tive prices.

When investors overprice properties and neighborhoods relative to other types of properties and neighborhoods, you should reorient your investment strategy.

In other words, don't just calculate market cap rates for any one type of property of neighborhood. Learn as much as you can about a variety of submarkets.

You can overpay for a property in two ways: (1) if you apply a cap rate that's below market given the property and neighborhood you're buying into; or (2) if you fail to realize that market cap rates, themselves, may sit too low relative to other types of properties or neighborhoods. On the other hand, often you can make extraordinary profits when you locate out-of-favor (high cap rate) properties that yield high rents relative to the price you have to pay (we will explore these points in more detail in Chapter 4).

SUMMARY

As we emphasized earlier, "market value" is not synonymous with the concept of "appraised value" or "sales price." Market value refers to the selling price of a property only when that sale conforms with the specified conditions of a market value transaction (see p. 65). Therefore, when you estimate the market value of a property based on the sales prices of other properties, first investigate the terms and conditions under which those properties have sold. Because a house down the street went for $100,000 does not necessarily indicate that a similar house nearby will sell for $100,000.

Also, by now you should realize that the market value of a property can be estimated with several different approaches. Yet, because you, an appraiser, or a real estate agent must work with imperfect data, those approaches won't all produce the same value estimate. You must decide in specific cases which approach best serves your purposes.

Moreover, the quality of your value estimate is directly related to how well you describe varying property features such that you can identify and consider "those differences (positive or negative) that make a difference." To make good investment decisions, you must learn as much as you can about properties, neighborhoods, construction costs, and lot values. Technique cannot substitute for knowledge and judgment.

Other Limiting Conditions

Besides the preceding cited limitations, also keep in mind that formally prepared appraisals by licensed real estate appraisers typically list a variety of other limiting conditions (see Figure 3.1). Most important for our discussion here are limitations 1, 2, 5, and 6 on the sample form used for Figure 3.1:

1. Appraisers do not guarantee title. They simply assume a property's bundle of rights are good and marketable. For a legal opinion of property rights, you should consult with a title insurance company.

2. Appraisers do not guarantee the boundaries of a site, nor do they necessarily note encroachments or other potential site problems. To accurately identify site dimensions, encroachments, and some easements, you need to employ a surveyor.

6. Appraisers note only the condition of a property that is visible through casual inspection. To assess the soundness of a property and its systems (HVAC, electrical, plumbing), always have a property inspected by professionally competent building inspection services and/or skilled tradespeople.

7. Appraisers gather much of their market information from secondary sources (real estate agents, public records, mortgage lenders, and others). For example, appraisers seldom see the interiors of the comparable properties that they include in their appraisal reports. Naturally, this reliance on nonverified secondary data sources means that appraisals often err in fact and interpretation. Consequently, use a professionally prepared appraisal as "for-what-it's-worth" information. But never accept it on faith as the one and only correct answer.

Valuation versus Investment Analysis

Although you should never buy a property without a good understanding of its market value, by itself, market value won't tell you everything you need to know to make sound investment decisions. Besides knowing what a property is worth today, you need to determine:

- Will the property generate adequate cash flows?
- Can the property be profitably improved?
- Can the property be expected to appreciate?

To answer these questions, we now turn to Chapter 4.

4 ANALYZING YOUR INVESTMENTS

As we have discussed in Chapter 3, prior to making a purchase offer, you should closely study the market and the property. The more you know, the more confidence you can place in your estimate of the property's market value. Except in unusual circumstances (discussed later), market value should set the upper limit for the price you are willing to pay.

Nevertheless, just because you can buy a property at a price equal to or less than its market value doesn't mean you should buy that property. Before committing yourself to a purchase, you should also ask:

- Will the property generate adequate cash flows?
- Will the property appreciate at an above-average rate?
- Will you be able to increase the value of the property through selective improvements?

WILL THE PROPERTY GENERATE ADEQUATE CASH FLOWS?

Market value appraisals typically calculate a rental property's net operating income (NOI), but unless you pay cash, NOI won't tell you how much money that property will put into your pocket each year. And even if you could buy the property for cash, you probably wouldn't want to because you would lose the potential benefits of leverage.

Therefore, for reasons of necessity and financial advantage, most real estate investors finance their purchases of rental real estate. This fact, though, creates another draw against the rental property's income stream. With a mortgage (or other type of financing) in place, you will have to make monthly payments. So now the question becomes not just how much NOI a property can be expected to produce, but also how much money (if any) will be left after you pay debt service. This remainder amount is called *before tax cash flow* (BTCF) or sometimes, *cash throw-off*.

As you may recall from Chapter 2, you can easily calculate BTCF as follows:

$$
\begin{array}{ll}
 & \text{NOI} \\
\text{less} & \underline{\text{Debt service (P/I)}} \\
\text{equals} & \text{BTCF}
\end{array}
$$

Now, let's bring forward the eight-unit apartment building example introduced in Chapter 3, where we calculated an NOI for this property of $47,121. Using a 10 percent cap rate, we then figured the property's market value at $471,210.

$$
\$471{,}210 \ (V) = \frac{\$47{,}121}{.10} \ \frac{(\text{NOI})}{(\text{R})}
$$

If we can assume that you could finance this property with an 80 percent L-T-V at 9.5 percent interest amortized over a term of 25 years, we can calculate your annual mortgage payments as follows:

$$
\begin{array}{ll}
\$471{,}210 & \text{Market value} \\
\underline{\quad\ \ .80} & \text{L-T-V} \\
\$376{,}968 & \text{Loan amount}
\end{array}
$$

On the mortgage terms specified (9.5%, 25 years), the monthly mortgage factor equals $8.74 per $1,000 borrowed. Since your original loan balance is $376,968, your monthly mortgage payments would equal $3,294 for an annual total of $39,536:

$$
\$376{,}968 \div 1{,}000 = 376.968
$$
$$
376.968 \times \$ \ 8.74 = \$ \ 3{,}294
$$
$$
12 \times \$3{,}294 = \$39{,}536
$$

Therefore, on the terms stated, this eight-unit property would provide you with an annual before-tax cash flow (BTCF) of $7,585:

$47,121 (NOI)
less   39,536 (Annual debt service)
$ 7,585 (BTCF)

To calculate your annual cash-on-cash return on investment (ROI), you would divide your down payment (original cash investment) into your annual cash return (BTCF):

$$\text{ROI} = \frac{\$7,585}{\$94,242} \quad \begin{array}{l} \text{(BTCF)} \\ \text{(Down payment)} \end{array}$$

$$= 8.05\%$$

Does this first year cash-on-cash rate of return look attractive? That would partially depend on the property's potential for improvement as well as its potential for market appreciation. If you rated the property strong in either or both of these areas, you might be willing to accept relatively low cash flows. On the other hand, for purposes of illustration, let's say that you're not happy with an annual BTCF of $7,585 and a cash-on-cash ROI of 8.05 percent. Does this mean you should give this property a pass? Not necessarily. Before rejecting a property that fails to yield adequate cash flows, look for ways to increase those returns:

- Could you arrange alternative financing with lower payments?
- Should you increase (decrease) your down payment?
- Can you buy at a bargain price?

Arrange Alternate Terms of Financing

It's amazing how you can improve the cash flows from a property by coming up with alternative ways to finance it. As explained in Chapter 2, sophisticated investors give as much attention to their financing as they do the price and other terms of their transactions. In our first run through the numbers for our eight-unit apartment building, we assumed a 9.5 percent interest rate amortized over 25 years with an 80 percent loan-to-value (L-T-V) ratio. To improve the cash flows, though, you could try to:

- Seek a lower interest rate.
- Increase the term of the mortgage.

- Use a balloon second mortgage.
- Combine several of these alternatives.

To arrange a lower interest rate, you could switch to an adjustable rate mortgage, ask for seller financing, buy down the interest rate, or perhaps, assume a seller's low interest rate mortgage. Here's how a lower interest rate of, say, 8.5 percent would boost cash flows:

Monthly payment per $1,000 @ 8.5%, 25 years = $8.05

376.968 × $ 8.05 = $3,035 mo. pymt.

12 × $ 3,035 = $36,415 annual pymts.

$47,121 (NOI)
less   36,415 (Debt service)
$10,706 (BTCF)

$$ROI = \frac{\$10,706}{\$94,242} \frac{(BTCF)}{(Down\ payment)}$$

= 11.36%

If this BTCF and ROI still fall short of your investment goal, extend the amortization period from 25 to 40 years (with a balloon at year 10 or 15, if necessary).

Monthly payment per $1,000 @ 8.5%, 40 years = $7.33

376 × $ 7.33 = $2,763 per month

12 × $2,763 = $33,158

$47,121 (NOI)
less   33,158 (Debt service)
$13,963 (BTCF)

$$ROI = \frac{\$13,963}{\$94,242} \frac{(BTCF)}{(Down\ payment)}$$

= 14.8%

Now, let's return to our first calculation where you were securing a new first mortgage from a bank at 9.5 percent interest with a 25-year term. Say the seller won't carry back the entire amount of the financing, but will give you a $100,000 balloon second mortgage due in 5 years, payable interest only at 6 percent. So you borrow $276, 968 from the bank on its terms, and $100,000 from the seller on his terms. Here's what your cash flow would look like under this financing arrangement.

276.968 × $8.74 × 12 = $29,048 (to the bank)

.06 × $100,000 = 6,000 (to the seller)

Total annual debt service = $35,045

$47,121 (NOI)
less   35,045 (Debt service)
$12,076 (BTCF)

$$\text{ROI} = \frac{\$12,076 \ \ (\text{BTCF})}{\$94,242 \ \ (\text{Down payment})}$$

= 12.8%

Although your cash flow under this financial scenario isn't quite as good as the completely seller-financed transaction, it still beats the baseline bank financing. Our point, though, is not to show that any one type of financing is best. Rather, we want to encourage you to calculate your returns under a variety of financial arrangements so that you can discover which (if any) financing might make a deal work for you and the sellers. Under just these few alternatives shown here the first year BTCF varied from a low of $7,585 to a high of $13,963. By changing the terms of financing, you can dramatically change the financial performance of a property.

Should You Decrease (Increase) Your Down Payment

You can also dramatically influence your cash flow and ROI by decreasing (or increasing) your down payment. Let's say that instead of putting 20 percent down ($94,242) on this eight-unit property, you swing the deal with just a 10 percent down payment of $47,121. You finance the balance of $424,089 at 9.5 percent interest for 25 years:

424.089 × $8.74 × 12 = $44,478 (Debt service)

$47,121 (NOI)
less   44,478 (Debt service)
$ 2,643 (BTCF)

$$\text{ROI} = \frac{\$2,643}{\$47,121} \quad \begin{array}{l} \text{(BTCF)} \\ \text{(Down payment)} \end{array}$$

$$= 5.6\%$$

In this case, reducing your down payment gives you a very thin margin of cash flow and drops your ROI to 5.6 percent. On the other hand, let's see what happens to cash flow and ROI, if you were able to buy with 10 percent down seller financing at 8.5 percent interest amortized over 40 years:

424.089 × $7.33 × 12 = $37,302 (Debt service)

$$\begin{array}{ll} & \$47,121 \text{ (NOI)} \\ \text{less} & \underline{37,302} \text{ (Debt service)} \\ & \$\ 9,819 \text{ (BTCF)} \end{array}$$

$$\text{ROI} = \frac{\$\ 9,819}{\$47,121} \quad \begin{array}{l} \text{(BTCF)} \\ \text{(Down payment)} \end{array}$$

$$= 20.8\%$$

Now this outcome looks attractive. When you combine the benefits of the lower interest rate seller financing with the benefits of higher positive leverage, you dramatically beat the returns realized with the hypothetical baseline bank financing (80 percent L-T-V, 9.5 percent, 25 years).

In some parts of the country with generally high housing prices, you may find that many well-kept properties (single-family houses, duplexes, fourplexes, small apartment buildings) produce negative cash flows. Say that our example eight-unit building is located in a prime neighborhood in high demand by both owner occupants and investors. Instead of a cap rate of 10 percent, properties in this neighborhood are typically valued with an 8 percent cap rate. So, instead of $471,210, these apartments are valued at $589,012:

$$\$589,012 \text{ (V)} = \frac{\$47,121}{.08} \quad \begin{array}{l} \text{(NOI)} \\ \text{(R)} \end{array}$$

If you finance with an 80 percent L-T-V, you'll put down $117,802 and secure a mortgage of $471,210. With a 9.5 percent interest rate and a 25-year term, your annual mortgage payment would total $49,420:

471.210 × $8.74 × 12 = 49,420 (Debt service)

$$\begin{array}{ll} & \$\ 47,121 \text{ (NOI)} \\ \text{less} & \underline{49,420} \text{ (Debt service)} \\ & \$\ -2,299 \text{ (BTCF)} \end{array}$$

In negative cash flow situations, your first remedy should be to search for alternative financing possibilities. If that doesn't work, then you could either cover the negative (feed the alligator) from your other income, or increase the amount of your down payment. With 30 percent down ($176,703) on a price of $589,012, you would borrow $412,308 and incur annual mortgage payments of $43,242:

$$412.308 \times \$8.74 \times 12 = \$43,242 \text{ (Debt service)}$$

$$
\begin{array}{ll}
& \$47,121 \text{ (NOI)} \\
\text{less} & \underline{43,242} \text{ (Debt service)} \\
& \$\ 3,879 \text{ (BTCF)}
\end{array}
$$

$$\text{ROI} = \frac{\$3,879}{\$176,703} \frac{\text{(BTCF)}}{\text{(Down payment)}}$$

$$= 2.19\%$$

At least the larger (30%) down payment converts your negative cash flow into a positive; but your ROI still looks anemic. You would want to buy such a property only if you knew it could be profitably improved or that neighborhood property values were about to escalate. Alternatively when facing a low return or a negative cash flow market, you can avoid the alligators by finding bargain-priced properties.

Buy at a Bargain Price

One of the best ways to increase your cash flow (or eliminate a negative) is to locate properties that can be bought at less than market value. While this technique requires hustle, knowledge, and creativity, you can do it if you work at it. Motivated sellers, lender-owned properties (REOs), foreclosures, tax sales, uninformed sellers, trade-in properties, and other sources of bargains routinely account for between 10 and 20 percent of property sales.

We discuss each of these types of bargains in later chapters. But our purpose here is simply to show how a below-market price can lead to higher cash flows.

Return to our eight-unit example that was valued with a 10 percent cap rate at $471,210. With the hypothetical baseline bank financing of 80 percent L-T-V and 9.5 percent, 25-year terms, the property produced a first-year cash flow of $7,585. But what if you could buy that property (or a similar one) at a bargain price (say 10% under market)? You would pay $424,089, put $84,817 down and borrow $339,271

(80%). Your annual debt service would fall to $35,582 and your cash flow (BTCF) would increase to $11,539:

339.271 × $8.74 × 12 = $35,582 (Debt service)

$47,121 (NOI)
 35,582 (Debt service)
$11,539 (BTCF)

Your first-year ROI would increase to 13.6 percent:

$$\text{ROI} = \frac{\$11,539}{\$84,817} \quad \begin{array}{l} \text{(BTCF)} \\ \text{(Down payment)} \end{array}$$

$$= 13.6\%$$

In markets where properties typically fail to give you the cash flows you want, don't necessarily give up your search. Instead try to ferret out a property you can buy at a bargain price.

Should You Ever Overpay for a Property?

Some books on real estate investing urge you to tell sellers that they can name the price, if you can name the terms. The idea is that you will agree to stroke the seller's ego by giving him a price he can brag about, but you'll still earn good cash flows and a high ROI because of the favorable terms of financing.

Staying with our eight-unit example property, say the seller takes you up on your offer and names the price at $525,000 (in contrast to a $471,210 market value). You say "Fine, here are my terms, $25,000 down, 6.5 percent interest, and 40-year amortization period with a balloon due in 12 years." This means that the seller would carry back a mortgage (or contract for deed) of $500,000. Here's a look at the numbers:

500 × $5.85 × 12 = $35,127

$47,121 (NOI)
 35,127 (Debt service)
$11,994 (BTCF)

$$\text{ROI} = \frac{\$11,994}{\$25,000} \quad \begin{array}{l} \text{(BTCF)} \\ \text{(Down payment)} \end{array}$$

$$= 47.9\%$$

On the surface, these numbers look very good. Compared with a market value price and bank financing, you've achieved three important objectives: (1) You've reduced the cash you need to buy the property; (2) you have increased your cash flow; and (3) you have lifted your ROI into superstar territory. You can readily see why some writers encourage this approach.

Nevertheless, you've got a problem. You owe more than the property is worth. Absent a strong increase in value, you will not be able to sell the property. Also, if market interest rates drop, you will not be able to refinance your outstanding mortgage balance. This "favorable" financing essentially locks you in for what could be a prolonged period of time (especially in slow markets when this type of deal seems to proliferate).

Therefore, to protect yourself if you enter such a deal, ask for two other conditions:

1. *The right to assign.* If your buyer can assume that low interest financing, you will dramatically add to your ability to sell the property without coming up with cash out of your own pocket.

2. *Right to prepay the mortgage at a discount.* To help you overcome the excessive mortgage problem, you could try to insert a pre-payment discount clause into the mortgage. If you paid the seller off within the first five (or whatever) years, the payoff balance would be discounted by say 5 or 7.5 percent, or even some higher figure. Sellers who are eager to cash out their debt interest in a property may agree to this discount clause. (Also, even when a mortgage does not include a prepayment discount clause, many sellers will later accept such offers.)

The "you name the price, I'll name the terms" buying strategy can work to decrease your down payment, increase your annual cash flow, and jack up your ROI. Yet, if these prices and terms leave you with an excessive mortgage balance, keep in mind the risks you face. Make sure you consciously decide that the benefits of the deal outweigh its drawbacks. Most importantly, don't simply assume within a few years market appreciation of 6 or 8 percent a year will eliminate the excessive mortgage problem. Maybe it will, but don't bet the ranch on it.

The Debt Coverage Ratio

Up to this point we have been emphasizing how the terms of your property transactions (price, interest rate, L-T-V, amortization period) can significantly increase or decrease your annual cash flows and ROI. Also remember that if you use lender financing, the lender may apply a debt coverage ratio (DCR) as one of its underwriting criteria. The lender may want to see that relative to annual debt service the mortgage property's NOI is large enough to provide a margin of safety. For example:

$$DCR = \frac{\$47,121}{\$39,536} \frac{(NOI)}{(Debt\ service)}$$

$$= 1.19$$

Among lenders who incorporate debt coverage ratios into their underwriting decisions, a DCR range of 1.1 to 1.3 is usually considered reasonable. Yet, if it turns out that your property's NOI fails to meet the lender's standard, go back to the drawing board. It's quite common for real estate investors not only to restructure their deals to meet their own cash flow requirements, but also to meet a lender's stipulated debt coverage ratio.

Numbers Change, Principles Remain

In the preceding sections, we've focused on the cash flows of an eight-unit apartment building with a variety of interest rates, L-T-Vs, amortization periods, cap rates, and purchase prices. However, even though the numbers used in these examples were derived from actual properties and financing arrangements, their primary purpose is to illustrate techniques and principles—not to suggest that any specific numbers are appropriate in your market or for your investment goals.

In the Dallas suburb of Denton, Texas, you can buy a good eight-unit rental property for less than $200,000. In San Francisco, you can easily pay in excess of $1,000,000 for a similar building. In Denton, I've seen cap rates of over 12 percent. In San Francisco, I've seen them at less than 8 percent. All markets are different. And even within the same urban area, you'll find wide variance among submarkets (e.g., types of properties, neighborhoods, gross rent multipliers, and typical terms of financing).

So whether you would like to buy condos, single-family houses, or small apartment buildings, you must search your local area. Look at properties. Talk to well-informed Realtors, mortgage loan officers, real estate appraisers, property managers, and real estate investors.

Then, once you learn the numbers that seem to apply within your area, work through them just as we have demonstrated in this chapter (and in Chapter 3). Making money in real estate doesn't just mean buying properties. Nor does it simply mean buying properties at a good price. To a large degree, investing profitably means *structuring* deals to yield good positive cash flows and high ROIs while avoiding foolish financial risk.

INCREASE RETURNS THROUGH APPRECIATION

In addition to the amount of yearly cash flows and cash-on-cash ROI, most real estate investors expect their properties to appreciate significantly. Over longer periods, even appreciation rates of 3 to 5 percent a year can add hundreds of thousands of dollars to your net wealth.

For example, assume you buy just one house at a price of $100,000 and finance it with a $90,000 mortgage at 8 percent interest and a 30-year term at an annual appreciation rate of 4 percent. After 15 years, that $100,000 house would be worth $180,000. Deduct your outstanding mortgage balance of $69,102 and your $10,000 down payment has grown elevenfold to $110,898. After 30 years, your mortgage would be paid off and the value of the house (at 4% yearly appreciation) would then total $324,340.

Buy just three or four $100,000 houses within the next several years and at retirement (if you're under age 50), your net wealth from those houses could easily total somewhere between $400,000 and $1,000,000. In addition, with even modest inflation in rents, your income from those houses could reach $7,000 to $12,000 a month. And that's from only three or four houses!

LOW INVOLVEMENT VERSUS HIGH INVOLVEMENT INVESTING

An investment strategy where you buy and hold three or four houses for income and appreciation over a period 15 to 30 years (or more) can be considered a low involvement investment strategy. Virtually anyone can come up with the limited time and money necessary to make this strategy pay off. On the other hand, if your goal is to build more wealth over a shorter period, then you may want to pursue a higher involvement appreciation strategy. Although this approach won't necessarily require more cash, it will require more time, effort, and knowledge. Generally, to beat the market averages, you first need to identify those communities, neighborhoods, and properties that are positioned for faster appreciation. This means that you or your real estate agent must astutely research various real estate markets. Second, within those markets that show the highest potential for appreciation, you need to search for bargain-priced properties whose market values can be increased through improvements.

Searching for Appreciation Potential

As most everyone now realizes, short-term appreciation of real estate prices is not guaranteed. Although you can always count on a long-term, buy-and-hold strategy to help you build large amounts of wealth, during the short term, local job layoffs, overbuilding, high interest rates, and myriad other factors can temporarily stall housing price increases.

Yet, this doesn't mean that you can't dramatically improve your chances of profiting from short-term appreciation gains. By looking for markets that signal strong potential, you can make good profits even when market averages are just crawling along. Here's how to find these future star performers.

Compare Relative Prices of Neighborhoods

An often cited cliche in real estate tells investors to "buy in the best neighborhoods you can afford; the best neighborhoods always appreciate the fastest." On closer inspection though, this advice makes no sense because no neighborhood or community can persistently outperform others. The law of compound interest proves the statement false.

Assume you can choose between a neighborhood of $100,000 houses (Affluent Acres) and a neighborhood of $50,000 houses (Modest Manor). Over the past several years, houses in the higher-priced neighborhood have jumped in value by 25 percent (say 8% a year). Houses in the lower priced neighborhood have moved up by only 10 percent (say 3% a year). Can these different rates of appreciation continue indefinitely? Not likely. A look at the projected home values shows why:

Future Appreciated Values

Years	$100,000 Neighborhood at 8%	$50,000 Neighborhood at 3%
3	$125,970	$54,635
6	158,690	59,700
9	199,900	65,200
12	251,820	71,250
15	317,222	77,900
20	466,100	90,300

When we first compared the relative prices of these two neighborhoods, homes in the better area cost twice as much as those located in the lower-priced area. But at different rates of appreciation, after 20 years the higher-priced homes would cost more than five times as much as their "inferiors." Unless some very rare market forces were at work in this example, such a situation could not result.

Long before such exaggerated price differences could occur, increasing numbers of potential home buyers would be priced out of Affluent Acres and would switch their buying to Modest Manor. Appreciation rates in Affluent Acres would slow. Appreciation rates in Modest Manor would accelerate.

The intelligent investor never assumes that neighborhood appreciation rates in the future will simply mirror the past. Rather, intelligent investors compare the prices and features of a variety of neighborhoods and communities and search for those that are relatively undervalued.

Undervalued Neighborhoods and Communities

At any given time and in any given urban area, no general statement about neighborhood or community appreciation potential ever holds true. Sometimes lower-priced areas may represent a great buy. On other occasions, higher-priced neighborhoods may look best. Sometimes new beats old; sometimes old beats new. Neither can anyone speak definitively about close-in versus far out, well-kept versus run-down, or lower-crime versus higher-crime neighborhoods. Most certainly, neither racial nor ethnic composition, household income level, or occupational status need necessarily correlate in one direction or another with neighborhood appreciation potential.

The neighborhood that offers the best appreciation potential is the neighborhood (community) where price and rent levels look good relative to the benefits offered.

Beverly Hills versus Watts (South Central Los Angeles)

By 1989, many home prices in prestigious Beverly Hills had shot up by 50 percent or more since 1985. On the other hand, during the same period house prices in the troubled neighborhood of Watts had barely budged upward. But by 1995, $5 million (1989) houses in Beverly Hills were selling at reduced prices of $3 to $4 million, whereas $85,000 (1989) houses in Watts were selling at the increased price of $125,000. Between 1989 and 1995, investors would have been much better off to have owned properties in troubled South Central Los Angeles than in the movie star haven of Beverly Hills.

Does this same relative potential exist today? Will Watts out perform Beverly Hills during the coming 5 or 6 years? My guess is no. Relative to other premier neighborhoods in world-class cities, homes in Beverly Hills now stand as terrific bargains. With the California economy at last climbing out of recession, house prices and rentals in Beverly Hills may now be positioned to hit new record highs.

Since I haven't recently studied either of these neighborhoods in detail, I am not making any firm predictions here. But that actually is the major point. Until you study neighborhood home prices relative to features, benefits, and buyer/renter demographics, you should not arbitrarily decide which neighborhoods or communities do present the best potential for appreciation.

Apart from relative prices, how should you compare areas? Here are some of the more important factors to consider:

- Demographics.
- Accessibility.
- Job centers.
- Taxes, services, and solvency.
- Construction and renovation.
- Land-use laws.
- Civic pride.
- Sales and rental trends.

Demographics

In most instances, when real estate investors refer to community demographics, they're referring to the income levels, occupations, education, ages, household size, and composition, and other characteristics of the people who live in an area. These data are readily available from U. S. Bureau of Census data and commercial market research firms.

However, you not only need to find out who now lives in the neighborhood, but even more important, you want to learn who is moving *into* the neighborhood. A historically lower income area that's attracting middle or even upper-middle income younger residents may signal appreciation potential. Similarly, a neighborhood where many residents are moving from government dependency to self-sufficiency is a positive sign.

To really learn about the people in a neighborhood, walk the neighborhood. Talk to people who are working in their yards or walking their dogs. Talk with realtors, mortgage loan officers, retail merchants, schoolteachers, and anyone else who would possess firsthand knowledge. Ask anyone and everyone how the neighborhood is changing and whether they see these changes as positive or negative. Then, based on what you hear, see, and research, form your own conclusions. Do you think the people moving into the neighborhood are likely to push up home prices and rental rates?

Accessibility (Convenience)

Neighborhoods don't change their physical position on the face of the earth, but nevertheless they can become more or less convenient relative to other neighborhoods and relative to their own past. Several years back, I chose to buy a home in the southeast part of town rather than the more popular northwest corridor. A primary reason was easier accessibility. Due to rapid growth and development, the freeway traffic leading to the northwest corridor was becoming increasingly clogged. What had been a 15- to 20-minute trip to town was now taking 30 to 45 minutes, and it looked as if the situation was going to get worse (which it did).

As a result, increasing numbers of home buyers decided (like me) that they did not want the hassle of fighting traffic everyday. So, they too switched their preferences to the east and southeast developments. Home prices in my neighborhood jumped 40 percent within 3 years.

Improved (Increased) Transportation Routes

As another accessibility factor, consider whether a neighborhood might become more convenient because of changing transportation routes. Are any new or expanded freeways or toll roads planned or under construction? What about bridges, ferries, subways commuter trains, or bus service? Will any type of new or expanded transportation facilities or services make travel to and from a neighborhood or community easier, cheaper, or more convenient?

Can you recall 5 to 15 years ago when some of those "outlying" developments were built in your area? Are they still outlying? More than likely they're now just minutes from shopping centers, office complexes, restaurants, and other commercial developments. So, in addition to investigating new or improved transportation routes, consider whether convenience might be coming to the neighborhood. Developments or communities that today sit miles from anywhere may tomorrow be located just minutes from everything.

Centers of Employment

Other things equal, most people would rather live close to their jobs rather than travel a long commute. So as another part of your search for appreciation potential, consider neighborhoods or communities that are located near employers or employment centers that are adding jobs to their payrolls.

During the late 1970s and 1980s when housing prices shot up in Boston, New York, Los Angeles, San Francisco, Washington, DC, and several other large cities, most "experts" said that the price increases were caused by millions of baby boomers flooding the housing market. Although that explanation was partly true, it was not *primarily* true.

Primarily, home prices shot up because these cities had very little developable land within an easy commute of the downtown areas where millions of square feet of new office space were being built. As these new office buildings filled with workers, tens of thousands of people began looking for homes and apartments close to their jobs. Those people with money (especially two-income career professionals) bid up the prices of desirable close-in properties. Those people with lower pay were pushed to the suburbs. Housing prices in both markets accelerated, but the close-in properties increased the most.

On the other hand, during the late 1980s and early 1990s, home prices stalled and retreated in these high-cost cities. Corporate downsizing took a toll. Plus, not only did construction of new office space stop, much that had been built remained vacant. Architects, mortgage lenders, leasing agents, construction workers, real estate lawyers, and accountants, and others employed in real estate related fields experienced job losses and lower incomes.

Now, though with the economy back on track, your task is to identify where in your area employment gains are most likely to grow. The greater the job growth and the less the amount of nearby developable land, the greater the appreciation potential.

Taxes, Services, and Solvency

Not long ago, Orange County, California, shocked the financial world. The county had lost $1.7 billion dollars by speculating in risky stock and bond derivatives. As a result, it defaulted on the payment of its outstanding municipal bonds and filed bankruptcy. Thousands of county employees were laid off, government services were cut back, and all new capital spending projects were put on hold.

Because California's Proposition 13 Constitutional Amendment limits property tax increases to about 2 percent a year, property owners in Orange County did not suffer a large hike in taxes. Nevertheless, the Orange County financial debacle did issue a warning to property owners and potential buyers throughout the United States: Governments can mismanage their finances. Governments can go bankrupt. And, governments can cut back or discontinue many types of services and programs (school, libraries, parks and recreation, public transportation, legal aid, housing assistance, trash collection, etc.).

Therefore, as you seek neighborhoods and communities (counties) in which to invest, check out the level of their property taxes, government services, and fiscal fitness. Does the community offer a high level of services and programs? Are the public finances of the community well managed? Does the tax/benefit ratio for the community (neighborhood) compare favorably with other areas? Considering all the taxes the residents pay, does the community government provide them relatively good value?

NOTE: Co-ops, condos, and other developments governed by homeowner associations may present special problems. *In a sense, a homeowner association is a government within a government. It issues rules and regulations; it provides services and recreational amenities; and it charges legally enforceable monthly fees. So if you are planning to buy into any type of housing development that's governed by a homeowners association, check out its "laws," services, fees, and fiscal solvency in the same way that you would check out a government.*

At one point during the early 1990s, 50 percent of the homeowner associations in the state of Massachusetts were insolvent. As condo prices collapsed, many unit owners stopped paying their monthly fees. This in turn caused higher fees for other unit owners. Of course, many of those remaining owners refused to pay. A vicious cycle ensued. Foreclosures mounted and all concerned lost money.

As of late 1995, new state laws have been passed to prevent a recurrence of this disaster. Homeowner associations in Massachusetts (and other states) have been given stronger powers to collect unpaid association fees before an association's finances get out of control. Even so, don't trust your financial fate to others. Before you buy, thoroughly review the operating rules, budget, and solvency of any homeowner association that will govern your property. (In most areas you can obtain this and other important association information by asking for a copy of the applicable "resale package".)

New Construction, Renovation, and Remodeling

Are neighborhood property owners (especially those who have recently bought into the area) upgrading their houses and apartment buildings? Are they painting exteriors, remodeling interiors, building on room additions, or adding amenities such as central heat and air, decks, patios, hot tubs, or skylights? Do you see homes being brought back to life after years of neglect? Check with building contractors, home improvement stores, and government building inspectors. Note trends in building permits for the area. Try to learn whether spending for property improvements is increasing.

Also, look for new construction of housing, office buildings, manufacturing plants, retail stores, or parks and recreational facilities. Not only does new construction create jobs, but if properly integrated into an area, it increases its desirability. Note, too, the prices or rental rates of any housing that's newly built or under construction. Is it noticeably more expensive than the existing homes and apartments in the area? If so, it indicates the neighborhood is moving up.

Beware of Overbuilding.   Be careful, though, if there's too much new housing under construction. Obviously, overbuilding can pull prices and rental rates down. Although everybody thinks "oil belt" home prices fell because of the collapse in oil prices, that's another partial truth. In fact, overbuilding (especially apartments and condominiums) was a leading culprit. In Houston, during the early to mid-1980s, for example, developers brought more than 100,000 new multifamily units to market. Apartment vacancy rates ran close to 20 percent. Rent levels for new luxury 2-bedroom apartments fell to less than $300 a month. Naturally, such low rents for apartments also brought down the prices of condominiums and houses.

New Construction at Historically Low Levels.   Since the early 1990s, lenders have severely tightened the financing for new apartment construction. Between 1991 and 1995, fewer new units were built than for any other 4-year period since 1945. Nevertheless, no one knows what the future holds. So, even though in general, limited amounts of new construction indicate neighborhood improvement and a healthy economy, before you invest in real estate, make sure that new apartment projects are renting without difficulty and that vacancy rates aren't teeming up into a danger zone.

Land-Use Laws

Land-use laws may include zoning, building codes, health and sanitation rules, occupancy codes, rent controls, environmental protection, historical preservation, architectural review boards, and many other types of laws, rules and regulations. In total, these laws may either encourage or discourage new development, but their major effect has been toward restricted growth and higher costs for development.

Therefore, to help you judge appreciation potential for a neighborhood or community, discover community attitudes toward growth. Do current (or pending) land use laws limit construction and drive up building costs? Is government artificially restricting supply? While debates rage between progrowth and no-growth forces, history shows that when no- or slow-growth attitudes prevail, rent levels and housing prices are pushed up.

When land-use laws become too restrictive, as they eventually did in California, businesses leave the state, employment falls, the economy sags, and real estate prices turn downward. So as another caution, if your area favors tight restrictions of growth, make sure those laws aren't pushing potential employers to start or expand their businesses elsewhere.

Civic Pride

Always remember two critical points: (1) You're not buying a neighborhood's past, you're investing in its future; and (2) you and others in the neighborhood can join together to enhance and improve the area. Civic pride, community spirit, and community action can change a neighborhood with a poor reputation into one that becomes "the place to be." Contrary to popular opinion, you can change and improve the location of a property.

So when evaluating neighborhood appreciation *potential*, evaluate the civic pride of neighborhood residents. Are they working individually and collectively to make their community a better place to call home? Are they cooperating with the people responsible for government services such as schools, libraries, public safety, street maintenance, parks and recreation, and public health? If there are specific problems such as crime, graffiti, school quality, traffic congestion, or unkempt public areas, are residents and public officials putting a plan into action to solve them?

Locate a neighborhood with possibilities for improvement and you've located a neighborhood with strong potential for appreciation. When you, other property owners, and tenants work together, civic pride and community action can make a world of difference.

Sales and Rental Trends

As emphasized earlier, conventional wisdom tells you to buy in the neighborhoods that have appreciated the fastest. Yet, that advice can easily fail. If price gains in one neighborhood have been outpacing those in somewhat similar neighborhoods for several years or more, the market could be set for a switch. So don't choose neighborhood or community by simply looking at the past. Instead, look for the market signals previously discussed. In addition, investigate sales and rental trends.

Sales Trends. Frequently, before prices begin to increase in a neighborhood, time on market data will show increasingly faster sales. In slow markets, properties may sit unsold for 180, 270, 360, days or even longer. On the other hand, as time on market falls from say, 270 days to 180 days to 120 days, you can bet prices are about to go up. Also, another important indicator of imminent price advances is a decreasing inventory of unsold properties. When sellers see the number of for sale signs coming down, they soon begin to raise their prices.

By all means, you should compare past neighborhood appreciation rates. But also compare time on market and unsold inventory data. Fewer homes that are selling faster point to a strengthening market.

Rental Trends. You should look at four important rental trends: (1) vacancy rates; (2) time on market; (3) annual rent increases (or rental concessions); and (4) rates of owner occupancy. Review the past 12 to 24 months. Are vacancy rates falling or increasing? How long do vacant apartments or rental houses sit vacant before they're rented? What types of units rent the quickest? Do any buildings or types of units have waiting lists? What are their characteristics?

Are rent levels increasing or stable? Or, are property owners giving concessions like one or two month's free rent for a 12-month lease? Also, are homes in the neighborhood or community primarily owner occupied or tenant occupied? In which direction is the neighborhood trending? Ideally, you would like to own rentals in neighborhoods where tenants are being squeezed out by homeowners. Increasing rates of owner occupancy signal higher home prices and higher rental rates for those relatively few rental units that remain.

Summing Up

To maximize your potential for appreciation gains, thoroughly compare neighborhoods on everything from relative selling prices to relative accessibility to relative civic pride, community spirit, and community action. Home prices and rent levels do not exist in a vacuum. Home buyers and tenants persistently shop neighborhoods and communities to discover the best *values*—not necessarily the best features in and of themselves. When you identify relatively undervalued areas, you're almost certain to benefit from price increases.

CAN YOU PROFITABLY IMPROVE THE PROPERTY?

As you compare neighborhoods and properties, keep your eye out for ideas you can use to improve the houses and apartments you do buy. Although most books and articles on real estate investing tell you to buy "fixer-uppers," remember, as I point out in my book, *Yes! You Can Own the Home You Want*, (John Wiley & Sons, 1995, p. 96) a fixer-upper is any home "that can be redecorated, redesigned, remodeled, expanded or romanced. The name of the home improvement game is profitable creativity. You can make nearly any home live better, look better, and feel better."

Don't think that only run-down houses and apartments fit the definition of a fixer-upper. Sure, poorly maintained properties may offer good potential for value-enhancing improvements. But to keen observers, even meticulously kept properties aren't immune to profitable change. When you stay alert to opportunity, you can always find ways to make a property more desirable to potential tenants. The following sections offer some value-creating suggestions.

Thoroughly Clean Your Properties

Many owners of small rental properties do not realize the basic necessity of spotlessly clean apartments or houses. Many owners seem to take the view, "Why clean the place thoroughly? The tenants will simply leave it like a pigpen anyway." But actually it's this attitude that often leads to this undesired result. When rental units aren't meticulously maintained, top-quality renters are turned off. They go elsewhere. On the other hand, those tenants who will accept units with dirt-encrusted windows and light fixtures, stained carpets, grease-layered stoves, or dust-laden window blinds are also the same tenants who are likely to treat your property as a pigpen.

If you display pride of ownership cleanliness, you will not only attract a better class of tenants, you'll demonstrate to your tenants the degree of cleanliness you expect. When I first became a landlord, I confess that I operated with the "why clean thoroughly" attitude. After seeing how badly tenants can wreck a property, it's easy to reduce standards. But, I soon learned that that's a self-defeating downward cycle. On the other hand, once I began to offer units that were head and shoulders above the competition, I was always able to choose the best tenants from a long list of applicants.

Add Pizazz with Color Schemes, Decorating Patterns, and Fixtures

Before you paint or redecorate your rental units, go out and tour several new home developments and new upscale apartment projects. Also look through a variety of home decorator magazines. Can you enhance the appeal of your units with more modern color schemes, wallpaper patterns, or special touches like chair moldings, mirrors, fancy plumbing, light fixtures, or patterned tile floors? You don't want to go wild with creativity or personal flair, but just the right amount of pizazz can make your units stand out from the crowd.

Create More Usable Space

Have you seen the ads of the California Closet Company or any of its imitators? This company took the simple idea that closet space could be used more efficiently and turned it into a $50 million a year business. Now, they're following the same principle with garages, workshops, and home offices. You can do the same thing. Figure out how to create more usable space and you've increased the value of your property.

But don't merely look to using existing space more efficiently. Maybe you should convert an attic, garage, or basement to additional living area. Or, you might consider enclosing a porch or patio, adding a second story, or building an accessory apartment. Keep asking yourself, "How can I use or create space to generate more income from these units?"

You might also think about "rightsizing" the living area within the units. "Rightsizing" the living area means reducing the size of large rooms by adding walls or separate areas. Or perhaps, combing small rooms to make larger areas. In other words, every storage and living area within a house or apartment should be proportionate to market tastes and preferences. When areas are perceived as "too large"or "too small," you can't get top rents. By rightsizing, you better fit the space to tenant needs.

In another sense, rightsizing can refer to making units themselves larger or smaller. For example, several years ago a Manhattan investor noticed that 2-bedroom apartments were a glut on the market and rent levels were severely depressed. On the other hand, those few buildings that offered 4-bedroom apartments had long waiting lists. So he bought a building of 2-bedroom apartments at a steep discount, combined the apartments into 4-bedroom units, and rented them all immediately at premium rent levels.

Create a View

Some years back when I was looking for a lakefront home in Winter Park, Florida, I discovered a basic flaw in homebuilding. Many builders had used stock building plans even when they built on view lots. As a result, the great majority of older lakefront houses I looked at failed to fully capture the view potential of the properties. Similarly, not long ago I was touring a new home development in northwest Albuquerque when I came across a home situated such that it could have offered spectacular views of the Sandia Mountain Range. But it didn't.

As I entered the house full of anticipation, disappointment soon set in. None of the rooms downstairs even had windows facing the mountains. Surely, though, the upstairs would be different. I imagined a master bedroom suite with large windows and perhaps a deck facing out to the mountains. But again, no. The master bedroom was situated to look straight at the house next door. And on the mountain side of the house was a small child's bedroom with no view window.

Capitalize on Builder Mistakes

If you can find older (or even newer) homes or apartments that fail to fully capture a potential view of a lake, ocean, mountain range, park, woods, or other pleasant surroundings, you may have discovered a great way to add value to a property.

What's surprising is that quite often the current owners of such properties have become so accustomed to the property as it exists, that they don't even realize its possibilities. After remodeling my home in Winter Park to achieve lake views from eight of the nine rooms in the house, the previous owners stopped by and exclaimed, "Wow! If we could have imagined these changes, we might never have sold the house."

NOTE: *This example emphasizes the overall point that profitable improvements begin with creative imagination. Don't rush into your property improvements without first considering a variety of possibilities. Too many property owners think property improvement means slapping on a fresh coat of white paint and laying new beige wall-to-wall carpeting. While such improvements may help, don't needlessly limit yourself to such routine ideas.*

Eliminate a Negative View

Some buildings suffer diminished value because their windows look out directly into an alley, another building, or perhaps a tangle of power lines. For such properties, your goal is to eliminate a negative view and convert it into a positive whenever possible. For example, can you change the location of a window? Can you plant shrubbery, bamboo, or leafy trees? Can you add decorative fencing?

At the Black Oak Bookstore in Berkeley, California, the owners have transformed an area that had looked out directly into a plain concrete block wall. To remedy this negative, the owners planted ivy to run by the wall, added hanging plants, a rock garden, and wooden lattice work. The results are quite pleasing and a 200 percent improvement over the plain concrete wall.

Enhance the Unit's Natural Light

Today, most home buyers and tenants prefer homes with loads of natural light. You can achieve this effect by adding or enlarging windows, changing solid doors to those with glass, or installing skylights. In addition to the positive influence of the sunshine itself, brighter rooms seem more spacious. To enhance this effect, determine if you can add volume to interior rooms by tearing out a false ceiling; or at times it can even pay you to eliminate attic area. When you add skylights and volume simultaneously, you can dramatically improve the way a home lives and feels.

Which Improvements Pay the Greatest Returns?

Newspaper and home improvement magazines frequently run articles that tell you a remodeled kitchen will pay back, say, 75 percent of its cost; a remodeled bath 110 percent of its cost; or a swimming pool may return 40 percent of its costs. Don't ever rely on any of these specific figures. Instead, you must evaluate every property and every project on its own merits.

Before you can accurately estimate potential returns, you must research competing properties and tenant preferences. Remember you are trying to achieve a competitive advantage. In addition, budgets for projects can vary enormously depending on who does the work, what materials are selected, and the skill and creativity with which the job is undertaken.

Plan Your Work, Work Your Plan

As a starting point for your research, inspect other rental properties. What are their strengths? What are their weaknesses? Talk to tenants. What complaints do they voice? What features do they consider essential? Next, talk with Realtors, property managers, and owners of rental properties. What insights can you pick up? Given what you've learned, now develop a plan to make your properties stand out from the crowd.

How Much Should You Budget for Improvements?

Before you finally choose the improvement projects you plan to pursue, though, try to develop a cost/benefit analysis. By studying market housing prices and rent levels, figure how much you can increase rents for each project you undertake. As a rule of thumb, every $1,000 you invest in improvements should increase your net operating income at least $200 a year. You can see the logic of this rule by applying the valuation formula we've previously disclosed:

$$\frac{NOI}{V} = R$$

Thus, if your improvements of $1,000 yield $200 more a year in income, you're earning 20 percent on your investment. Of course, you can develop whatever return criterion you think is appropriate. Some investors I know use 10 percent; others may go as high as 40 percent. The exact rate you use is not so important. What matters is that before you charge ahead to renovate a property, temper your enthusiasm with a realistic look at the amount of increased rents your investments of time, effort, and money are likely to produce.

Beware of Overimprovement

Generally, the improvement budgeting process is intended to keep you from overimproving your property relative to its neighborhood and relative to the rent levels your tenants are willing and able to pay. To look at the problem from this perspective, survey the top rental rates in the neighborhood for the size and quality of units you intend to rent. If $850 an month is tops and your present inferior units rent for $700 a month, using the 20 percent rule, you should spend no more than, say, $6,000 to $9,000 per unit for improvements. These figures assume that after renovations you could raise your rents to $800 or $850 a month and pocket another $100 to $150 a month in income:

$$\frac{\$1,200 \ (12 \times \$100)}{.20} = \$6,000 \text{ cost of improvements}$$

$$\frac{\$1,800 \ (12 \times \$150)}{.20} = \$9,000 \text{ cost of improvements}$$

Again, these numbers won't necessarily apply in your market. But, it's the methodology and thought processes that count. You want to run through the numbers so that you satisfy yourself that the market actually will support the rent level you intend to charge, and furthermore, that that rent level will give you an adequate return for your investment.

Other Benefits besides Rent Increases

On some occasions, you may want to invest more in your improvements than rent increases would seem to justify. For besides higher rents, your renovated units should attract a better quality of tenant, reduce apartment turnover, and cut losses from bad debts and vacancies. Nicer units also give you greater pride in ownership. Not withstanding these points, however, you still must work the numbers. Good tenants and pride of ownership are a worthwhile blessing only if you're collecting enough rents to pay your mortgage and other property expenses.

No-No Improvements

Nearly all real estate investors have developed their no-no lists of improvements. In a recent article Robert Bruss, for example, says, "Smart fixer-upper homebuyers and investors look for properties with 'the right things wrong.' " To Bruss, the right things wrong primarily include cosmetic improvements such as painting, landscaping, carpets, and light fixtures. On his list of no-nos are roofs, foundations, wiring, and plumbing.

While Bruss is clearly right, in general, remember, you're dealing in specifics. Whether you can profitably improve any specific property primarily depends on the price you pay for the property, the amounts you spend to improve it, and its value (or rent levels) after you've completed the work. By this standard, cosmetic fixers can be overpriced, and serious fixers may be underpriced. No universal rule applies. You must always analyze the financial details.

I know of a house that sat on the market for nearly a year because of serious foundation problems. No one wanted it. Eventually, though, an investor bought the property at a steep discount. He then jacked the house up 12 feet, repaired the foundation, built a new first story, set the old house (renovated) back on top, and resold the completed two-story house for a $42,000 profit. Not bad pay for 3 months of work.

How to Finance Your Improvements

As part of your property fix-up strategy, you must decide how to finance your improvements. One good possibility for one- to four-unit properties is the FHA 203(k) mortgage discussed in Chapter 2. Another good FHA program is the Title 1 property improvement loan. You can use this loan to finance improvements for either single-family houses or two- to five-unit rental buildings. For multifamily properties, you can borrow $12,000 per unit up to a total of $60,000. Generally, for loans up to $15,000, you do not need to have built any equity in your property. Above $15,000, you'll need equity at least equal to the amount of Title 1 funds you intend to borrow. (For a list of Title 1 lenders in your area and current program details, call FHA at 800-733-4663.)

Seller Financing. If you have a sound property improvement plan, you also might be able to persuade a seller to carry back financing. In lieu of a down payment, you could agree to complete a fix-up strategy within, say, 2 to 4 months. In this case, your "sweat equity" would enhance the value of the property and protect the seller's security interest. In fact, you can actually combine 100 percent seller financing and the use of a Title 1 loan up to $15,000. This is an excellent way for cash-short buyers to get started in real estate investing.

Absent Title 1 money, you could finance your improvements with cash from your savings, credit card purchases, or open credit accounts at building materials and home improvement suppliers. Once your fix-up work is completed and you've increased the value of the property, you could refinance your charges into a long-term second mortgage or a new first mortgage. In these situations, lender loan-to-value ratios will relate to the property's new market value, not the price you paid.

Example. Say you locate a fixer-upper that you can buy for $60,000 (100% seller-financed). Besides your own work on the property, you plan to spend $15,000 (Title 1, credit cards, open accounts) for materials and several skilled tradespeople (plumbers, electricians). After completion of the improvements, recent sales of comparable properties confirm that your property will have a market value of $100,000. You then could borrow, say, $75,000 on a new first mortgage, pay off the $60,000 you owe the seller, and pay off your borrowed $15,000 of improvement expenses. As compensation for your work and creativity, you now own a property with equity of $25,000.

SUMMARY

Throughout the 1970s and much of the 1980s, many naive real estate investors came to believe that to make money in real estate, all you had to do was buy it. Inflation would take care of the rest. But that view was just as wrong then as it is today. To successfully build wealth in real estate, you must carefully analyze and compare properties, neighborhoods, and communities. Before you invest, answer these four questions:

1. What is the market value of the property (Chapter 3)?
2. Will the property generate adequate cash flows (Chapter 4)?
3. Will the property appreciate at an above-average rate (Chapter 4)?
4. Will you be able to increase the value of the property though selective improvements (Chapter 4)?

If you apply your intelligence to ferreting out answers to these questions, your real estate investments will richly reward you. Although it may be true that a rising tide lifts all boats, there's absolutely no reason for you to cast your financial fate with the sun, the moon, and the winds. Follow the principles and techniques of value analysis explained in these past two chapters and (regardless of the movement of the tides) you will achieve financial security.

5 HOW TO FIND BARGAINS

In real estate—unlike the stock market—you not only can make money when you sell, you can make money when you buy. Whereas in the stock market, it's virtually impossible to buy a stock for less than its market value, in real estate such transactions occur every day. If Ford Motor Company is selling at 47⅛, no one would tell Merrill Lynch to try to find a Ford stockholder who will sell 100 shares at a price of $40 a share. But if you want to buy a $250,000 house for $200,000 to $225,000, it's quite possible that you or your real estate agent can locate a seller who will oblige you.

WHY PROPERTIES SELL FOR LESS (OR MORE) THAN THEIR MARKET VALUE

Recall from Chapter 3 that a market value transaction presumes these five conditions:

1. Buyer and seller are typically motivated. Neither is acting under unusual time pressure.
2. Both buyer and seller are well-informed and knowledgeable about the property and the market.
3. The market period and property promotion efforts are sufficient to reasonably inform potential buyers of the property's availability.
4. There are no special terms of financing (other than those typically available).
5. No unusual sales concession is made by either the seller or the buyer.

As you read through these market value conditions, you can see that when owners are in a hurry to sell, they may have to accept a price lower than market value. Similarly, an FSBO (for sale by owner) who doesn't know how to market and promote a property may not receive top dollar. Or, say the sellers live out of town and either don't have good recent information about sales prices, or don't recognize the potential improvement possibilities of their property (or maybe the neighborhood).

Owners in Distress

Every day people hit hard times. They are laid off from their jobs, file for divorce, suffer accidents or illness, experience setbacks in their business, and run into a freight train of other problems. Any or all these calamities can create financial distress. For some, their only way out of a jam is to raise cash by selling their home (or other real estate) quickly at a bargain price.

Some investors do find it distasteful and unethical to prey on the down and out. Yet, I suspect that a majority of sellers who find themselves in financial distress are quite anxious to get rid of their sleepless, toss-and-turn nights. If that means selling their property for "less than it's worth," then that's what they're willing to do. For these people are not just selling a house, they are buying relief.

Under these circumstances, as long as the sellers believe they have gained from the sale more than they've lost, it's a win-win agreement for both parties. If you are willing to help someone cope with a predicament—as opposed to taking advantage of the person—seeking out distressed owners could give you the good deal you want.

The "Grass Is Greener" Sellers

One day Karla Lopez was sitting in her office and in walks the executive vice-president of her firm. "Karla," she says, "Stein in the Denver branch just gave us two weeks' notice. If you want the district manager's job you can have it. We will pay you $12,000 more a year plus a bonus. But you have to be relocated and on the job within 45 days."

"Do I want it?" Karla burst out. "Of course I want it. Hope for a promotion like this is why I've been working 60- to 80-hour weeks for these past four years." Now in this situation, does Karla think, "Well, the first thing I must do is put my house up for sale and go for top dollar?" Hardly. More than likely Karla will be willing to strike a deal with the first buyer who gives her any type of offer she can live with.

Karla's got her eyes on the greener grass of Denver. Optimistic about her career and facing a time deadline, first and foremost, Karla simply wants to get her home sold as quickly as possible.

Grass is greener sellers stand in contrast to the financially distressed. Whereas distressed owners sell on bargain terms or price to relieve themselves of pain, grass is greener sellers are willing to accept a less than top dollar offer so they can quickly capitalize on better opportunities that lie elsewhere.

On one occasion where I was a grass-is-greener seller, not only did I give my buyers a slight break on price but, more importantly from their perspective, I permitted them to assume my below market interest rate first mortgage and carried back a personal note for virtually all their down payment. On at least three occasions I've bought from sellers who were eager to pursue better opportunities elsewhere. Each time, I negotiated a good (if not great) price and quite favorable financing.

If looking for distressed owners doesn't appeal to you, turn your search in the opposite direction: Sellers who are moving to greener pastures (especially under a deadline of time) are frequently the easiest people to work with and the most accommodating in price and terms.

Stage-of-Life Sellers

When shopping for bargains, you can also find good deals among stage-of-life sellers. These sellers are typically people whose lifestyle now conflicts with their property. They may no longer enjoy keeping up a big house or yard, collecting rent, or dealing with tenant complaints. They may be eager to move to that condo on the 14th green at the Bayshore Country Club. Or, perhaps these sellers would rather not go through the trouble of updating and repairing their current property(ies). Whatever their reasons, stage-of-life sellers are motivated to get on with their lives.

In addition, and this makes these sellers good prospects for a bargain price or terms, stage-of-life sellers typically have accumulated large amounts of equity in their properties. Further, because they're older, they also may have substantial sums in savings or other investments. In other words, stage-of-life sellers can be flexible. They don't need to squeeze every last penny out of their sale.

Just as important since they often don't have a pressing need for cash, stage-of life sellers make excellent candidates for some type of "owner will carry" (OWC) financing. Not only will OWC terms help them sell their property more quickly, an installment sale can reduce or postpone the capital gain taxes that a cash sale might otherwise require. As another advantage, OWC financing—even when offered at below market rates—will bring the sellers a higher return than they could earn in a savings account or certificate of deposit.

NOTE: *As a college student who wanted to invest in real estate, I sought out stage-of-life owners of rental houses and small apartment buildings. These people were tired of managing their properties. Yet, at the same time, they liked a monthly income and didn't want to settle for the meager interest paid by banks. They also didn't want to sell their properties and get hit with a heavy tax bill for capital gains.*

Their solution: Sell on easy OWC terms to an ambitious young person who was willing to take on the work of rental properties in exchange for an opportunity to start building wealth through investment real estate. This technique remains valid today. Because properly selected, well-managed rentals will pay for themselves, a buyer who is willing to work can substitute ambition and perseverance for a large down payment and high monthly wages.

Seller Ignorance

Some sellers underprice their properties because they don't know the actual prices that similar homes have been selling for. Or they may not know of some unique advantage their property has that would favorably distinguish it from other properties. I confess that as a seller, I have made this mistake of selling too low because I was ignorant of the market.

In this particular case, I was living in Palo Alto, California. The rental house I decided to sell was located in Dallas, Texas. A year earlier, the house had been appraised for around $110,000, which at the time of the appraisal was about right. So, I thought, I'll ask $125,000. That price is high enough to account for inflation and still leave room for negotiating.

The first weekend the house went on the market, three offers came in right at the asking price. Immediately, of course, I knew I had underpriced. What I didn't know but soon learned was that during the year I'd been away, home prices in the Dallas market had jumped 30 percent. After learning of my ignorance, I could have rejected all the offers and raised my price. Or, I could have put the buyers into a "bidding war." But I didn't. I just decided to sell to the person with the cleanest offer (no contingencies). I was making a good profit why get greedy?

Although not necessarily an everyday occurrence, this type of mistake does happen. So stay on the lookout for this potential opportunity.

If a good deal drops in your lap, be prepared to act. Good deals generally don't last long.

Not All Bargain Prices Are Bargains

Although good deals go fast, always remember that not all "bargain-priced" properties are good deals. You have received a good deal only if you can sell the property for substantially more than you have put into it. So, beware of underestimating fix-up expenses; beware of hidden defects; beware of environmental problems (e.g., lead paint, underground storage tanks, asbestos, contaminated well water); and beware of improving a property beyond the rent level that tenants are willing and able to pay.

Always temper your eagerness to buy a bargain-priced property with a thorough physical, financial, market, and legal analysis. Especially in cases of very attractive seller financing, many beginning investors jump at a "great" deal without subjecting it to rigorous scrutiny. While sometimes you must act quickly, keep in mind the less you know about a property, the more you assume without verification or inspections, the greater your risk. At least until you obtain greater real estate knowledge and experience, don't let a seller's apparent eagerness to sell become your pressure to buy.

Finding Bargain Sellers

In many ways, finding bargain sellers is like panning for gold. Even when you know a stream is loaded with nuggets, more than likely, you still must sift through a ton of mud and rock before you find the treasure that makes the entire search profitable. Therefore, when trying to locate bargain sellers, expect to work at it. It is true that as you gain experience and reputation as a real estate investor, deals will start coming to you. But as stock speculator Gordon Gekko (Michael Douglas) tells Bud Fox (Charlie Sheen) in the movie *Wall Street*, "Kid, I look at 100 deals a day. I may choose one." So, as a starting point for locating bargains, prepare yourself mentally for substantial effort.

Furthermore, never forget that among the many properties that are promoted as bargains, most are overpriced money traps. Conversely, through skillful negotiation and financial structuring, you can sometimes transform an apparently mediocre deal into a true winner. Except in cases of pure luck, putting nuggets in your pocket will require time, effort, intelligence, knowledge and analysis.

WHAT KIND OF BARGAIN DO YOU WANT?

As a practical matter, you can't look at every possible property in an area. And even if you could, you still wouldn't be interested in buying every bargain property that came to your attention. So, before you begin your search, narrow down what you are looking for:

- What neighborhoods look most promising (see Chapter 4)?

- Do you want a single-family house, condominium, co-op, townhouse, or multiple-unit rental property? If multiple units, how large of a property will you accept?

- Do you want a property for owner occupancy as well as an investment? If owner occupancy is important, how does this fact limit your choice of properties?

- How much repair, renovation, or remodeling work are you prepared to take on?

- What types of improvements are you willing to undertake? Structural? Cosmetic? Environmental? Fire damaged? Earthquake damaged? Other?

- Which is most important? A bargain price or bargain terms? Would you buy a property with negative cash flows? If no, what is your minimum cash on cash ROI?

- Would you accept a property that is occupied by problem tenants?

- How much risk are you willing to tolerate? When buying fixer-uppers, your repairs and renovation costs may exceed your estimates. If you buy into a turnaround neighborhood, the turnaround may take longer than you expect. How much cash or borrowing power do you have to sustain you through a period of weak rent collections (vacancies, bad tenants)? What's the minimum time period you would accept on a balloon mortgage?

By narrowing your search to those properties that match your requirements, you eliminate the wild goose chases that steal the time of many beginning real estate investors. Also, by asking yourself questions such as the preceding ones, you reduce the temptation to grab a deal just because it is a deal, rather than because the property well suits your abilities, finances, and inclinations.

Okay, now that you have developed your screening criteria, how do you start meeting potential sellers? Here are five techniques:

1. Networking.
2. Newspapers and other publications.
3. Cold call owners directly.
4. Real estate agents.
5. Information highway.

Networking

Some time back I was leaving the country for several years and decided that I wanted to sell my house with a minimum of hassle. Coincidentally, the PhD student club at the university where I was teaching was looking for a faculty member to host the upcoming faculty-student party. Aha, I thought, what better way to expose my house to more than 100 people. So I volunteered. The week following the party, I received two offers and accepted one of them.

The buyers got a good price and excellent financing. I avoided the hassle of putting the property on the market and did not have to pay a real estate commission. We both were satisfied.

This personal example shows the power of networking. What's surprising though, is that so few buyers and sellers consciously try to discover each other through informal contacts among friends, family, relatives, coworkers, church groups, clubs, business associates, customers, parent-teacher groups, and other types of acquaintances. So, don't keep your search a secret. Tell everyone you know. Describe what you're looking for. Why do it alone when you can enlist the help of hundreds of others?

Newspapers and Other Publications

To most people looking for real estate means perusing the real estate classifieds with a highlighter, calling owners or Realtors, getting basic information, and when something sounds promising, setting up an appointment. While this method can work reasonably well, it also can fail for two reasons: (1) If a property isn't advertised, you won't learn about it; and (2) if the ad for a property you might be interested in is not written effectively, you may pass it by without serious notice.

To at least partially overcome these drawbacks, run your own advertisement in the "wanted to buy" column. By describing the type of property and terms you're looking for, you invite serious sellers to contact you. When I began buying real estate, I used this technique to locate about 30 percent of the properties I bought.

As another way to use the newspaper, read through the "houses for rent," "condos for rent," and "apartments for rent" ads. Not only will this help you gauge rental levels, quite often you'll see properties advertised as "lease-option" or "for rent or sale." These kinds of ads generally indicate a flexible seller.

To search for potential bargain sellers in the newspaper, you need not limit yourself to the classified real estate ads. You might also locate names of people from public notices: births, divorces, deaths, bankruptcy, foreclosure, or marriage. Each of these events can trigger the need to quickly sell real estate. If you contact these potential sellers before they have listed with a real estate firm, you stand a fair chance of buying at a bargain price.

Cold Call Owners

Most successful real estate agents develop listing farms. A listing farm is a neighborhood or other geographic area that an agent consistently cultivates to find sellers who will list their homes for sale with that agent. Agent cold call techniques typically include telephoning property owners with names gathered from a criss-cross directory, walking the neighborhood and talking to residents, circulating flyers by mail or doorknob hangers, and by taking part in neighborhood or community-sponsored events. By cultivating a farm, an agent hopes to become known in the area and to position himself or herself to be the first person to learn of a contemplated sale.

You might take a lesson out of the real estate agent's book and similarly try to cultivate a farm in the neighborhoods or communities where you would like to buy. You could circulate a flyer, for example, that reads:

> Before you list your home for sale, call me. I am buying properties in this neighborhood directly from owners. Let's see if we can structure a transaction to benefit both of us.

If property owners can save time, effort, and money selling direct, they may be willing to offer you a favorable price or terms.

Vacant Houses and Out-of-the-Area Owners

Undoubtedly, your farm area will include some properties (vacant or tenant occupied) that are owned by people who do not live in the neighborhood. These owners may not see your flyers, nor will they be listed in a criss-cross directory. Therefore, to learn how to reach these potential sellers, you may have to ask neighbors of nearby properties or talk directly with tenants in the units occupied.

If this research doesn't reveal the owners' names and addresses, you can next contact the county property tax assessor's office. There, you can learn where and to whom the property tax statements are being sent. It's not unusual to find that out-of-the-area property owners are actually "sleeping sellers." That is, they would like to sell, but haven't as yet awoken to that fact. With luck and perseverance, you could be their alarm clock.

Broker Listings

For any one of a number of reasons, many properties listed with real estate agents do not sell during their original listing period. When this situation occurs, the listing agent will try to get the owners to relist with his or her firm. And quite likely, agents from other brokerage firms will also approach the sellers. However, here's what you can do to cut them off at the pass and perhaps arrange a bargain purchase.

When you notice a listed property that looks like it might fit your requirements, do *not* call the agent, and do *not* call or stop by to talk to the owners. Instead write the owners a letter stating the price and terms that you would consider paying. Then ask the owners to contact you *after* their listing has expired. (If a seller goes behind his agent's back and arranges a sale while the property is listed, the owner is still legally obligated to pay the sales commission.)

For example, consider this scenario: The property is listed at $200,000 which is a reasonable estimate of its market value. The listing contract specifies a 6 percent sales commission. The sellers have told themselves that they will accept nothing less than $192,500, which means that after selling expenses they would net around $180,000. Your offer is at $175,000. Would the sellers accept it? Or would they relist, postpone their move, and hold out for a net of $5,000 to $10,000 more?

It would depend on the sellers' finances, their reason for moving, and any other pressures they may be facing. But you can see that even though your offer is low relative to the value of the house, it still provides the sellers almost as much as they could expect if their agent found them a buyer. (Naturally, your letter offer would not formally commit you to the purchase. It would simply state the price or terms that you have in mind.)

Nothing I have said thus far is meant to imply that you should not rely on a real estate agent to help you find your investment properties. A good agent can provide valuable assistance in many different ways. It is a basic fact of life, however, that agents deserve to be paid for the services they provide. So, if you're planning to buy at a bargain price or buy on bargain terms (especially with low or no down payment financing), where's the agent's fee going to come from? If you want to pursue the best deal possible, at times you may have to forgo an agent's services and do your own legwork.

Agent Services

Before you decide to go it alone though, consider these words of experience form career real estate investor and renovator, Suzanne Brangham. In her excellent book, *Housewise*, Suzanne says:

> Real estate agents are invaluable. You need them as much as they need you. After you have narrowed your choice to one or two neighborhoods or towns, enlist the aid of an expert. Your real estate agent will be your guide so you can sit back, take out your notebook, ask questions, and learn. . . . Good agents know what properties are selling for, which areas are strong, and which neighborhoods are getting hot . . . .
>
> If you let your agent know that you plan to buy and sell several properties over the next few years, he (or she) will do everything short of breaking and entering to show you the properties that are available. . . . I'd been lusting after a beautiful two-unit building, but it had never been up for sale. My agent called me the minute it was listed and I bought it in less than an hour. In fact, I soon become notorious for signing offer forms on the roof of her car. When there's a race to get in your bid on a particularly juicy piece of property, a faithful agent who knows exactly what you want can make all the difference. (Harper Collins, 1987)

In addition to showing you properties and neighborhoods, a good agent can assist with many other tasks:

- Suggest sources and techniques of financing and help you run through the numbers.

- Research comp sales and rent levels so you can better understand values.

- Act as an intermediary in negotiations.

- Recommend other professionals whose service you may need (lawyer, mortgage broker, contractor, designer, architect, property inspectors).

- Handle innumerable details and problems that always seem to pop up on the way from contract to closing.

- Clue you in on what type of interest and market activity has developed around various properties.

- Give you an insider's glimpse into an area to let you know who's doing what and where.

- Disclose negatives about a property or neighborhood that otherwise might have escaped your attention.

In a real sense, your agent will become your partner. He or she will help you sort through your neighborhood and property trade-offs, suggest possibilities for value creating improvements, and help persuade sellers to accept your price and terms. Overall, as Suzanne Brangham points out, "A good agent, one who really listens when you explain what you want, is likely to take you directly to the buried treasure you've been looking for."

Tell Agents What You Expect.   If your sole experience with real estate agents has only brought you into contact with the run-of-the-mill variety, you may think that the preceding discussion of agent services is fantastically exaggerated. But it's not. Since most relatively new real estate investors don't expect much from their agents, they tend to tolerate mediocrity. Then they complain that "agents are underworked and overpaid."

To avoid this self-fulfilling prophecy, you first must accept responsibility for specifying the types and quality of services you expect to receive. As you talk with agents, tell them the information you'll need and the types of questions you will be asking. Test them with substantive inquiries. Do they rattle off answers as if they're a walking almanac of community information? Or do they repeatedly respond, "I don't know, but I can find that for you if you really want me to."

Certainly, no agent can know or anticipate all the information your neighborhood and property analyses might require. But if an agent repeatedly waits for you to ask questions before doing the spade-work necessary for you to make intelligent decisions, then you need to find a more knowledgeable agent.

NOTE: *Real estate agents (like everyone else) must constantly guard what they say out of fear of lawsuits. For example, if you should ask, "What's the quality of the schools in this neighborhood?" the agent may hedge an an-swer if, say, forced integration has created white flight, and corresponding achievement test scores have fallen.*

Similarly, if the changing ethnic or racial composition of a neigh-borhood is affecting property values (either up or down), the agent would probably prefer to avoid any discussion along those lines. The U.S. Department of Justice and the U.S. Department of Housing and Urban Development (HUD) have decreed that neither ethnic, religious, nor racial demographics affect property values. Hence, any real estate agent (or appraiser) who disagrees with HUD or DOJ can be held civilly and criminally liable for damages.

In a fit of excess, agents have even been warned against using terms such as "exclusive neighborhood," "walk-in closet," "beautiful view," "master bedroom," and "walking distance to school." In Berke-ley, California, HUD sued a group of neighbors for speaking against the placement of a home for the mentally retarded in their neighbor-hood. In today's climate of victimhood, any statement that in any way might give offense to some "protected" group can land a real estate agent in court and out of a job. So don't expect candid answers to any of your questions that may even remotely transgress someone's idea of civil rights.

A second area of concern to agents is property condition. "How's the roof?" you ask. The agent answers, "As far as I know, it's 8 years old and hasn't had any leaks." You buy the property and 3 months later the roof begins to leak. On the basis of the agent's statement, you sue him or her for misrepresentation and fraud. Even though the agent was telling the truth so far as he or she knew it, many judges or juries would still find the agent liable.

In other words, agents have been sued so many times for giving "to the best of my knowledge" answers concerning property condi-tion, that many simply avoid such questions and will refer you to ap-propriate specialists and inspectors. In one major precedent-setting case in California, an agent was held liable for not informing his buy-ers that their property was located in a mudslide area—even though the agent did not know that the area was risky. In response to this case, the California Association of Realtors convinced the California legislature to enact a seller disclosure law. More than 20 other states now have followed California's lead (more on disclosure statements later).

To confirm your belief that you're buying at a bargain price, you need full and accurate information about neighborhoods and specific properties. A top real estate agent will be able to provide you with much of this knowledge. But not everything. So in addition to knowing what types of information you should rightfully expect from your agent, also keep in mind your agent's practical and legal limitations.

Experience and Professional Education.   If you plan to invest primarily in single-family houses, condos, or townhomes, you can safely rely on an experienced and knowledgeable agent who specializes in residential sales. As a further criterion, you can look for those agents who have achieved the GRI (Graduate Realtors Institute), the CRS (Certified Residential Specialist), or the CRB (Certified Residential Broker) designation. Each of these designations require experience and advanced professional education. For example, although the National Association of Realtors had approximately 600,000 members, only 32,000 of these agents have met the experience and education standards required for the CRS designation.

If you plan to buy income properties of four units or more, you might consider using an agent who has earned the CCIM (Certified Commercial Investment Member) designation. To meet the standards for this professional credential, agents must complete advanced courses in market analysis, economics, statistics, taxation, financial analysis, and other topics related to real estate investing. Most CCIMs work exclusively with buyers and sellers of apartment buildings, office buildings, and shopping centers.

Beyond professional education and experience, you want an agent "who is sophisticated, hardworking, fun, fast, and smart—a person who knows the town inside and out and makes a lot of deals," advises Suzanne Brangham. I agree. In my book, *Yes! You Can Own the Home You Want,* I speak of agents who are skilled in "possibility analysis." These agents demonstrate a "we can make it happen" attitude. Rather than tell you what you can't do, they show you how to get over, under, or around whatever obstacles stand in your way. These agents know how to get deals structured and closed.

Buyer Loyalty.   For every real buyer they work with, most agents come in contact with another dozen pretenders—people who are quite willing to steal an agent's time and knowledge, but feel no obligation to buy from that agent. Or if they do buy, the first thing they do to make a deal work is to try to cut the agent's commission. This is not the way to build a lasting and mutually beneficial relationship. For best results, once you find a top agent, demonstrate buyer loyalty.

Overall, when you're loyal to your agents, they will see you as a real buyer who will give them repeat business (as well as referrals). As a result, they will give you preferred treatment and make sure that you're among the first to learn of those "juicy deals" as soon as they hit the market, and sometimes even before the listing goes into the MLS (Multiple Listing Service).

Law of Agency.   Up until the early 1990s, the great majority of real estate agents who helped buyers find properties actually worked as agents or subagents for the sellers. This system had worked well for more than 100 years. More recently though, lawsuit-happy lawyers and self-proclaimed consumer advocates have widely publicized claims that such a system cheated buyers by denying them their own representation. Furthermore, since many buyers did not know "their" agent was really a subagent of the sellers, all too frequently these buyers unwittingly disclosed personal confidential information to the agent who then passed it onto the sellers to use against the buyers during negotiations.

While undoubtedly a few agents did abuse their buyers' trust under this subagency system, most did not. Of the tens of millions of real estate transactions that have occurred over the years, only a very small percentage has resulted in serious complaining. Furthermore, under the previous system, "seller's" agents often disclosed to buyers valuable tidbits of information such as, "The sellers are asking $160,000, but they're going through a bitter divorce and are pressed to sell. They will probably accept something around $140,000. Would you be interested at that price? Let's write up an offer and see what happens."

Notwithstanding this reality, it was a buyers' class action lawsuit against Edina Realty in Minnesota that sent shock waves throughout the real estate industry. Even though Edina's agents were not proven to have acted against their buyers' interests, Edina Realty suffered a $250 million judgment for having "insufficiently emphasized and explained their role as sellers agents or subagents."

In self-defense, Realtor groups throughout the country pleaded with the courts and state legislatures to clarify their respective lawful duties to buyers and sellers. Although this area of law is still evolving, nearly all states have now enacted mandatory agent disclosure. As a rule, these laws compel buyers to explicitly choose the type of agency relationship they want to enter into with their real estate agents. Generally, these four choices are available:

1. You can work with an agent or subagent of the sellers.

2. You can elect a dual agency. Under this arrangement, an agent may help both buyers and sellers, but he or she also agrees not to pass along confidential information that could benefit either a buyer or a seller at the expense of the other party. (Many agents now refuse to act as dual agents because they believe the risk of liability is too great.)

3. Some agents are holding themselves out as facilitators. In this role, they do not advocate or represent the interests of either the buyers or the sellers. Instead, they act as mediators helping buyer and seller structure an agreement that both parties are happy to live with.

4. The fastest growing type of agency relationship is called "buyer's agency" or "buyer's brokerage." Although any licensed real estate agent may serve as a buyer's agent, a true buyer's brokerage firm only represents buyers. Such a firm will not accept listings from sellers.

In most situations, you will probably want to choose a buyer's agency or buyer's brokerage relationship with your agent. In that way, the agent is free to research, inquire, and discover any type of information that could be helpful to you without worrying about any conflicting duties or loyalties that he or she owes to a seller.

On the other hand, there are two reasons that on some occasions you might want to work with a seller's listing agent. First, although I am generally against asking agents to cut their commission, working with a listing agent presents a possible exception. For if the listing agent does not have to split the sales fee with your buyer's agent, why not "split it" with you.

While the agent may not legally be able to give you a cash kickback, he could pass along the savings to the sellers who then would reduce their price accordingly. For example, say the listing agreement specifies a sales fee of 6 percent of the selling price. You have offered $97,000 tops. The seller's bottom dollar is $100,000, which after paying a $6,000 sales fee will leave a net of $94,000. If the agent gives up 3 percent of the fee that would have gone to your buyer's agent, the sellers can meet your price without losing anything from their net of $94,000. Because now, they'll pay a sales commission of around $3,000 instead of $6,000. You, the sellers, and the agent benefit.

A second possible reason to work with a listing agent is to obtain information about the sellers. When you're trying to negotiate a bargain price, you must learn all you can about the sellers' personal situation, their finances, their motivation for selling, and anything else that might help you structure an offer that will gain their approval.

In today's litigation climate, you may find that listing agents are more tight-lipped than they used to be. Still, it doesn't hurt to ask. And in many instance, it's actually in the sellers' interests for their agent to at least disclose enough information to tempt a buyer into making an offer. If the sellers really need to sell, an honest admission often sets the stage for productive negotiations.

Agents: Summing Up. Most experienced real estate investors buy their properties through real estate agents. Although on occasion, they might save some money by dealing directly with property owners, they would also lose a great deal of time and valuable help. So most investors delegate the legwork to someone who knows their requirements, knows how to find properties, and knows how to push a deal through to closing. Top real estate agents are out talking to buyers, sellers, investors, lenders, politicians, merchants, employers, and government agencies, every day, all day. Put one of these agents to work for you and you may be offered more good deals than you could ever hope to buy.

The Information Highway

In addition to driving neighborhoods, you can now cruise the information highway to look for properties. America On-Line, CompuServe, and Prodigy now list properties for sale and many providers of realty services. Also, the World Wide Web on the Internet includes a rapidly growing number of home pages that post properties for sale. In Dallas, Texas, in what may be an emerging trend, property buyers (or browsers) can directly access the Realtors' MLS through their personal computers.

There is also a budding entrepreneurial industry of network providers who are accumulating specialized listings of everything from foreclosures to distressed properties to FSBOs (for sale by owners). Going on-line you can locate investors looking for money—or money looking for properties. Virtually all real estate information that in the past has been available from Realtors, public records, newspaper ads, newsletters, and other sources is now (or soon will be) accessible to anyone with a PC.

Or, maybe you won't even need a PC. Consumer electronic companies are working hard to develop and market "Internet information appliances" that will sell for less than $400. These devices will operate without hard discs or built-in software. Instead, they will be able to pull software and any needed data or information right off the Internet for display through the home television set. Acorn Computers, Inc., is already shipping its version at a retail price of $399.

Nobody today knows exactly where technology will lead us tomorrow. But within a short period (2 or 3 years?), some form of electronic shopping for real estate almost certainly will make the MLS book an obsolete artifact.

Will Realtors Become Obsolete, Too?   The ongoing revolution in information technology has not escaped the attention of organized real estate groups. The question is repeatedly asked, "Since the primary stock in trade of real estate agents is information, will anyone need a Realtor when prospective buyers and sellers can communicate directly with each other over the information highway?" Most agents believe the answer to that question is yes for two reasons.

First, much of the information, knowledge, and assistance Realtors provide is personal, informal, analytical, and creative. Information technology hasn't yet been able to replace these human characteristics.

Second, Realtors aren't standing around watching the World Wide Web pass them by. They have created their own on-line network called RIN (Realtors Information Network). Technologically sophisticated Realtors are using RIN and advanced software designs to prepare reports for prospective buyers that detail and map out neighborhoods, population demographics, home prices, school districts, property tax records, environmental hazards, and many other statistical and geographic data that can assist home buyers and real estate investors.

While access to most of the RIN data is limited to Realtors who subscribe to this service (the Blue Network), the system also includes a consumer access portion (the Green Network) which is linked into other major on-line networks. Through the Green network, buyers can review selected properties from 2 to 3 million advertisements. Although not yet available, in the future RIN may permit you to use video technology to do a "virtual" walk-through of such properties.

Will the Information Highway Make Buying Easier?   In one sense, the information highway could make buying properties easier, but buying *bargain-priced* properties more difficult. As information becomes more widely dispersed and less costly to obtain, sellers may be less likely to underprice their properties (as I did with my Dallas house while I was living in Palo Alto). Also property owners who need to cut their price to sell quickly will be able to simultaneously inform literally thousands actually (millions) of potential buyers. With greater market exposure, bargain-priced houses may sell faster and with smaller discounts.

On the other hand, astute investors may actually find it easier to locate bargains. If the information networks homogenize market data, run-of-the-mill investors will simply act on that data as it is presented. As the stock market illustrates, a greater flow of information encourages and accents fads. The stocks of popular companies or investors get bid up beyond reason. Other currently out-of-favor companies become undervalued.

Warren Buffett, the titan of stock market investors, built his $10 billion net worth by applying the principles of *value investing*—not by following "market trends" and popularly held notions. With or without the information highway, you can build your real estate wealth in a similar manner.

Always critically examine conventional wisdom. Look at market information from a variety of perspectives. Constantly ask yourself what does this fact mean for the future? Focus on property and neighborhood details, make reasoned interpretations. Discipline your intellect to apply the value principles explained in Chapters 3 and 4. Remember, you find and create good deals through work, intelligence, and creativity. Yes, information is important. But without effort and intelligence, information is worth no more than yesterday's newspaper. Keep these lessons in mind, and like Warren Buffett, you will stand head and shoulders above most other investors who obsess over information but are strangers to knowledge and insight.

SELLER DISCLOSURES

When buying property, quite often what you see is not all that you get. That house you bought at a bargain price may not seem like such a great deal after you learn the roof leaks, the foundation is crumbling, and termites are eating away the floor joists. Moreover, if the next-door neighbors behave like an unruly mob of loud ruffians, you also may find that you can't keep your property occupied with quality, rent-paying tenants.

As a first line of defense against such unwanted surprise, you must thoroughly inspect the property, talk to existing tenants, walk the neighborhood, and make sure you're working with a knowledgeable and trustworthy real estate agent. As a second line of defense before you buy, get the property checked out by a property inspector, a structural engineer, a pest control expert, or other specialists who can attest to the condition of the property. And third, ask the seller to complete a seller's disclosure statement.

The Disclosure Revolution

As briefly mentioned earlier in this chapter, most states now require sellers to complete a seller's disclosure statement that lists and explains all *known* problems or defects that may plague the property. But even if your state doesn't yet mandate seller disclosure, you still should obtain a disclosure form (most major realty firms keep blank copies on hand) and ask the sellers to fill it out. However, in reviewing a completed disclosure statement, keep in mind the following:

- Sellers are not required to disclose facts or conditions of which they are unaware.

- The disclosure is a statement of the past, not a guarantee of the future. By completing the statement, the seller is not warranting the condition of the property.

- Many questions require somewhat subjective answers. Are playing children a neighborhood "noise" problem? Is a planned street widening an "adverse" condition?

- Disclosure statements may *not* require the sellers to disclose conditions that are readily observable.

- Pay close attention to any seller (or agent) statements that begin, "I believe," "I think," "as far as we know," and other similar hedges. Don't accept these answers as conclusive. Make a written note to follow up with further inquiry or inspection.

Seller disclosure statements materially reduce the chance for unwelcome surprise after you take possession of a property. But even so, you still should try to independently check out the property to satisfy yourself that you know what you are buying.

Income Properties

Most seller disclosure laws only apply to one- to four-family properties. If you're buying a larger income property, the seller may not be required by law to fill out a disclosure statement. If in this situation the seller refuses, you should offset this additional risk by downwardly adjusting the top price you're willing to pay.

Additionally, with income properties make sure you verify rental income and operating expenses. As a minimum, ask the sellers to sign a statement whereby they swear that the income and expense figures that they have reported to you are true and factual. Beware of owners who put friends, relatives, and employees into their buildings at inflated rent levels. These tenants don't really pay the rents stated (or if they do, they get kickbacks in cash or other benefits), but their signed leases sure look attractive to unsuspecting prospective buyers.

SUMMARY

Keep in mind that the great majority of real estate deals involve negotiated transactions. Every buyer or seller has his or her own personal needs, pressures, time constraints, financial worries, capabilities, interests, knowledge, and objectives. In addition, every property has its own unique physical features, location, and potential for improvement. Moreover, past real estate sales prices are frequently difficult to interpret without full information about the parties involved and the property itself.

To use the jargon of the economists, all these facts mean that real estate trades in an imperfect, inefficient market. As a result, those investors with superior information, knowledge, and perseverance can earn superior returns. Shop carefully, compare properties systematically, seek out motivated or uninformed sellers, and negotiate skillfully. You will be able to find and create many great deals that offer a bargain price, bargain financing, or maybe both.

6 FORECLOSURES: HOW TO BUY REAL ESTATE IN DISTRESS

Another potentially profitable real estate investment is distressed property that is in foreclosure. One of the best buys I ever made was a 19-unit apartment building in foreclosure. Distressed property has always been a popular investment, especially since it is often sold substantially below market value.

Real estate in foreclosure is a specialized market. There is a lack of detailed material written about the subject, yet most people know about this market. Foreclosure property, then, can be compared with the famous lost Dutchman Mine: investors are aware of it, but few know where it is.

Fortunately for me, years ago while I was working as an appraiser for a large savings and loan, I was transferred to the REO department because of my previous property management experience. REO means "Real Estate Owned," which is real property owned by an institutional lender and acquired through foreclosure proceedings.

This particular savings and loan needed all the help it could get in the REO department because numerous bad loans on its books had been acquired during the time when this lender became so large (35 branches) by buying out smaller companies. The department eventually had to foreclose on over $4 million worth of real estate, and it was my job to manage and dispose of this property. This inventory consisted of dilapidated single-family homes in the midst of riot-torn Watts and 40-unit, rat-infested apartment buildings without windows or parking facilities. Trust me when I say these properties were a landlord's nightmare. But we eventually sold most of them.

From this experience I would like to make two key points about distressed real estate:

1.   If you plan to buy foreclosure property, remember . . . what you see is not always what you get. Property that has been foreclosed on is usually in more disrepair than first meets the eye. It is unlikely that the owner who is delinquent in loan payments has been adequately maintaining the building for several years. The last thing a financially troubled owner does is get behind in loan payments (but the first thing he'll do is defer maintenance), otherwise he knows that the lender will foreclose. Often the maintenance is neglected for years before the actual act of foreclosure occurs.

Therefore, if you happen to be interested in a foreclosed property, estimate the costs to repair the building, then, just to be safe, add another 25 percent to cover you for any unforeseen expenses that are likely to show up after you own the building.

2.   Do not, under any circumstances, leave a vacant property unattended for an extended period. While I worked for the savings and loan, we made sure that the day we took title to a property was the day that that particular property was secured. Regardless of the quality of the neighborhood, we immediately sent out a crew to board up all windows and doors. Without properly securing the property, we would have risked viewing the following scenario: In one night I have seen an entire house gutted from top to bottom; vandals ripped all the plumbing fixtures from the walls, including tubs and sinks, built-ins, anything even of marginal value. A glass windowpane without a protective board over it is a likely target for a stone-throwing juvenile delinquent. Teenage gangs have been known to make unsecured houses their operational headquarters, and the homeless have also been known to hole up for months in such accommodations.

Finally, when you buy a boarded-up foreclosure, if the property is unattended, keep all the boards up until you finish with the renovation. If you purchase the property unboarded and you plan to renovate it without anyone living there, board it up until it's renovated and you have tenants for it. This way you'll avoid the frustration of witnessing all your renovation destroyed by malicious people.

THE THREE PHASES OF FORECLOSURE

The process of foreclosure goes through three phases, and an investor can purchase the distressed property in any one of these phases.

1. A property owner who defaults (fails to make payments when due) on a loan is notified by the lender that it is initiating legal procedures that will eventually lead to a foreclosure sale.

2. Unless the payments—including late fees and penalties—which are in arrears are made, the property goes up for sale at public auction. The lender who is foreclosing initiates the bidding, usually at the price which represents the lender's financial interest, including late fees and penalties. The highest bidder pays off the loan (in cash) and claims the property.

3. If no one outbids the lender, the property ownership reverts to the lender, and if that lender happens to be a financial institution, the property then becomes REO.

Purchasing real estate during the first phase of foreclosure can often get you a real bargain. However, the many difficulties associated with such property can often lead you to something you never bargained for. There may be liens against the property and you may find that, although you were able to purchase the property quite easily, you must also buy it back from the IRS, county tax assessor, or some other entity that has attached a lien to the property. Unless you do exhaustive research before getting involved in a foreclosure property, you could get stuck having valuable working capital tied up waiting for liens against the property to be cleared up or for a title search to be conducted. In the end, your so-called bargain may cost a lot more than you had contemplated.

Should a property have problems, you automatically assume them when you purchase it. Property purchased during the first phase of foreclosure requires much research and time, and even then you may end up with your funds tied up in escrow for an extended period.

When you purchase property in the second phase—at public auction—you're faced with similar problems, and you must thoroughly investigate the property before you bid. Furthermore, you are required to pay cash for the property.

It is in the third phase—when the institutional lender has title to the property as REO—that the property may emerge as an attractive venture for the investor. But before going any further, you should realize an institutional lender's attitude toward REO: They don't want anything to do with it!

Institutional lenders are in the business to earn money by lending out their funds, and in so doing to earn interest and fees. They take in savings deposits then lend these funds on long-term real estate loans. The property itself is used as collateral to secure the loan against the possibility of default by the borrower. Occasionally they are required to foreclose on a property when a loan goes sour. The property is essentially unwanted. The lender would prefer to sell the REO and use the proceeds to fund another loan; therefore, institutional lenders will usually offer attractive terms to an investor to relieve the institution of the unwanted property once it's on the books as REO.

Acquiring Property in the First Phase

Should you decide to invest in distressed property before the actual foreclosure sale, it will be necessary for you to deal directly with troubled owners. The following procedures are required to be successful:

1. Learn the terminology.
2. Acquaint yourself with the sources.
3. Select a territory in which to operate.
4. Prepare a list of potential acquisitions.
5. Prepare an investment analysis.
6. Meet and negotiate with the owner.
7. Estimate the costs.
8. Gather all the data.
9. Close the deal.

Now we can examine each procedure in more detail.

Learn the Terminology

Investing in foreclosure property is a specialized business. Some of the terms and phrases associated with it are unique and it is imperative that you learn the proper phraseology and procedures so as to portray yourself to property owners as a knowledgeable person. Thus you will function more efficiently and effectively at acquiring worthwhile properties.

What is foreclosure? It is the procedure where property pledged as security for a debt is sold to pay that debt in the event of default in payment and terms. The process of foreclosure varies from state to state throughout America, but the basic procedure is similar nationwide. The primary difference is between states where lenders use a mortgage instrument as security and those states that use a deed of trust.

Mortgages and trust deeds (or deeds of trust) are written instruments that create liens against real property. Should the borrower default on the loan, these instruments allow the lender to sell the secured property to satisfy the loan obligation.

Mortgages.   A mortgage instrument involves two parties: One is referred to as the *mortgagor,* who is the borrower or property owner, and the other as the *mortgagee,* who is the lender. A mortgage has two parts: the *mortgage note,* which is evidence of the debt, an the *mortgage contract,* which is security for the debt. The note promises to personally repay the loan, while the contract promises to convey title of the property to the mortgagee in case of default.

Should the mortgagor fail to make payments, the property can then be sold through foreclosure in a court action. ("Court action" is not required under a deed of trust, and this is the primary difference between the two instruments.) To initiate foreclosure proceedings, the mortgagee must first obtain from the court a foreclosure judgment ordering the sheriff to sell the property to the highest bidder. The property is then put up for sale at public auction.

Once a successful bid is made, the bidder receives from the sheriff a document known as the *certificate of sale.* In some states, the bidder must then hold the certificate for one year. He then receives a deed to the property if the mortgagor does not pay the outstanding debt. In many states, the mortgagor who pays the outstanding debt during this period then retains ownership of the property and the foreclosure sale is nullified. The mortgagor's privilege of redeeming the property during this period is referred to as the mortgagor's *equity of redemption.*

Deed of Trust.   A deed of trust is similar to a mortgage instrument except that an additional third party is involved and the foreclosure period (without court action) is much shorter.

Under a deed of trust, the borrower or property owner is called the *trustor,* and the lender is the *beneficiary.* The intermediate party, whose function is to hold title to the property for the security of the lender, is called the trustee. Should the trustor default on the loan obligation, the subject property will be sold by the trustee at public auction through a "power-of-sale" clause contained in every deed of trust.

Foreclosure is initiated by a *notice of default,* which is recorded by the trustee, with a copy sent to the trustor. After a statutory period such as 3 months, a *notice of sale* is posted on the property, and an advertisement for sale is carried in local newspapers for, say, once a week for 3 weeks. If during this grace period the trustor fails to pay the beneficiary sufficient funds to halt the foreclosure (overdue loan payments plus interest, penalties, and late fees), the sale will be conducted by the trustee. Proceeds from the foreclosure sale are disbursed first to the beneficiary, then to any other lien holders, and then any remainder to the trustor.

The following are additional terms that are often used in connection with foreclosed properties:

- *Assignment of mortgage (or deed of trust).* A written financial document transferring the rights of the beneficiary (mortgagee) under a mortgage or deed of trust to another party.

- *Substitution of trustee.* A written document, usually found on the reverse side of a deed of trust, that transfers trusteeship. Transfers, or substitutions of trustees, are made for reasons of convenience or for better personal service. Legally the beneficiary can also be trustee. The purpose of doing so is to gain control of a trustee sale.

- *Notice of action* (lis pendens). The legal term for a notice that a lawsuit is pending on the subject property is lis pendens (litigation pending). It gives notice that anyone acquiring interest in the subject property after the date of notice may be bound by the outcome of the pending litigation.

  Obviously, you should be concerned when such a notice is attached to a property you're interested in. Unlike most other liens and attachments, a foreclosure sale may not wipe out this pending litigation.

- *Recision.* The act of nullifying the foreclosure procedure, usually because some requirement of due process was violated.

- *Power of sale.* A power-of-sale clause is written into every deed of trust giving the trustee the right to advertise and sell the secured property at public auction should the trustor default on the loan. This clause enables the trustee to sell the secured property without court action. When the sale is completed at the public auction, the trustee will convey title to the purchaser, use the funds from the proceeds to satisfy the beneficiary, then return surplus monies, if any, to the trustor. Once this is accomplished, the trustor is divested of the property.

Acquaint Yourself with the Sources

You have four available sources to learn of properties in various stages of foreclosure.

1. The REO listings of institutional lenders.
2. Legal newspapers (in states where such published notice is required).
3. Fee subscription services that publish defaults and foreclosure sale notices either in newsletters or via computer on-line.
4. The county recorder's office, which records notices relevant to foreclosure.

Services that provide such information vary throughout the country with each state's legal requirements. Some states require that the notice of default be publicized in a legal publication, while many legal newspapers publish such notices routinely as a community service. Further, some companies make available public-record services on a fee-subscription basis. Both the legal publications and the fee-subscription sources obtain their information directly from the county recorder's office. Their published information is rearranged into a less complicated and easier-to-read form. The cost of the convenient fee-subscription service is substantially higher than either that of legal publications or the information available at no cost from the public records or the county recorder.

You also can acquire these data on recorded defaults directly from the county recorder, where this information is recorded daily and is for public use.

Once the default has been recorded and the grace period has elapsed, the notice of sale is published. But this legal notice may not be found at the county recorder's office, because the trustee is usually required only to publish, not to record, this notice. This is where the subscription services, legal newspapers, and local newspapers come into play. They are authorized to publish such notices. In addition, you'll often see these postings on bulletin boards in your county courthouse.

Keep in mind that services which publish notices of default are not liable for the accuracy of the information. You may find incorrect addresses or other incorrect information published by such services. The only data that can be deemed reliable are the actual recordings found in the county recorder's office.

These published services do not state whether the instrument in default is a first, second, or third mortgage. To determine which of the liens is in default, you'll have to make a personal visit to the county recorder's office and look it up yourself.

Occasionally, these legal notices of default omit the exact street address of the property. If this is the case, the correct address can be obtained by consulting the map books available while you're at the county recorder's office. Match the legal description given with the address in the map books.

After you obtain the required information about a distressed property and drive by for a personal inspection of it, you'll note an interesting phenomenon. Property in foreclosure, 99 times out of 100, always has the same appearance. You can literally spot the neglected property a block away. It's probably the only house on the block with a dried-out, unmowed lawn with debris scattered about. You'll probably notice a broken window or two and it probably requires paint. This neglected house, which once was a nice home, stands out in the neighborhood like a sour grapefruit in a crate of fresh red apples.

At one time, the trustee would offer necessary information about the default to the public as a professional courtesy. This service is no longer given so freely, primarily because of the increasing popularity of investing in foreclosures, which has developed into a nuisance for the trustee. Today the trustee is obligated only to provide information regarding date, time, and location of the sale.

Select a Territory in Which to Operate

To be most effective, restrict your operations to a specific area within your city. One appropriate area may be the surrounding neighborhood in which you live. Working within a designated area close to home will make it easier to develop contacts and to ascertain property values. Furthermore, the area you select should have a potential for an increase in property values.

Once you choose the designated territory, begin accumulating information relevant to events occurring in that area. Obtain a large map of the area, then note sales prices of homes, location of schools, and specific streets where resales offer higher value per square foot of house. In addition, note particular areas that show signs of declining value that might be the result of crime, poor land planning, or traffic congestion.

To make your search easier, you might limit your operational zone to an area not to exceed, say, 2,000 homes. Obtain a large map of the area from the county assessor's or county clerk's office. As trends and events occur, note them on your map in pencil. Include positive or negative trends and events that may have an economic impact on your designated area.

After you gain some experience and are somewhat of a specialist in distressed property, you no longer have to confine your activities to single-family residences. Get to know values of multiunit buildings, raw acreage, and office or industrial projects.

Prepare a List of Potential Acquisitions

After you're acquainted with the territory and the sources of distressed property, you can then begin to narrow down the total supply of foreclosures from the information compiled. Start with all available Real Estate Owned from your meetings with REO managers. Then compile available property through the sources mentioned earlier (legal publications, subscription services, and the county recorder's office).

Write down all pertinent data on each property on the Property Information Form (Figure 6.1). This form lists the vital information you need to make a preliminary financial analysis and close the deal successfully.

Additional potential investments can be developed while you're acquainting yourself with the designated territory. If you're alert, you can often spot signs of property that eventually, if not immediately, will be in distress. Run-down homes with debris scattered about are often rented out by absentee landlords and frequently are abandoned by tenants; the absentee landlord should be contacted immediately to procure a sale.

Absentee landlords often board up vacated property, especially in declining neighborhoods, to protect doors and windows from vandals. If you spot a boarded-up house that is not already on your list, find out who the owner is and attempt to make a deal.

Prepare an Investment Analysis

Now that you have listed potential investments, it's time to prepare a financial analysis of those properties deserving further consideration. From the Property Information Form, you can gather more detailed information and an estimate of the property's market value after renovation. Now you're prepared to contact the troubled owner.

Meet and Negotiate with the Owner

Bear in mind that the purpose of your visit to the property is not only to make a good investment but also to maintain a proper attitude which will aid the troubled owner in this distressed situation. If

Lot # _____ Block # _____

Map page # _____

Owner's name: _____

Property address: _____

Phone: (home) _____ (work) _____

Date default action taken: _____ Final date to correct: _____

First Loan Data

Lender's name: _____ Loan #: _____

Type: _____ Is it assumable? _____

Interest rate: _____ Original principal owing: _____

Balance as of: _____ is _____

with monthly payments of _____ and annual taxes of _____

Second Loan Data

Lender's name: _____ Loan #: _____

Type: _____ Is it assumable? _____

Interest rate: _____ Original principal owing: _____

Balance as of: _____ is _____

with monthly payments of _____.

Loan payments in arrears:

First loan $ _____ # of months at _____ _____

Second loan $ _____ # of months at _____ _____

Third loan $ _____ # of months at _____ _____

Total late charges   _____

Total default and foreclosure fees   _____

Grand total of amount in arrears as of _____ _____

(Continued)

Figure 6.1 Property Information Form

Figure 6.1   *(Continued)*

Description of other liens:

1. _____ as of _____ total owing
   including penalties is _____ .

2. _____ as of _____ total owing
   including penalties is _____ .

Sq. footage of livable area _____ Lot size _____

# of bedrooms _____ # of baths _____ Dining _____ Garage _____

Estimated cost to repair interior (describe rooms and work required) ____

_____

_____

Total estimated cost of interior and exterior _____

Property location factors (good, average, below average):

Lot _____ Shopping _____ Public transportation _____

Schools _____ Parks and other _____ Freeways _____

Preliminary cost estimates:

Preliminary cost of all delinquencies   _____

Title and escrow expenses   _____

Loan transfer or origination fee   _____

One month's P&I + taxes and insurance   _____

Cash required for additional   _____

Total cash required to make current   _____

Total interior and exterior repair costs   _____

everything goes according to the plan, the owner will receive cash for some of his or her equity, the person's credit will be salvaged, and you will acquire title to the property.

Refrain from phoning until after you have personally met with the owner. This avoids a brush-off over the phone. A personal visit is not only more businesslike but also allows you to look over the property.

Begin with a simple introduction of who you are and why you're there, suggesting a mood of mutual assistance. Mention that you have discovered through your sources that the property might be for sale. If in fact the property is for sale, you can immediately get into details of the transaction. However, if the owner does not have the property up for sale, a different approach is required.

Time is on your side when you are negotiating to purchase property in foreclosure. Pressure is on the troubled owner to remedy the situation so as not to lose the property and good credit rating. It is to your advantage to mention that, while you're interested in making a good investment for yourself, it will also be a good decision for the owner, who can realize some cash and prevent a serious blemish on his or her credit rating.

During these periods of stress faced by homeowners in foreclosure proceedings, it is important to remember that they often disguise the truth about certain matters. Understandably, the loss of home and property is a horrible event. Therefore it's essential to verify all details about the property.

Should the owner miraculously remedy the troubled financial condition and bring delinquent payments up to date, be happy for the person. But at the same time continue to keep in touch, because now the homeowner is faced with an additional problem: how to keep up with the existing house payments, plus paying back the additional funds borrowed to cure the initial crisis. Chances are, if you continue to stay in touch, the opportunity to buy the home will arise once again.

The following are suggested approaches to stimulate negotiations with an owner in foreclosure:

- "If you'll allow me to make a complete financial analysis of the property, I can be back within 24 hours with a firm offer that will solve your current dilemma."
- "My purpose in being here is to offer you cash for your equity, which you would lose in a foreclosure sale. Therefore, by

working with me you can salvage your credit, drive away much better off, and start all over again."

- "Please allow me to see the documents on your home. Do you have the deed, the title policy, and the loan payment record?"

As a professional investor, you can act faster and offer more results to a troubled owner than anyone else. Do not be concerned with cosmetic damage to the house as long as it is structurally sound, for a run-down house usually presents more opportunity for the investor. In fact, the more run-down, the better. Every defect offers profitable opportunity to the shrewd distressed property investor and renovator.

Each defect must be noted; then an accurate cost estimate must be made to correct such defects. Your deal with the owner will then be made on the basis of the estimated repair cost, plus a reasonable profit for you. Once you acquire the property, make every effort to renovate it within the budget arrived at under your repair-cost estimate.

You need not be a jack-of-all-trades and repair everything yourself, but it's essential to be accurate at discovering problems and at knowing how much it will cost to repair each problem. You must know what the renovated home will sell for in that particular neighborhood. It is obviously poor judgment to invest in a property if the total cost of renovation plus purchase price is greater than its subsequent market value.

By thoroughly checking out the entire property, carefully analyzing it, then honestly evaluating the sales price once renovation is complete, you can feel confident that your risk has been minimized and you will realize a profit.

If you've analyzed the numbers carefully and the total costs of renovation and acquisition are more than the resale value, don't entirely abandon the project. Go back to the troubled owner and reopen negotiations. Point out that it is necessary for you to make a reasonable profit, but if you're still unable to arrive at a reasonable transaction, then, indeed, it's time to look elsewhere.

Estimate the Costs

The least complicated way to acquire property in foreclosure during the first phase is to assume the existing loan while making up all loan payments in arrears, then purchasing the deed, and finally taking possession of the property. Very neat and clean. But, more often than not, you'll be required to involve yourself with details that tend to complicate matters involving distressed property. To simplify matters, use the Cost-Estimate Form (Figure 6.2). It considers all the items relevant to investing in foreclosed property.

Purchasing the Deed.   Check the *grant deed* or the *title insurance policy* to make certain that the owner has the property vested in his name. If neither of these is available, check the escrow documents from when the owner purchased the property. If none of these is available for verification, check the official records at the county recorder's office.

You must know the difference between a grant deed and a *quit-claim deed.* An owner of real property who issues a grant deed is warranting that he has marketable title to the property. A quitclaim deed simply releases any interest the grantor may have in the property. A grantor who has no interest in the property is not releasing anything. For example, assume you give me a quitclaim deed on the Golden Gate Bridge. If you have no interest whatsoever in the Golden Gate Bridge, you're simply executing a statement saying, "I convey to you all the rights I have in the Golden Gate Bridge, whatever those rights might be." Obviously, since you have no ownership interest in it, you're conveying nothing. If you accept a quitclaim deed, it's imperative that the grantor have an interest to convey to you.

Real Estate Taxes.   Delinquent property taxes assessed against a property, occasionally up to three years' worth, could have accumulated, as is often the case when the lender fails to provide for an impound account for hazard insurance and property taxes. With an impound account, the borrower pays a prorated share of these expenses monthly into a trust, out of which the lender pays these expenses.

The best method of making sure that property taxes have been paid is to get information directly from the county tax collector. All that is required is a phone call to the county tax collector, with you providing the complete legal description of the property.

Bonds and Assessments.   Most frequently, bonds and assessments show up in less than fully developed areas where sewers and sidewalks have not been completed. To fund the construction of sewers and sidewalks, the county will usually assess property owners for the construction of these items and attach a lien to the property until the amount assessed is paid in full. Be careful of these liens against real property because they do not always appear on the title report. These liens are recorded against real property and are written in a way to allow the homeowner to pay them off monthly over a period of years.

Address _____

Cost of acquiring property:

    Purchasing the deed $ _____

    Delinquent taxes   _____

    Bonds and assessments   _____

    Delinquencies on first loan:

    _____ months at $ _____

    Total late charges and fees   _____

    Advances   _____

    Pay off second loan (include all

    delinquencies, advances, and fees)   _____

Preliminary cost estimates:

    Title and escrow expenses   _____

    Loan transfer or origination fee   _____

    1 month P&I + taxes and insurance _____

Total cash to purchase   _____

    Balance of all loans after purchase _____

    Other encumbrances   _____

Total property cost (before repairs) _____

Cost of repairs needed:

    Paint_____ Plumbing _____ Roof_____

    Electrical_____ Termite_____ Fencing _____

    Landscape _____ Floors _____ Carpeting _____

    Wallpaper _____ Fixtures _____ Hardware _____

Total cost of repairs   _____

Total property cost (after repairs)   _____

Figure 6.2   Cost-Estimate Form

However, in some states, these liens may have to be paid in full when the property is sold.

To verify whether any bonds or assessments are outstanding, or to learn any other details about them, call the tax department or the county treasurer.

Existing Loans.   Probably the most important consideration in purchasing a property in foreclosure is the existing loans. Because there are a variety of ways the property could have been financed, you should be familiar with all the methods described in Chapter 2.

Non-qual assumable VA and FHA loans offer the foreclosure investor much more flexibility than do conventional loans, since they require no credit qualification, and the interest rate cannot be changed. Unfortunately, very few of these simple assumptions are now available through foreclosure.

If the property you're interested in has a conventional loan, then it is likely the new borrower will have to qualify and the interest rate may be adjusted upward if the current market is higher. Furthermore, conventional lenders may charge a 1 to 2 percent assumption fee on the unpaid balance.

Conventional lenders vary substantially in their methods of handling delinquencies. However, they're normally stricter than government-backed loans on the matter of allowing a borrower in a conventional loan to fall in arrears. On conventional loans, they usually record a notice of default if the borrower falls 60 to 90 days overdue. On VA and FHA loans, they're usually more patient with the borrower and may often wait up to 6 months before recording a notice of default.

In addition, conventional lenders normally charge higher late charges on a delinquent loan than lenders who fund VA and FHA loans. These late charges can run as high as 5 percent of each monthly payment.

The law provides the borrower a period for reinstatement of the loan, which means that within a certain period the loan can be brought up to date. This occurs when all monies in arrears, including all penalties, are paid in full. This period of reinstatement varies from state to state.

A homeowner who allows a home loan to go into arrears to the extent that the lender records a notice of default and foreclosure proceedings begin is now required to pay a sizable sum to make the loan current. Because the amount is substantial, the troubled homeowner will likely have to sell or allow the lender to foreclose.

Therefore, when you invest in a distressed property that has a VA or FHA loan attached, you'll benefit from the following:

- In some (increasingly rare) cases, you may assume the existing loan without credit qualification.
- You can assume the existing loan for a small incidental fee.
- You won't be charged a prepayment penalty when you sell.
- The interest rate remains unchanged throughout the term of the loan.
- You can allow the next buyer to assume all the same benefits, or you can wrap the existing loan at a higher rate of interest.

If you invest in a distressed property that has a conventional loan with a due-on-sale clause, you'll have to:

- Be prepared to qualify for the loan.
- Pay a higher rate of interest if the existing rate is below the current market rate.
- Possibly pay a prepayment penalty fee when you sell.
- Be prepared to pay off the existing loan, or get a new loan if the lender decides to exercise the due-on-sale clause.

Gather All the Data

What do you do after having located a property that appears profitable, made an appraisal, evaluated all the costs to renovate, and arrived at a price range you're prepared to offer? The next step is to answer the following questions:

- What are the names of the mortgagor and mortgagee or the trustor, trustee, and beneficiary?
- Is the loan in foreclosure a first or a second loan?
- When was it recorded, and for how much?
- If the loan in foreclosure is a second, who holds the first?
- Is the loan a conventional loan or a government-backed loan that may be assumed?
- How much is each loan in arrears?

- Are the taxes delinquent, and if so, how much?
- Are there other liens against the property?

You can find answers to most of these questions in the office of the county recorder where the subject property is located. All documentation involving real property is kept open to the public in the county recorder's office.

The recording process dates back to before the American Civil War. Now, as then, it provides the public a notice of important documentation in regard to real property. When it's time to verify pertinent data on a property in foreclosure, note that a first mortgage recorded has priority over liens recorded subsequently. In other words, except for tax liens, the first in line is first in right to any claims on the property.

The actual recording is done by the county recorder. When a mortgage is recorded, the county recorder will file a copy of that mortgage in the official records.

Close the Deal

Before the troubled owner is prepared to make a deal, you must set the stage. The owner has to be convinced that you are a knowledgeable specialist in the field of real estate. You accomplish this during the initial stage of negotiations by demonstrating knowledge about the foreclosure process and by showing the owner what will happen if the borrower's default is not remedied. The owner is also informed that it's too late to list the property for sale, and possibly too late to borrow additional funds. You can add that selling to you now can remedy the pending crisis. The owner will salvage a decent credit rating, and leave the burdensome property behind while departing with some cash in hand. Otherwise, the lender will acquire the property and everything will be lost, including credit rating and accumulated equity.

Troubled owners appreciate the investor's interest and feel relieved that help is near at hand. These troubled homeowners feel they can speak openly because their financial difficulties are now out in the open. For that reason, they no longer feel someone is intruding and have no need to disguise their troubled financial condition. Troubled owners are prepared to act. Time is running out, and they have been alerted to the consequences. An owner in this predicament knows that you can remedy the situation better and faster than anyone else, and he or she is prepared to make a deal.

Price Declines with Time.   Time is money. In no other realm of business can this fact be stated more emphatically. During the typical span of a foreclosure proceeding in which a property can still be reinstated under a deed of trust, offers to the troubled owner will vary. Offers during the first 30 days would be considerably higher than those made during the final days of redemption.

By the time a property reaches the final days of the reinstatement period, additional unpaid monthly installments have accumulated, and attorney fees and late charges have increased. Alert the owner to these facts; the quicker the owner acts to resolve the problem, the more he or she will get out of it.

Verification of Names.   It's imperative that the seller's name on the deed be correct—if his legal signature is Anthony Thomas Jones, it's necessary to put down the name exactly as it is shown, not Tony Jones, or A. T. Jones—and that all the information on the deed transferring the property exactly match that on the original deed the seller received from the lending institution.

Once the owner has signed over the grant deed, you should immediately have it recorded at the county recorder. Later you can submit a copy of the grant deed to the title company. Immediately recording the grant deed assures you that liens recorded against your newly acquired property will be invalid, as long as they're recorded after your name, and not before. However, contract or liens for unpaid work recently performed at the property may be valid even after you take title if they are filed within the allowable statutory period. So, if the owner has hired out any work within the past 6 months, verify that no outstanding bills remain unpaid.

Finally, ask the seller to sign an Equity-Purchase Agreement, which will give you, the buyer, control of the property (see Figure 6.3). This will be accomplished after completing final negotiations and checking that the property is actually transferable. Then the grant deed can be executed, signed by the seller, and properly notarized. Again, be sure that the grant deed is filled out exactly as the previous grant deed was. Once the grant deed is properly executed and notarized, take it to the county recorder to be recorded. The discussion in this chapter and the sample Equity-Purchase Agreement Form are general in nature. So, before you enter into an agreement to buy property in foreclosure, make sure you consult with legal counsel in your area to learn your local laws and customs.

Investing in foreclosures during the first and second phases requires much tedious research and preparation to complete a successful

(This agreement is to be filled out in triplicate, with one copy issued to the seller, to the buyer, and one to the buyer's file records.)

Date _____ Address of subject property _____

_____ Lot# _____ Block _____ Tract _____

Lender's name _____ Loan # _____

Seller's name _____ Address _____

Buyer's name _____ Address _____

     Buyer agrees to purchase and seller agrees to sell the equity in the above-described real property for the sum of _____ net to the seller, receipt of which is hereby acknowledged by the seller.

     Buyer agrees to take title to the above-described property subject only to existing liens and encumbrances not exceeding _____

_____.

     It is also mutually agreed that: _____

_____.

     Seller is to deliver possession of subject property on or before _____, 19_____ . If the property is not transferred to the buyer by the above-agreed date, all payments and further expenses incurred from that date forward shall be deducted from the net amount due to the seller at closing.

     Buyer will pay all escrow, title, loan transfer, and closing costs.

     Monthly payments on the above loan including, principal, interest, taxes, and insurance are _____ .

     Impounds for taxes and insurance, if any, are to be assigned without charge to buyer. Any unforeseen shortage in the impound account will be deducted from the net amount due seller at closing.

     Seller will immediately execute a grant deed in favor of buyer, which the buyer has the right to record.

     Seller will not remove any fixtures from the real property and will leave premises reasonably clean and in good condition.

     Seller will allow buyer access to property for any reason prior to date of possession of the buyer.

     Buyer will pay the balance of all funds due seller at closing after checking title, liens, and that the property is vacated.

     Additions to this agreement: _____

_____

Buyer _____ Seller _____

Buyer _____ Seller _____

Figure 6.3 Equity-Purchase Agreement

transaction. A much less complicated source of foreclosure property is available through institutional lenders, as described in the following section on REOs.

INVESTING IN BANK REAL ESTATE OWNED (REO)

Bank REO is real property that has been foreclosed on and that failed to sell to a private bidder (investor) at public auction. The financial institution now owns the property. One aspect of REO which makes it an attractive investment when compared with property in the other two phases of foreclosure is that all clouds on the title have been removed through the act of foreclosure. In the process of acquiring the property, the financial institution has eradicated all outstanding liens. Except for possibly back taxes which have yet to be paid, the lender now owns the property free and clear. If you acquire REO, it will be free of encumbrances, except for deferred maintenance. You can usually buy REO property with a small down payment. The purchase can sometimes be financed at interest rates below conventional rates, especially since the lender is also the seller and eager to unload the property. Sometimes it's possible to defer the monthly principal and interest payments up to 6 months, which will allow you time to renovate the property and generate some income before the first payment is due. Also, it's not uncommon for the REO buyer to acquire an additional loan to pay for the cost of such renovation. And the financial institution will usually absorb most of the closing costs.

The important thing to remember is that everything is very negotiable. Nothing is carved in stone regarding standard procedure for the buying and selling of lender REO.

To succeed at investing in REO, you need a special technique for dealing with lender REO managers. This is not an easy task because there has been a great deal of public interest in foreclosure property in the past 10 years, and potential REO buyers are constantly inquiring.

Typically, an inquiry from an uninformed member of the public is in the form of phone calls to REO departments, asking if any foreclosure property is available. So many people phone in that REO departments may now give a stock reply: "Sorry, nothing available."

REO will usually be sold through an established real estate broker and to known investors who are personal friends with whom the lender has done business before. Thus, if you want to invest in REO, approach the REO department in person and meet its manager. Establishing such a personal relationship is the only viable way to have access to these potential bargains.

SUMMARY

Each year nationwide, hundreds of thousands of property owners hit financial hard times. Divorce, job loss, accident, illness, business failure, and other setbacks render people unable to make their mortgage payments. Rather than effectively deal with their problems as soon as default is imminent, most owners hang on too long hoping for a miracle to bail them out. Since miracles are rare, most of these people end up staring foreclosure in the face.

At that point, you may be able to help them salvage their credit record and part of their home equity and at the same time secure a bargain for yourself. Faced with pressures of time and money, these property owners may be willing to accept a quick no-hassle sale at a price less than market value.

However, there's no magic system for successfully buying a property from owners approaching foreclosure. They are typically contending with myriad financial troubles, personal anguish, and indecisiveness due to depression. In addition, they probably have already been attacked by innumerable foreclosure vultures, speculators, bank lawyers, and recent attendees of "get-rich-quick" foreclosure seminars. These owners are living with the shame of a very public failure. For all these reasons and more, they are not easy people to deal with.

Nevertheless, if you can develop a sensitive, empathetic, problem-solving approach with someone suffering foreclosure, you may be able to come up with a win-win agreement. Just keep in mind that more than likely you won't be the only investor who pays them a visit. A "Here's my offer. Take it or leave it" approach will undoubtedly antagonize the owners and will not distinguish you from a dozen other potential buyers. So develop your offer and negotiations to preserve what little may be left of the owner's dignity and self-esteem. Perhaps you can share personal information about setbacks you have lived through. Above all, emphasize win-win outcomes. Dire straits or not, no one wants their home (property) stolen from them.

Absent success in dealing directly with owners, you can bid for properties at the foreclosure auction. However, because of potential title problems and because generally to execute your bid you must pay for the property in cash, we do not recommend this approach for most beginning investors. In fact, because of these drawbacks, most foreclosed properties are not bought by investors. They are "bought" by the lender who has prosecuted the foreclosure action.

Once a foreclosed property becomes a bank REO, you may then enter into negotiations with the lender—either directly or through the lender's real estate agent. Since lenders do not want to hold property, let alone manage it, they are usually eager to sell at a favorable price or on favorable terms. Moreover, every day a lender holds a property, it is losing interest earnings on the money tied up in the house. And, if the house is vacant, the lender runs the risk that the property will be wrecked or pillaged by vandals.

As you can see, lenders (if they're smart) will do whatever they can to get an REO off their books. Through skillful negotiating, you can turn a lender's problem into your investment advantage.

7 HUD/VA HOMES AND OTHER SOURCES OF BARGAINS

In addition to REO property held by local banks, savings and loans, credit unions, and other mortgage lenders, two of the largest sources of REOs are the U.S. Department of Housing and Urban Development (HUD homes) and the Department of Veterans Affairs (VA homes). Other sources of potential bargains that you might investigate in your area include REOs of Fannie Mae, Freddie Mac, and private mortgage insurers; probate sales; sheriff's sales; and private auctions.

HUD HOMES AND OTHER PROPERTIES

Each year the FHA (Federal Housing Administration), a division of HUD, insures hundreds of thousands of new mortgage loans. (Nationwide, the total number of outstanding FHA mortgages runs into the millions.) Typically, FHA loans are originated by banks, savings institutions, mortgage bankers, mortgage brokers, credit unions, and other types of mortgage lenders.

If borrowers fail to repay these lenders as scheduled, the lender may foreclose the property and take possession of the property. However, rather that retain the property in its own REO portfolio, because of the FHA mortgage insurance, the lender turns in a claim to HUD (FHA's parent). HUD then pays the lender the amount due under its mortgage insurance coverage and acquires the foreclosed property. In turn, HUD next puts the property (along with all the others it has acquired in similar fashion) up for sale to the general public.

In some cities such as Atlanta, Georgia, HUD has been selling several thousand properties a year. In the San Francisco Bay Area, though, HUD's annual sales may total less than 150 homes. So, depending on where you live, the available selection of HUD properties will vary considerably. Still, every area can be counted on to have at least some HUD homes.

Like all other sources of bargain properties, HUD presents opportunities for investors, but you cannot buy one of these homes blindly and expect to get a great buy. Nevertheless, many investors and home buyers who have done their homework (through neighborhood and property value analysis) have been able to buy properties for substantially less than their market value (after fix-up work).

Also, as is explained in this chapter, HUD only sells its properties through HUD approved licensed real estate agents. In fact, many of these agents make HUD/VA homes their specialty. For example, Memphis realtor Jamiel Rivers has run the following advertisement in the *Memphis Commercial Appeal:*

> I specialize in non-qual equities (assumptions), THDA (Tennessee Housing Development Agency), and HUD & VA foreclosures.

Because HUD homes vary so much in price, condition, and fix-up potential, and because HUD sets detailed bureaucratic buying procedures, you should only deal with a real estate agent who really knows the ins and outs of buying HUD properties. Although HUD is best known for selling houses, you actually may be able to buy any of the following types of HUD properties:

- Vacant lots.
- Single-family detached residences.
- Duplex or two units on one lot.
- Triplex—three units.
- Fourplex—a four-unit building.
- PUD—A Planned Unit Development.
- Condominiums.

Now, let's look more closely at HUD's practices and procedures.

SALES POLICY

HUD sales policy is to sell to anyone regardless of race, color, creed, family status, disability, or sex who can meet the down payment, credit, and certain other requirements. Plus, HUD sells to investors as well as owner occupants.

HUD lists properties for sale on an "open basis" with HUD-approved licensed real estate brokers. Offers to purchase are submitted by brokers on behalf of prospective purchasers, and HUD pays the broker's commission at closing. Showing properties to potential buyers, preparing the HUD-9548 Standard Real Estate Contract and Addenda, and following up on all paperwork required for closing a transaction are the primary responsibilities of the selling broker. Buyers may not submit offers directly to HUD except in circumstances where they cannot obtain the services of a licensed broker.

Buy Property in "As-Is" Condition

All HUD properties are sold as-is, without warranties. There will be no further alterations or additions made by HUD, and no statements or representations made as to the condition of the property will be binding on HUD. It is the buyer's responsibility to determine the condition of the property.

Financing the Sale

HUD properties are listed for sale, either with or without FHA mortgage insurance. For those properties listed "with FHA insurance," the buyer may seek an FHA-insured loan from a private lender and use the mortgage proceeds to buy the home from HUD. For properties listed "without insurance," the terms are all cash to HUD in 30 days, with no contingencies for financing. As a rule, if you do not complete the sale, you lose your earnest money deposit.

Mailing List

Real estate brokers wishing to be placed on the mailing list for the Broker's Information Package to participate in the sales of HUD properties must certify on the Public Information Mailing List Request (HUD-9556) that they will comply with Federal Fair Housing Laws and Affirmative Marketing Regulations. A broker's executed Form

HUD-9556 must be on file at the HUD office before any offer or contract will be accepted from that broker.

Access to Properties

A HUD master key and lock box key can be obtained from any of the Area Management Brokers by HUD-approved sales agents.

BROKER LISTING AND ADVERTISING PROCEDURES

Listings

Local HUD offices mail out weekly new listings of HUD properties directly to brokers on the HUD mailing list. Listings include list price, property description, bid opening date, and deadline date. The listing price of each property is an appraiser's estimate of market value. HUD will accept offers less than the listing price; however, in competitive bid situations, some buyers even offer more than HUD's asking price. Also, HUD's "market value" estimate may be substantially more or less than a property is actually worth. Since HUD sells its properties in as-is condition, whether the property proves to be a good deal depends on how much time, effort, and money a buyer must put into the property. The key to getting a good deal often turns on finding underpriced properties whose repair and renovation costs are actually much less than HUD's estimates.

Broker Advertising

Broker advertising is encouraged by HUD as long as it's done according to the following guidelines:

- Price listed with broker cannot be any price other than the HUD-listed price.
- Broker cannot advertise until the property is officially listed by HUD.
- Context of broker advertising cannot be worded in such a way as to indicate that it is a distress sale.
- Brokers cannot word advertising to indicate that they are the sole source of HUD property data or that they have a favored listing advantage.

- Advertising must include the statement, "Properties are offered for sale to qualified buyers without regard to the buyer's race, color, religion, sex, or national origin."
- All advertising has to comply with the Truth-in-Lending Act.

Generally, rather than advertise specific homes, most agents who specialize in HUD properties advertise their services (as in the preceding example). Since agents do not have exclusive listings on HUD properties, many work primarily to help their buyers get a good deal on a HUD home, not on a specific property. Often buyers bid a number of times before achieving a winning bid.

"For Sale" Signs

No signs or business cards are allowed to be placed in or on the property unless authorized by HUD. Only HUD's "For Sale" sign can be posted on the property. A "Sold" sign may be installed by the selling broker only after the broker is notified of the acceptance of the sales contract.

Open House

Brokers can hold an open house provided HUD receives and approves a letter of request from the broker. The open house is limited to two consecutive days, and property must be on the market at least 15 days before such an open house can be held.

Conflict of Interest

Although most HUD-approved agents will work hard to help you get a good deal, be aware that a potential conflict of interest does arise in the sale of HUD homes. First, if you do not submit a winning bid, your sales agent does not earn a commission. Thus, an unethical agent could pressure you to raise your bid even if the value of the property does not justify a higher price. Second, sales agents may submit bids from competing buyers of the same property. If you bid $80,000, an agent could tell another buyer to bid $80,100 to knock your bid out of consideration. Third, HUD typically pays brokers who submit a winning bid a full 6 percent sales commission, plus on occasion a $500 (or more) selling bonus for designated properties. Again this creates a financial incentive for the agent to push you into bidding high. With these issues in mind, make sure you discuss with an agent the quality of representation and services that agent is willing and able to provide you (see discussion of agents in Chapter 5).

AVAILABLE SALES PROGRAMS

HUD sells properties under two different programs, each of which has different terms and conditions. The following are features of each program.

As-Is Sales—All Cash Transactions

This program offers properties for sale in an unrepaired, or as-is, condition for cash. Under this program, the sale will not be contingent on the buyer's ability to obtain financing. The following conditions apply:

- *Property condition.* The property is unrepaired and currently does not meet HUD's minimum standards for mortgage insurance. In addition, it may have local code violations. HUD does not allow repairs or modifications, even at the buyer's expense, on properties listed as-is before closing.

- *Warranty.* Buyers should be cautioned that HUD provides no warranty, and that the property may have code violations.

- *Financing.* HUD does not permit buyers of uninsurable HUD homes to use the standard FHA 203(b) mortgage insurance program. However, contrary to implication, many "uninsurable" properties may be financed by either owner occupants or investors under the FHA 203(k) rehabilitation loan (see Chapter 2). In addition, regardless of the source of financing (if any), HUD will typically pay some or all of the closing costs incurred in the sale of "uninsurable" HUD properties.

- *Earnest money deposit.* Real estate brokers will collect the earnest money deposit, regardless of the method of sale. Generally, the amount of this deposit will run $500 for properties priced at $50,000 or below, and $1,000 or $2,000 for properties priced above $50,000. Delivery of the deposit, along with sales contract and addenda are the responsibility of the selling broker.

- *Down payment.* When the sale is all cash to HUD there is no down-payment requirement. However, if conventional financing is arranged, then, of course, the lender's requirements apply. With FHA 203(k) financing, owner occupant down payments generally run 3 percent or less of the purchase price. For investors, the down payment is 15 percent of the purchase price.

- *Tie bids.* In the event of tie bids, owner occupants are given priority over investors. Among tying owner occupants, a public drawing will resolve bids determined to be equally advantageous to HUD.

- *Time allowed for closing the sale.* Buyer is allowed 30 days to close the sale after HUD's signing of the sales contract.

Insured Sales—Insured Financing Available

This program offers properties that are eligible for FHA 203(b) mortgage financing. Such financing requires the buyer to have acceptable mortgage credit, and the sale is contingent on the buyer's being approved. FHA-insured financing is not required and buyers may obtain other financing. However, if the buyer uses another form of financing, then the purchase is treated as an "all cash" transaction.

The following conditions apply:

- *Property condition.* Properties that HUD selects for sale with FHA-insured financing appear to meet the intent of HUD's minimum property standards for existing dwellings, based on available repair estimates. Regardless, HUD does not certify that the property is without defects, and buyers are cautioned to verify the property's condition before they submit an offer.

- *Insured with repair escrow.* Sometimes when an as-is HUD property does not meet the standards of an FHA 203(b)-insured loan, it will be listed as "insured with repair escrow." In these cases, HUD will approve the use of the FHA 203(b) program, if within 10 days after closing the buyer brings the property up to FHA standards. To pay for these repairs, HUD typically places part of purchase price (usually less than $5,000) into a repair escrow account the buyers may draw on. If the buyers perform much of the work themselves to save on labor costs, then those savings can be credited toward reducing the buyers' outstanding mortgage balance.

For example, say you buy a HUD home that's been approved for an $80,000 FHA 203(b) mortgage that includes a $5,000 repair escrow. You pay $2,500 for materials and supplies and provide $2,500 of your own labor. If the house passes HUD's inspection, your loan balance will be reduced to $77,500. You will have earned "sweat equity" of $2,500 plus any other instant equity that has resulted because your improvements have boosted the market value of the property above your purchase price. Here's how the numbers might look:

Date of Closing

Purchase price	$82,500
Loan balance	80,000
Equity	2,500

After Value-Boosting Renovation and Sweat Equity Credit

Market value	$87,500
Loan balance	77,500
Equity	10,000

As you can see, bought right and strategically improved, an "insured with escrow" HUD home can help you quickly build home equity wealth.

- *Warranty.* Buyers are cautioned that HUD provides no warranty whatsoever pertaining to condition of the property. Moreover, HUD typically assumes no responsibility for damage that may occur to a property between the date of your winning bid and the date of closing. As a rule, if vandals break in, trash the house, and steal the furnace, that's the buyer's loss, not HUD's.

- *Disclosures.* Although HUD may provide prospective buyers with a list of needed repairs for each of its properties, do not confuse these lists with seller disclosure statements that often are required by law of most private sellers. Congress has exempted HUD from these state disclosure laws. Along these same lines, buyers usually have almost no chance of winning a lawsuit against HUD for misrepresenting the condition of a property or for failing to disclose known (or unknown) problems or defects.

- *Earnest money deposit.* Real estate brokers usually are required to collect a minimum $500 deposit, or 5 percent of the listing price not to exceed $2,000. Sales of vacant lots require 50 percent of the listing price as a deposit.

- *Down payment.* Ordinarily, with FHA financing, owner-occupant buyers are required a down payment of 3 percent of the list price. Investors are allowed to finance only 85 percent of the sales price. Although these down payment amounts are typical, HUD frequently runs low or no down payment "specials." For example, recently all HUD-owned, FHA-insurable properties throughout the state of Georgia were being financed under either FHA 203(b) or FHA 203(k) with just $300 down. Usually, though, down payment specials only apply to owner occupants. Check with HUD-approved sales agents in your area to see what deals HUD may be offering.

- *Time allowed for closing the sale.* The buyer is responsible for making sure that loan application information and verifications are received by HUD as soon as possible after acceptance of the offer. Generally, the sale must be closed within 60 days after HUD's acceptance of the offer.

- *Other incentives.* In addition to low or no down payment specials, HUD local offices may also run other types of incentive programs for buyers of HUD properties. For example, to encourage quick closings in Indianapolis, HUD was offering a $2,000 early closing bonus (less than 30 days) to investors and owner occupants. In Chicago, HUD had offered a renters' rebate up to $1,000 to renters who buy a HUD home for owner occupancy. In Boston, HUD was recently offering a 5 percent purchase price credit on certain designated properties, a $250 bonus to buyers who had arranged a lender's preapproval, and a $675 early closing bonus (less than 45 days). In Baltimore, the early closing bonus was $900, but settlement had to occur within 15 days of contract acceptance. On occasion, to reduce its inventory of unsold homes, HUD offers "clearance sales" at deep discounts. Several years ago in Houston, HUD ran a huge "turkey day" sale on Thanksgiving.

  As you can see, HUD authorizes its regional and local offices to modify (loosen) HUD's overall financial requirements. If HUD properties are accumulating unsold in Chicago, for instance, you can bet that HUD will increase buyer incentives for its Chicago-area homes. Similarly, when sales are booming in a given city and HUD has relatively few properties available, HUD is not only reluctant to offer incentives, but it may refuse to accept bids at less than a property's list price. Generally, you can drive the best deal on HUD properties in down markets. But regardless of the market, it's always worth your time to at least investigate the HUD opportunities that may be available in your area.

- *Owner occupants versus investors.* HUD biases its sale of properties toward owner occupants. As a rule, investors may be offered less favorable terms of financing and fewer incentives. In addition, often investors are precluded from bidding on some properties until after owner occupants have been given first chance to submit an acceptable bid. Also, HUD may offer some properties as "affordable homes" or "homes in revitalized areas." For these properties, HUD may offer low-to-moderate-income buyers or not-for-profit community housing groups particularly attractive terms not available to the general public.

PROCEDURES FOR BIDDING

HUD properties are offered for sale on a competitive-bid basis. Should the property fail to generate a bid, or if all the bids are rejected, then the listing period will be extended for a specified time. Appropriately marked and sealed envelopes are used for offers submitted under this procedure (these forms vary in each region, so call your local HUD office for information on the correct form).

HUD accepts those bids that produce the greatest net proceeds to HUD. Greatest net return is calculated by deducting from the bid price (1) the dollar amount of financing or sales incentives that the buyer requests; and (2) the sales commission HUD agrees to pay.

For as-is sales without insured financing, the deduction figure contains the sales commission and financing costs that are paid by HUD. Closing agent fee, deed recording fees, and owner's title policy are not included in the deduction.

For as-is sales with insured financing available, the deduction figure contains the sum of the sales commission and an amount that the buyer will expect HUD to pay toward the closing costs. At buyer's request, HUD will pay for loan-origination fees, discount points, and a credit report. HUD will not pay costs that in HUD's judgment are not reasonable or customary.

Selling brokers are required to prepare HUD-9548 Sales Contract showing the sum of costs the buyer expects HUD to pay and deducting this total from bid price to determine net return to HUD.

Closing of the sale will be conducted by HUD's closing agents, one of whom will be assigned to each sale. HUD will pay the closing agent's fee. The cost of this fee is not to be included in the calculation of the best-offer deduction on the addendum to the sales contract.

Bid Example

As an example, let's assume that a property is listed for $50,000 on an insured-sale basis. HUD receives two bids on this particular property. The following example illustrates how HUD determines which of the two offers it will accept:

Bid 1, a selling broker investing for himself:

Bid price	$50,000
Deduction (credit report)	50
Net to HUD	$49,500

Bid 2, an owner-occupant buyer:

Bid price	$52,000
Deduction (commission, loan fees, and closing costs)	5,300
Net to HUD	$46,700

In this illustration, the greatest net return to HUD came from bid 1, although bid 2 offered more for the property. Bidder 2 requested that HUD pay the 6 percent sales commission of $3,120 and $2,180 in loan fees and closing costs, for a total deduction of $5,300. Bidder 1 is requesting HUD to pay $50 for a credit report; however he does not request HUD to pay for financing costs. Also, Bidder 1 is a real estate broker, and in this case he elects to waive his commission, thus improving the competitiveness of his bid.

To help prospective buyers improve the net to HUD, some real estate agents voluntarily reduce their sales commissions, or where legal, offer to rebate part of their commission to their buyers. Even if an agent doesn't volunteer this fee reduction, you can still ask for it. Especially where your bid price is low, a reduced commission may give your bid the competitive edge.

Bid Period

Generally, most HUD offices will accept sealed bids from prospective buyers beginning the day after the property is listed. The bid cutoff date is indicated on the listing; however, HUD reserves the right to change the bid period.

Sealed-Bid Envelope

Figure 7.1 shows a sample bid envelope. *Each individual envelope is to contain only one bid.* Bids are required to be in sealed envelopes, with the following information on the outside:

- Name and address of selling broker.
- "SEALED BID—DO NOT OPEN." This statement is to be prominently displayed in the lower right-hand corner.
- Address of the property and FHA case number on the lower left-hand corner of the envelope.
- Date of bid opening.

Ace Realty Company
3985 Elm Street
Las Vegas, NV 89107

                          Dept. of Housing & Urban Development
                          Address of your local HUD office
                          where bids are accepted goes here.

Bid opening date: June 1, 1987
FHA # 367-754948-201
457 Main St   SEALED BID
Las Vegas, NV 89118
Mike Smith (Buyer) owner occupant   DO NOT OPEN

Figure 7.1   Sample of Sealed-Bid Envelope

- Name of buyer and whether he is an "investor" or "owner occupant." If the buyer is not distinguished between the two, the bid will be treated as though from an investor.
- If the bid pertains to an "extended listing period," prominently note this expression on the envelope.

The Bid

The formal bid is to be completed on Form HUD-9548 Sales Contract. Attached to it is the addendum completed by the selling broker. The addendum contains the following information: property address, amount of the bid, requested total amount of selling costs to be paid by HUD, and the net to HUD after the deduction of these selling costs. Also indicate on the bid whether the buyer is an investor or owner occupant.

To establish the highest bid received, those bids containing other than whole dollar amounts will be reduced to the nearest whole dollar amount. *Do not submit earnest money deposit with the bid.*

Bid Deadline

Bids must be in that particular HUD office by a specified time on the advertised cutoff date unless otherwise indicated in the listing. *Bids must be hand delivered.*

Opening of Bids

The day after the deadline for submitting bids is usually the day most HUD offices conduct the bid opening. The opening of bids is a public event, and the time and place are announced in the weekly listings.

Winning Bid

The winning bid is that which provides the greatest net return to HUD after considering the bid price and cost to HUD. Bids may be accepted that are less than stated list price. The winning bid is announced at the bid opening and the representing broker is immediately notified. He will then be required to submit within one working day all sales documents and earnest money to the respective escrow closing agent.

Should the required documents from the winning broker fail to reach the escrow closing agent within the specified time, the bid will automatically be rejected. In the event only one offer is received by HUD and the representing broker fails to comply, the property will be relisted.

Submission of Sales Package

Include the following forms:

- Standard Retail Sales Contract HUD-9548, complete 5 parts.
- Original and 4 copies of Addendum 21 Net Sheet.
- Original and 4 copies of Addendum 18 Earnest Money Certification.

HUD requires that all submitted forms be typed or printed legibly. Furthermore, the earnest money collected by the representing broker must be in the form of a cashier's check or money order made out to the broker.

Bids submitted under the "extended listing period" shall remain available for sale for three working days from the date of regular bid opening. Bids submitted under this procedure are to be marked "Extended Listing Period" and are to include the appropriate forms listed previously.

The highest net bid, provided it is acceptable to HUD, will be formally accepted on this same date. If identical net bids are received, a drawing of lots will be conducted on all cash sales. And the owner-occupant offer will receive priority over the investor offer.

ACCEPTANCE AND APPROVAL OF SALES CONTRACTS

Acceptance of all offers will be announced by a HUD official at the time of bid opening. At that time, copies of the Sales Contract, Net Sheet, and Earnest Money Certification will be handed over to the broker representing the winning bid. The broker must then submit these copies along with the Earnest Money Deposit to the respective title company within one working day. Failure to comply within the allotted time will cause the offer to be voided and the Earnest Money Deposit to be forfeited while the property is relisted.

On acceptance of an as-is, all cash transaction, the buyer is required to close the sale within 30 days. If the closing does not occur within this time, the Earnest Money Deposit will be forfeited to HUD.

On acceptance of an as-is with insured financing transaction, it is important that the buyer and lender immediately get copies of the Sales Contract so as to secure financing. The buyer has the responsibility to get financing from a HUD-approved lender and is required to close the sale within 60 days. It is the lender's responsibility to submit a complete credit package to HUD as soon as possible. If the closing does not occur within 60 days, the Earnest Money Deposit will be forfeited to HUD.

Payment of Broker

Broker's commission will be paid from the sale proceeds at the time of closing. Sales commission to the broker is 6 percent of sales price (or less, if the agent accepts a fee reduction).

Extension of Closing

In the event of unforeseen circumstances preventing the escrow from closing within the prescribed time frame, the broker, on behalf of the buyer, may ask HUD to extend the closing date of escrow. The appropriate form is "Request For Extension of Closing Date and Fee Certification." This request also incorporates the fee certification, currently at $13.50 per day, which can be granted for 15 days maximum. Before these requests for extensions can be implemented, they must be approved by a HUD official.

Cancellation of Transaction

Should a transaction be canceled, the Notice of Cancellation will be forthcoming from the title company. This can only occur after HUD's review and determination to cancel.

Mortgage Credit Approval

A firm commitment will be sent by HUD to the title company and their Mortgage Credit Branch will send a firm commitment to the lender as well. No other notifications will be issued by HUD. It is the broker's responsibility, on receipt of the closing instructions, to notify the buyer that the loan application was approved, and that a closing date has been set.

Mortgage Credit Rejections

Generally, HUD refunds the earnest money deposit to bid-winning owner occupants if they are subsequently turned down for their mortgage loan when attempting to buy an "insured" or "insured with escrow" HUD home. However, to avoid (or at least reduce) this problem, many HUD offices are now recommending (or requiring) that buyers submit a lender preapproval letter with their contract offer.

Furthermore on cash as-is properties, owner-occupant buyers who fail to close because they can't arrange financing (or for any other reason) generally lose their deposits. Similarly, investors who after winning a bid fail to close their intended purchase on *any* property typically forfeit their deposit. The only exceptions to this policy are instances of "great hardship," which must be petitioned and are reviewed by HUD on a case-by-case basis. To be safe and minimize postbid uncertainty, try to get your financing lined up before you submit your offer to buy a HUD property.

Multiple Offers

Brokers are allowed to submit offers from different buyers on the same property.

- *Owner-occupant buyers.* In some HUD regions, brokers may submit bids by the same owner-occupant buyer on several properties subject to the same bid period. If all of the offers submitted by a single buyer are on properties that others have also bid on, the first bid from that buyer accepted as highest eliminates the rest of the person's bids from consideration.

- *Investors.* Brokers may also submit offers by the same investor on numerous properties subject to the same bid period. Should one of the offers submitted by the investor submitting several offers be the only one received on a particular property, its acceptance does not eliminate the other offers from consideration.

Bidding Integrity

HUD does not permit prospective buyers and brokers to engage in practices designated to reduce the dollar return to HUD. In the event such practices are discovered, they will be referred to the Office of Inspector General for investigation. An example of such practice is the submission by one person of several offers under different names (usually names of other family members) to purchase the same property at different bid amounts.

SALES CLOSING

Broker's Role

Throughout the preclosing process winning brokers must help buyers overcome any difficulties encountered with HUD. Submission of information from the buyer should be prompt so as to avoid unnecessary delays. Contact with the HUD sales staff to resolve any problems should be made by the broker, not the buyer. All telephone calls to HUD from the buyer will be referred to the broker.

Buyer

Other than the down payment, the buyer is required to pay at closing: prorated taxes, mortgage insurance premium, prepaid interest, home owner fees, and any other costs above those which HUD has agreed to pay. The broker should fully explain to the buyer all financial requirements regarding HUD home purchases at the time of initial application.

Extensions

HUD will consider a request for extension of closing date which does not exceed 15 days. An extension fee of $13.50 per day is charged and payable at time of request. This amount is made payable to the respective title company and must be certified funds.

Obtaining Financing

It is solely the buyer's responsibility to obtain financing for all sales.

Time to Close

Sales closing of an as-is, all cash transaction, must be accomplished within 30 calendar days of HUD's acceptance of the sales contract.

Sales closing of an as-is, with insured financing transaction, must be accomplished within 60 days of HUD's acceptance of the sales contract.

Closing Agent

HUD will assign a closing agent to conduct each sale. The assigned closing agent will notify the broker of the location, date, and time of closing.

FHA MORTGAGE INSURANCE PROGRAMS AVAILABLE

The FHA has several programs available to finance HUD homes listed under the Insured Sale Program. A buyer can obtain an FHA loan from an institutional lender and use the loan proceeds to buy property from HUD. FHA-insured financing is available under any of the following four programs:

Section 203(b) Mortgage

This is the most common and popular 30-year, adjustable or fixed-rate mortgage. Under current law, all newly originated FHA loans may be assumed by subsequent purchasers of the property as long as they meet FHA's qualifying standards.

Section 245: Graduated Payment Mortgage (GPM)

This loan program offers the borrower lower monthly payments initially, but they gradually increase over the term of the loan. Down-payment requirements may be higher than Section 203(b) requirements; however, this program allows the borrower to qualify at lower income levels. This program takes into consideration the borrower's future income growth potential and the ability or inability to handle higher loan payments in the future.

Note that under a GPM "negative amortization" occurs, which means that during the early life of the loan, the borrower will actually owe more than originally borrowed. (This is the opposite effect of a standard "amortizing" loan, which reduces the outstanding principal as each payment is made.)

Five payment plans are available under the Graduated Payment Mortgage program. They are:

Plan I   Monthly mortgage payments increase 2.5 percent each year for five years.

Plan II   Monthly mortgage payments increase 5 percent each year for five years.

Plan III   Monthly mortgage payments increase 7.5 percent each year for five years. (This plan is the most popular because it has the lowest initial monthly payment.)

Plan IV   Monthly mortgage payments increase 2 percent each year for 10 years.

Plan V   Monthly mortgage payments increase 3 percent each year for 10 years.

Section 245(a): Growing Equity Mortgage (GEM)

Under this loan program, scheduled increases in monthly payments during the early years are applied directly to principal reduction. Therefore, unlike the GPM, there is no interest deferral or negative amortization associated with a GEM. As a result, GEMs have a much shorter term than the GPM or level-payment mortgages. This result of a shorter term substantially reduces the total cost of the loan to the borrower.

The down-payment requirements for the GEM are the same as Section 203(b) requirements. Payment Plans IV and V of the GPM are the only two plans used for the GEM.

For additional details on how to submit offers under these different financing programs, contact a mortgage company or institutional lender of your choice.

Section 203(k)

At present, the only newly originated FHA loan generally available to investors to buy HUD properties is the FHA 203(k) rehabilitation mortgage which is discussed in Chapter 2. Investors may use this loan to purchase insured properties that will be improved at a cost in excess of $5,000, or many "uninsured cash only" properties. Owner occupants may also finance their HUD homes with the 203(k) mortgage.

OTHER PROCEDURES AND POLICIES

Keys to Acquired Properties

HUD properties are equipped with keyed-alike locks, and only one master key is issued to each realty firm registered with HUD. Brokers who are issued a master key from HUD are required to make duplicate copies for their sales staff. Brokers are not to release master keys to prospective buyers, and buyers must be accompanied by a salesperson when entering HUD-owned properties.

No Preshowing before Listing

Showing of HUD properties prior to listing is prohibited.

No Occupancy before Closing

Buyers are prohibited from occupying or working on a HUD property before a sale is closed.

False Certification of Intent to Occupy

Buyers, other than investors, must certify their intent to occupy the purchased property. If FHA mortgage insurance is sought, buyers other than investors are also required to certify their intent to occupy on the Mortgagee's Application and Firm Commitment (HUD-2900). False certifications from buyers are in violation of the law and may result in criminal prosecution.

HUD May Reject an Offer

HUD reserves the right to reject any bid, offer, or contract that is incorrectly drawn or that is submitted as a result of an incorrect listing or other error.

Contract Revision

Should a broker wish to revise a contract offer already submitted, he must deliver a letter of request to HUD. This letter must be signed by the buyer, stating reasons for the revisions together with a revised contract complete with attachments and addenda. After review by HUD, the broker will then be advised on whether such revisions will be allowed.

Cancellation of Bid Offers

Buyers may request cancellation of their bid by submitting a written request, which includes reasons for cancellation, through the selling broker. The request will then be forwarded to HUD by the selling broker along with any other pertinent information not disclosed by the buyer. HUD will then determine whether to refund the earnest money deposit.

In the event a buyer requests cancellation of "All Cash, As-Is" contract at any time, or cancellation of an insured sale after acceptance by HUD, the earnest money deposit will be forfeited to HUD. Exceptions will be made only in extreme cases and require full documentation and submission to HUD for final decision.

Procedures after Closing

All boarded-up material (all wood and hardware) becomes the property of the buyer after closing. It is not HUD's responsibility to remove boarded-up material, regardless of the type of sale. The padlock or lockbox is to be returned to the HUD Area Management Broker by the selling broker as a condition of receiving his or her commission check.

VA HOMES

The U.S. Department of Veterans Affairs guarantees the payment of home loans for eligible veterans. This guarantee permits veterans to finance their home with 100 percent (zero down payment) loans. However, just as FHA-insured mortgages are subject to foreclosure, lenders foreclose when VA borrowers fail to make their payments as scheduled. In return for a loan payoff, lenders turn foreclosed homes over to the Department of Veterans Affairs. The VA next tries to sell these homes as quickly as possible.

VA financing differs from FHA in three notable areas:

1. The VA guarantees single-family home mortgages up to $184,000; whereas depending on the area of the country, FHA maximum home loans (not including two- to four-family properties) range between $75,000 and $151,000. In lower priced cities, some VA-financed properties are upscale homes in quite desirable developments. In addition, because of the higher price range, you can find VA-owned homes even in costly areas such as San Diego and Washington, DC.

2. Most VA homes are offered to the general public with low interest rate financing and down payments of zero to $1,000.

3. The VA tends to welcome investors much more warmly than does FHA. The VA still prefers owner occupants, but it does not exclude some properties from investors as does the FHA. Also, VA has typically offered financing to investors with low interest rates and down payments ranging between zero and 10 percent.

Where Do You Learn about VA Homes?

The VA advertises all its homes in selected local newspapers by the VA. These ads will generally state the Property Management (PM) number which is VA's way of identifying each of its properties, the address of the property, the list (asking) price, down payment (if any), and a room count (e.g., 6-3-2, which would stand for 6 rooms, 3 bedrooms, 2 baths). These ads frequently are placed in the real estate sections of the Sunday paper, but not always. So, you will need to inquire when and where ads are placed in your area.

Like HUD, the VA only sells its properties through licensed real estate agents. In fact, many of the agents who are most knowledgeable about HUD homes frequently deal with VA homes too. Contact one of these specialty agents who follows HUD/VA listings and he or she will gladly take you through any of the homes that you would like to see. Also, on occasion, VA-registered sales agents may sponsor open houses at VA properties. Although any licensed real estate agent may sell a VA home, you're generally wise to work with an agent who is experienced with the ins and outs of VA policies and procedures.

Property Condition and Disclosures

The condition of VA properties runs the gamut from nice to disaster area. As with HUD homes and other foreclosures that stand vacant, vandals sometimes break into VA homes and destroy anything that they can't steal. To inform prospective buyers of a home's problems, VA posts a property inspection record inside each house. In addition, VA requires buyers to initial a checklist of ARs (Acknowledgment Required) that explicitly points out certain enumerated defects in a property such as lead paint, sewage problems, dry rot, termites, and foundation damage.

Nevertheless, even though VA attempts to disclose property defects to potential buyers, it offers no guarantees, warranties, or promises of any other sort about the condition of a VA home. As with HUD properties, buyers of VA homes must accept them as is. If the property turns out worse than anticipated, the buyer bears the expense. On the other hand, if repairs and renovations can be handled in a cost-effective, value-enhancing manner, the buyer can earn substantial profits.

This reemphasizes that buyers *earn* their bargains through superior knowledge of values and astute methods of creative improvement. Foreclosures typically present greater risks than properties purchased through traditional channels; but they also offer the possibility of large and fast rewards.

The Bidding Procedure

Like HUD, VA only accepts buyer bids through licensed real estate agents, and frequently the bidding process is highly competitive. This means that you can't count on getting any house you want. Instead, most investors play a numbers game. They figure how much they can afford to put into each house they're interested in and still turn a good profit. They then submit bids on a variety of properties. For example, one investor submitted 75 bids, yet won the right to buy only two houses. Yet, at the low price he paid, those houses yielded more than enough profit to make the effort worthwhile.

Owner occupants may also submit bids for more than one property; but as soon as a person wins a bid, all other offers from that bidder are dropped from consideration—even if one or more of the bids would have prevailed. You can't win multiple bids and then select the property that looks like the best deal.

Unlike HUD though, the VA accepts backup offers. HUD typically puts bid properties that fail to close back into its list of advertised properties and solicits new bids. In contrast, when a VA bid contract falls though, VA may select the next best offer without putting the property up for bid. In response to this policy, some investors low ball their bids not expecting to win, but rather wanting to get a place in line as a backup offer.

Whose Bid Wins?

Like HUD, VA evaluates bids according to how much money VA will net from the sale after it pays its share of settlement expenses and sales commissions. Therefore, if your real estate agent will accept a fee of less than 6 percent, you can improve the competitiveness of your bid. In addition, though, VA incorporates other factors into its bid-ranking system, including buyer creditworthiness; whether the owner occupant versus investor, veteran versus nonveteran, cash versus VA financing, and compliance with stipulated bid forms and procedures (bids that don't conform to VA rules are tossed out regardless of their financial merits). Overall, VA will select those bids that seem to best serve VA's interests.

VA Finances Its Buyers

As noted earlier, most VA homes are offered with seller financing on very attractive terms. The VA will finance owner occupants and investors with low or no down payment finance plans. Neither owner occupants nor investors need ever to have served in the military or to have acquired VA eligibility in any other way. VA wants to sell its homes as quickly as possible to anyone who will buy them (subject to various relatively easy standards for income, employment, and credit history).

As another advantage, VA loans are assumable (on credit approval) by a subsequent purchaser of the property. As of late 1995, the VA interest rate was 7.5 percent on a 30-year fixed-rate note. VA financing may be prepaid without penalty. To obtain this financing, borrowers pay a $300 application fee and 1 percent of the amount borrowed as a funding fee. Although VA financing is typically available to buyers, buyers may elect to pay cash or arrange their financing elsewhere if they so desire. For example, for VA properties that need substantial rehabilitation, a buyer might choose to finance the purchase and repairs all within an FHA 203(k) loan.

Closings

Once the VA accepts a bid, it expects to move to closing without delay (usually within 45 days). Moreover, the buyer may be given only 22 days to produce any income, employment or other verifications and documentation that VA requests. Failure to meet VA-imposed deadlines may result in automatic rejection of the bid and a forfeiture of the buyer's earnest money deposit (usually $500 to $1,000). Given these time constraints, buyers of VA homes should get with their real estate agents prior to submitting a bid and get their records organized so they can move forward quickly should the VA accept their bid. In fact, in some areas of the country, VA requires buyers to submit their applications for VA financing at the same time they submit their offers.

Summing Up: VA Homes

As with HUD, the Department of Veterans Affairs prices and sells its homes according to somewhat different procedures in different parts of the country. The VA recognizes that local real estate markets vary in strength and in the number of VA homes that remain unsold. Periodically, the VA also places some of its homes into the "no reasonable offer refused" category. Although ferreting out the junk VA properties from those that offer significant potential requires knowledge, effort, and perhaps a little luck, the search can pay off with nice rewards. Kevin Black, a former university student of mine, told me that he recently paid $8,000 for a VA home that needed only cosmetic renovation. Other similar houses in this south Dallas neighborhood were selling in the range of $25,000 to $40,000. Bargains like this don't pop up every day. But they are possible for those who persevere.

FANNIE MAE, FREDDIE MAC, AND PMI FORECLOSURES

Fannie Mae (the Federal National Mortgage Association) and Freddie Mac (the Federal Home Loan Mortgage Corporation) are the two largest players in the nation's secondary mortgage market. These mortgage companies do not make loans directly to home buyers, but they do buy nearly 50 percent of the mortgages that are made by banks, savings and loans, credit unions, and other institutional mortgage lenders. Sometimes when these loans go bad, Fannie (or Freddie) will force the lender to buy back the loan, and the lender ends up with a foreclosed house in its REO portfolio. However, lenders who have followed all of Fannie's (or Freddie's) underwriting guidelines when originally making these mortgages may require Fannie (or Freddie) to take ownership of such foreclosed houses.

Fannie Mae Foreclosures

Although its practices are subject to change, generally Fannie Mae has put its foreclosures in top condition, hired crack agents to sell them at good (though not necessarily bargain) prices, and offered both home buyers and investors low down payment financing. Fannie Mae (or Freddie Mac) foreclosures aren't easy to find. Whereas HUD and VA widely advertise their properties and permit most licensed real estate agents to submit bids on behalf of buyers, Fannie Mae markets its homes through exclusive right-to-sell listing agreements.

Fannie's listing agent may run small classified newspaper ads to promote a specific property, but you will seldom see the big display ads associated with HUD or VA homes. So to find Fannie (or Freddie) foreclosures you will need to telephone real estate brokerage firms and ask for the name of the firms that list the Fannie (or Freddie) foreclosures in the neighborhoods where you are interested in buying. Frequently, these houses are available through any MLS-member brokerage company, but you're better off contacting the listing firm directly. That way you can ask to be called as soon as any new Fannie listings come onto the market.

As caveats, you should note first that although Fannie tries to put its houses in top condition, it offers no guarantees or warranties. Like other sources of foreclosures, Fannie sells as is. If appearances deceive, that probably will be your loss. So while a Fannie house may look good, you still want to get it checked out by qualified structural, environmental, and pest (termite, etc.) inspectors.

Second, although Fannie offers attractive terms of financing, its underwriting (qualifying) standards are tighter than those of FHA or VA. Therefore, ask the real estate agent to prequalify you if you think you might have some past credit or employment problems that could create an obstacle to loan approval.

Private Mortgage Insurers (PMIs)

Most mortgage lenders who offer low down payment real estate loans on one- to four-family properties require their borrowers to buy private mortgage insurance. As discussed in Chapter 2, this insurance protects lenders against loss when insured borrowers fail to make their scheduled mortgage payments. Typically in response to a borrow default, a PMI will take one of two actions: (1) intervene before a foreclosure sale and try to arrange a PMI-assisted presale; or (2) wait for the lender to foreclose, reimburse the lender for its loss, and then take ownership of the foreclosed property and try to sell it. You may be able to work an advantageous deal with a PMI at either of these stages.

At present, eight major PMIs operate throughout the United States. Each of these insurers has its own policies and procedures for dealing with foreclosures in different local markets, and rarely do they widely publicize their foreclosed properties. So, as with Fannie Mae, to locate available PMI foreclosures in your area, you might call a variety of real estate firms and mortgage lenders. Ask whether they know of any PMI-owned properties and how you might go about inspecting and buying one (or more) of them. By getting on the inside track through a diligent search effort, you might discover that, "the deal on the purchase may be excellent," says foreclosure lawyer James Wiedemer.

SHERIFF SALES

Earlier we mentioned that investors could buy foreclosed properties "on the courthouse steps" at the foreclosure auction. Along these same lines, you should also take notice of sheriff sales or other legally mandated involuntary property sales. These include the sale of properties to satisfy tax liens (property, state income, IRS), court judgments resulting from civil lawsuits, and bankruptcy creditors.

Because of the specialized and frequently local nature of these types of forced sales, we can't go into the details here that relate to specific sales procedures or the relative possibilities for finding bargain prices. Here, we're reduced to saying nothing more than "It all depends." Nevertheless, if your goal is to leave no stone unturned in your attempt to locate good deals in your area, you should talk to lawyers, courthouse officials, foreclosure speculators, and others who are in the know about these sales. Since these sales take place under less than ideal marketing methods, it's only natural to expect sale prices that fall substantially below the property's market values.

BUY FROM FORECLOSURE SPECULATORS

Because of the risks involved in buying properties on the courthouse steps, you should proceed with caution until you learn the ropes for buying in these situations. One good way to profit from these sales without actually bidding is to buy from the winning bidder immediately after the sale.

For example, say a foreclosure speculator puts in a winning bid of $65,000 on a property that would appear to have a market value of $95,000 if it were subjected to market amounts of fix-up work and effective marketing through a good real estate brokerage firm. After the sale, you offer the speculator $80,000 (or whatever). To minimize your risk, however, you attach several contingencies to your offer that permit you to get the property thoroughly inspected, evict any holdover owners or tenants, clear up title problems, clear up and seek title insurance, and arrange financing. If the property then checks out satisfactorily, the sale closes and the speculator makes a quick $15,000 (or so) without having to lift a finger. You get the property at a significant discount without having to risk the costly surprises that can turn a "good" foreclosure buy into a heavy loss.

PROBATE AND ESTATE SALES

Estate sales are another source of bargain properties. When owners of properties die, quite frequently the property must be sold to satisfy the deceased's mortgagee and other creditors. Even where the deceased has sufficient wealth in cash to satisfy all claims against the

estate, heirs still normally prefer to sell the property rather than retain ownership themselves.

Probate

Some have suggested caustically, "Probate is a cumbersome and usually unnecessary (but legally required unless prior to death specific
steps are taken to avoid it) process whereby lawyers try to divert as
much money as possible into their own pockets and away from the deceased's intended heirs." Therefore, to buy a property through probate, you generally will have to submit a bid through the estate's
administrator (usually a lawyer) or executor, and then all bids received
will be reviewed by the probate judge assigned to the case. Depending
on local and state laws, the judge may then select a bid for approval, or
reopen the bidding in court proceedings. Because of the legalistic procedures and delays, bidding on probate properties can require stamina
and perseverance. Because the judge has substantial discretion in deciding when and whether to accept a bid, you can never tell for sure
where you stand.

   Robert Irwin tells of a probate property that came up for sale in
an area of $150,000 homes. The probate administrator listed the house
for sale at $115,000. A flurry of bids came in that ranged from a low of
$105,000 up to a high of $118,000. Several months later the judge looked
at the bids, announced the high bid at $118,000, and then solicited ad-
ditional offers. Eventually, the judge approved the sale at a price of
$129,850 to someone who had not even been involved in the first round
of bidding.

   Yet, it must be pointed out, that after all was said and done, the
successful buyer did achieve a bargain price—providing the property
held no unpleasant surprises. (Unlike forced sales "on the courthouse
steps," buyers in probate sales generally can enter and inspect the
properties prior to submitting a bid.) To learn about probate in your
area, contact probate lawyers and also investigate which local newspapers are typically used to announce upcoming probate sales.

Estate Sales

In some situations, an estate's assets need not be dragged through the
probate process. You may be able to buy directly from the heirs or the
executor of the estate. Although it sounds macabre, or perhaps ghoul-
ish, some buyers of estate properties simply follow the obituary notices and then contact heirs directly. To succeed in this approach and

still maintain your credentials as a human being, you would need to develop a sensitive and empathetic demeanor.

Apart from contacting heirs directly, you could also follow the estate sale announcements in the legal notices section of your local newspapers. Estate sales can produce bargains because heirs are often anxious to sell. The may eagerly want the cash so they can put the money to use for their own personal purposes. They may need the cash to pay off a mortgage, other creditor, or estate taxes. Or they may not want to hold a vacant property for an extended period while a top-dollar buyer is sought. Once again, you can see that pressures of time or money can lead to sale prices that fall below a property's market value.

PRIVATE AUCTIONS

Increasingly, many sellers who want to liquidate their properties quickly are turning to private (as opposed to government sponsored) auctions. For example, during the recent economic downturn in California, banks and thrifts were pooling their REOs and jointly auctioning off dozens (sometimes hundreds) of properties at a time. New homebuilders, too, have dramatically increased their use of auctions. Sometimes these involve closeout sales where the builder simply wants to get out of an old project so he can devote time and energy to his next new development. On other occasions, a homebuilder's auction may be a last desperate attempt to raise cash to head off project foreclosure or company bankruptcy. In Dallas recently, a wealthy homeowner tired of trying to sell his $1.6-million-dollar home (listed price) through a brokerage firm and eager to move into his newly built $4.4-million-dollar home, hired an auctioneer. On a pleasant Saturday morning, hundreds of people showed up and, within minutes of the opening bid, the home had a new owner. The winning price: $890,000.

Preparing for an Auction

Attending a major real estate auction can be fun. Often a band is playing, food and drinks are served, and a generally festive mood prevails. The auction company wants to do everything possible to make the potential bidders feel good. But beyond this display of cheer, never forget the auction company is pursuing one chief goal: get every property sold at the highest possible price. Auctioneers get paid a percentage of the day's take, plus perhaps a bonus for exceeding a certain level of sales.

To score a bargain, you must not get so caught up in the festive mood that you abandon your good sense (as some bidders do). Instead, you must go into the auction armed with information and prepared to walk out a winner—not simply a buyer. Here's how you can make that happen:

1. *Always thoroughly inspect a property.* During the weeks before most private auctions, the auction company will schedule open houses at the properties to be sold. If you can't visit an open house, contact a licensed real estate agent and ask for a personal showing. Today, most auction companies will cooperate with realtors, and if an agent brings a winning bidder to the auction, that agent will be paid a 1 or 2 percent sales commission. Sometimes auction properties sell cheap because they are nothing but teardowns waiting for a bulldozer. Or, they may suffer any of a number of other problems. In fact, even new properties aren't necessarily defect free. So, before you bid, first make sure you have verified the property's condition.

2. *Appraise the property carefully.* Even if free of defects, you can't assume value. You must figure it out by studying comps. Along these same lines, don't count on list price to guide you. Buying a property 25 percent below its previous listing price doesn't mean you have bought at 25 percent below the property's market value.

3. *Set your maximum bid price.* Remember, you're looking for a bargain. Market value tells you what a property might sell for if fixed up and marketed by a competent and aggressive real estate agent. Market value *does not* tell you the price you should bid. So, prior to the auction, set your maximum bid price. Don't let the auctioneer or one of his or her "boosters" cajole, excite, bamboozle, or intimidate you into going higher.

4. *Review the paperwork that will accompany a successful bid.* Avoid surprises. Before the auction begins, review the property tax statements, environmental reports, lot survey, legal description, and the sales contract you'll be asked to sign if your bid is accepted.

5. *Learn what type of deed the seller will use to convey the property.* With a general warranty deed, the seller guarantees clear title subject only to certain named exceptions. Other types of deeds

convey fewer title warranties. Don't accept a deed without an understanding of its limitations (liens, easements, encroachments, exceptions, missing heirs, etc.). All in all, title insurance is your best guarantee. If a property's title is uninsurable, consult a real estate attorney to obtain an opinion of title.

6. *How much deposit is required?* To become eligible to bid, you must register with the auction company prior to the auction. Upon showing a cashier's check, you will be issued a bid card which will signify to the auctioneer that you are an approved bidder. Without a bid card, the auctioneer won't recognize your bid. Generally, you will need a separate $2,000 check to hold each property you successfully bid on; but depending on the value of the properties and the policy of the auction company, this amount could run more or less. Sometimes, too, $2,000 will get you a bid card, but holding a property may require anywhere from 5 to 20 percent of the bid price.

7. *Is financing available?* Often auction companies will prearrange financing on some or all of their properties, If so, find out the terms and qualifying standards, if not, determine how much time the auction company will give you to arrange your own financing. Unlike most government-run auctions, private auction companies do not typically expect their successful bidders to pay cash for their properties.

8. *Know auction terminology.* Usually auction properties are either offered absolute or with reserve. If absolute, a property is sold no matter how little the top bidder offers. With a reserve price, the top bid must exceed this amount or the property is pulled out of the auction. On occasion, the owner of a property may "nod" to the auctioneer and approve a bid that does not meet the reserve price.

How to Find Auctions

Most auction companies heavily advertise their upcoming auctions in local and sometimes national newspapers (e.g., the *Wall Street Journal*). Auction companies not only want to attract as many bidders as possible, they want to draw large crowds so they can create a sense of anticipation, of excitement and tension. In addition to advertising, most auction companies will place your name on their mailing lists.

Your local auction companies will be listed in the yellow pages of the telephone directory. However, large-scale local auctions are frequently handled by auction companies that operate nationwide. These include Fisher Auction Company, Hudson & Marshall, JP Kink, Kennedy-Wilson, Larry Latham, NRC Auctions, Ross Dove & Company, and Sheldon Good & Company. Even if you decide not to bid, big auctions are great fun to attend. Try one. You'll like it. Plus, you can't help but learn as you watch the professional auctioneers and investors vie with one another.

SUMMARY

Good deals come in all kinds of packages, and for all sorts of reasons. But whether you're bidding at a private auction or buying an REO from a local mortgage lender, don't jump at an apparent bargain price. Unless you lead a charmed life, always look a gift house in the mouth. Neither a below-market price nor favorable terms of financing automatically puts you into the good deal category. Before you commit, ask these questions:

1. How much is the property's price being discounted from what it would sell for through normal marketing effort? Buyer frenzy, for example, can actually push the price of "bargain properties" above their fair market values.

2. Does the seller guarantee the quality of title? Will a title company insure it? If available, who pays for title insurance? Other closing costs?

3. Can you inspect the property to discover its defects and accurately estimate the cost of repairs? Who bears the responsibility for damage that may occur between the date of your offer and the date of closing?

4. Is the seller obligated to disclose a property's defects? Will the seller allocate an escrow allowance for repairs? Are you buying as is, without legal warranties or representations?

5. Will the seller provide financing? If so, on what terms? What qualifying criteria apply? Who is eligible?

6. Will the seller provide a buyer's warranty that will cover certain specified repair costs after you've bought the property? These "insurance policies" may be purchased from private warranty companies such as Homeowners Marketing Services (HMS).

7. How much deposit is necessary to put the property under contract? Are personal checks accepted? Or must you bring a cashier's or certified check? What other bid procedures apply?

8. If for some reason a transaction doesn't close, do you get your deposit back?

9. Is the property currently occupied by tenants, the previous owner, or squatters? Should any occupants not leave voluntarily, does the law permit you to evict them with a minimum of delay and legal expenses?

10. Weighing the answers to these questions, does the property look like a good deal? Are the price and terms of financing discounted enough to offset any risks of, say, title problems, property condition, or unmovable occupants?

Every type of bargain property is packaged differently. Fannie Mae typically offers homes in good condition, with great financing, and at prices as high as the market will bear. HUD/FHA frequently puts properties on the market that need major renovations. These homes can sell at very steep discounts. For its foreclosed one- to four-family properties, the VA has offered buyers no down payment loans (remember, you do not have to be a veteran to buy a VA foreclosure or to obtain VA financing to buy it). Lender REO departments try to get a good price for their properties, but will usually offer favorable terms of financing and easier qualifying.

You can get a good deal—even a great deal—on a home or income property. But you have to research your market. Talk to realtors who are experienced in the various types of bargain properties. Talk with personnel at HUD and VA. Talk with the REO departments of lenders. Talk with home buyers or investors who have bought from FHA, VA, Fannie Mae, private auctions, or other sources of bargain properties. When it comes to buying bargain properties, knowledge counts. So ask questions, investigate, look at properties, and make offers (bids). With knowledge, perseverance, and maybe some luck, you can knock tens of thousands of dollars off the cost of buying and financing your home or investment properties.

8 MAKING YOUR OFFER

At this point, assume that you're bargain hunting. You're searching the local want ads, talking to Realtors, and cruising neighborhoods looking for a good buy. Finally, you find one that looks promising. It's for sale by owner and has all the ingredients of a good buy (fixer-upper, assumable financing, low interest rate, and the seller appears motivated). Now what do you do? Negotiations begin right here, but wait . . . The most important time you'll ever experience investing in real estate is the next hour you spend talking with the seller. The first person to mention a number loses. If you're patient (probably the greatest virtue of a good negotiator) and wait long enough, the seller will mention a number, thus freely giving up his set position. A motivated seller becomes even more anxious in the presence of a patient negotiator.

The scenario of initial negotiations between you and the seller could begin like this: The seller might say "How much would you give me for the property?" If the buyer replies with a price, he loses. Because, the price the buyer offers might be substantially above what the seller is willing to accept. Consequently the buyer has just overbid for the property.

The information you require from the seller is the lowest price (or best terms) the seller would be willing to accept. But how do you find this out? You could open negotiations by saying, "What is the least amount you will accept for the property?" When the seller replies with a price, you then have a lower figure from which you can bargain further.

Whatever you and the seller finally agree on, you are going to have to live with. So it is absolutely imperative that you be fully informed of comparable values and bargain for a good deal.

Before initial negotiations even begin, you must establish the maximum dollar amount you would pay for the property. This price represents your final offer. Anything above this price is not worth paying, because then the property is no longer a bargain. The price you actually pay should be substantially below your set maximum, for then you've definitely made a good buy.

NEGOTIATING PRICE AND TERMS

Ideally, negotiations are simplified when the seller is highly motivated, wanting to sell for any number of reasons. You already know the seller's asking price and terms. You know, from your homework, that similar homes in the area sell for between $62,000 and $84,000, and the seller is asking $80,000. Now you have a basis to work from.

If at this point the seller initiates negotiations with a statement like, "The least I would take is $75,000 with a $10,000 down payment," you reply with patient silence. Now at least you know the seller is flexible. You could accept this price and terms, but there is definitely more room for negotiation. The seller starts getting anxious and says, "Well, I guess I could take $72,000, but not a penny less." Notice that you haven't said a thing, and already the seller has come down in price from the original asking price of $80,000, to $75,000, and now to $72,000. Let the seller do the talking. The silence is working beautifully and weakening the seller's position.

Bargaining to reach agreement is what negotiating is all about. Unless you're prepared to pay all cash, and at the seller's asking price, you will be bargaining for price and terms. As a general rule, if a seller is firm on price, then negotiate terms. If the seller is firm on terms, then negotiate price. If the seller is firm on neither, then negotiate both. If he or she is firm on both, then start looking for another investment. (Of course, sometimes the asking price is just too good to pass up. This doesn't happen very often, but when it does, grab it with a reluctant demeanor. Don't act as if you think the seller is giving the property away.)

Consider at this point what you can offer the seller in terms of a down payment. A total cash down payment is not always necessary to consummate a sale. Personal property items, such as vehicles, boats, recreational vehicles, furniture, and appliances may be used instead of cash. During earlier negotiations with a seller, you might have noticed that he's going to retire shortly; he might therefore consider a boat or RV for his equity in the property. Or instead of looking for cash he might be looking for income, which means you could offer a secured mortgage for his equity in the property. Your available cash is a valuable asset; it's working capital, and without it you're out of business. Don't forget the principle of leverage: the less you have invested in the property, the more leverage you will have, and the greater your return on investment will be (absent negative cash flows, that is).

MORE NEGOTIATING STRATEGY

The preceding discussion simply gives a quick overview of negotiation basics. To get an even better bargain, here are 15 other negotiation pointers for you to consider:

1. Perhaps the first rule is to find a common ground of interest that can start the negotiation. Don't just jump into talk about price and terms. Use some chitchat to warm up the relationship before you get down to business. Also avoid getting into a competitive spirit or a win-the-game attitude about the negotiation. You win the game when you buy a property at a good price, not when you drive off a potential seller because you failed to yield on a relatively minor point.

2. Recognize that negotiation is a cooperative enterprise; it is an emotional experience with both parties having needs, wants, and feelings that have to be considered.

3. A successful negotiator can feel tension building and can recognize the proper time to stop. Pushing the negotiations for that last dollar in purchase price or that last concession has killed many sales. Also beware of pushing so hard that you destroy the trust of the relationship. If the parties lose trust in each other, negotiations become much more difficult to maintain on a win-win basis.

4. Listen carefully to the objections and arguments of the seller. Try to determine what the person really wants. Often people will seek things in a roundabout fashion; if what a person actually wants is brought forth, the negotiations will tend to be fruitful. Many times, disagreements arise simply because two parties are not communicating what they think they are communicating.

5. Use questions in negotiations as a means of identifying needs. But phrasing the questions can be just as important as knowing what questions to ask. For example, an old story goes that a clergyman asked his superiors "May I smoke while praying?"

Emphatically, permission was denied. Another clergyman, though, used a different approach and asked, "May I pray while I am smoking?" Of course, you know the answer. A skilled negotiator should be adept at phrasing questions to identify a seller's needs without causing offense.

6. Give logical and practical reasons for supporting your particular viewpoint. And similarly, seek explanations for what the seller is wanting.

7. Do not say no too quickly to a proposition of a seller even when you might feel the offer or the proposition of terms is ridiculous. Take time to think about it such that the seller gets the feeling that what he or she has to say is important. Always try to come back with a compromise which seeks a common ground.

8. Keep the seller aware of all the property's negative features. But do so in a way that does not give offense—especially if you are negotiating with a homeowner. Speak in terms of the market, or the features or decorating schemes that tenants prefer. Don't insult the seller's tastes or handiwork. Say, "Tenants usually prefer neutral carpet colors such as beige or earth tones." Don't say, "How could you possibly think I could rent out this place with that awful orange shag and that pink foil wallpaper?"

9. Since many sellers expect to negotiate as opposed to agreeing flat-out with all your demands or requests, leave room in your offer for bargaining. Remember too, that even though price and terms may be the most critical points of negotiation, you should be willing to trade off a somewhat higher price for more favorable terms. Also, possession date, closing date, personal property, repair escrow, and other issues can present trade-off points.

10. Be realistic. You may be functioning in a seller's market or a buyer's market. You may have a very timid seller or a very assertive one; you may meet sellers where the wife is dying to sell the house, but the husband couldn't care less. Each negotiating situation is different. So you must keep in mind the realities of the transaction in which you are participating. This brings us to another important point. Usually the only party that benefits when two or more people are competing to buy an individual property is the seller. Try to avoid getting involved when other buyers are making offers on the same property. The influx of

the additional competition usually makes it too difficult to procure a good buy. Besides, why bother with competition when other potential bargains are available down the street? You only need to locate them.

11. Do not be overeager or too anxious to make concessions. A sophisticated seller will use this advantage in the negotiations.

12. Beware of oral concessions. Oral concessions may tip your hand to higher price or other unfavorable terms that you are willing to accept. Or, they may be used as a ploy to get you to orally commit to a price; once the seller feels you are committed that far, he or she will write the offer up for an even greater amount. Therefore, each time you are offering or counteroffering, make sure the terms are written. Utilize the original contract of sale form and simply change the relevant terms that are subject to the negotiation with each party initialing those changes.

13. Recognize the risks of negotiating. If you reject a counteroffer from a seller, that counteroffer is dead unless the seller chooses to revive it. Similarly, a counteroffer on your part is the same legally as a rejection of the seller's offer. Also, the seller is free to withdraw an offer at any time before your acceptance. Seller or buyer may withdraw an offer without any obligation even if the person has stated that the offer will remain open for a certain period.

14. Stockpile information early. The more you learn about a seller's financial capabilities, family situation, likes and dislikes, priorities, time constraints, available options, previous offers (accepted or rejected), past real estate experiences, perceptions about his property's condition and value, and any other factors that might bear on the transaction, the better you can adapt your offer and negotiating strategy to the sellers' situation and personality. You not only need to secure this information, you need to secure it as early as possible while you are in the relationship-building stage of your negotiations.

   If you jump into a hot and heavy debate over price and terms before you've built an information stockpile, you will generally find that the sellers will clam up. They will guard their disclosures much more closely. As another point, most sellers aren't stupid or naive. They may have their own information agenda in terms of what they would like you to believe. So don't accept the information you obtain as unvarnished fact. Look for nuggets of truth, but also keep your BS detector finely tuned.

15. Control the reference points of the negotiation. All sellers base their asking price and other terms on certain reference points. For example, the seller may believe that "comparable" properties have sold with a gross rent multiplier of 125, or maybe a capitalization rate of 9.5 percent, and will therefore apply those norms to figure a "fair price" for his property.

To negotiate effectively with this seller, then, you must learn the norms the seller is using, and why. Once you gain this information, you next should attempt to explain why those norms aren't applicable and why the reference points you've selected are "fairer" or "more appropriate." For example, you might point out that the comps with cap rates of 9.5 percent are much newer (better location, more stable tenants, better condition, etc.) than the seller's property. In fact, true comp to this property, have typically sold with cap rates in the range of 11 to 11.5 percent.

Similarly, the seller may know the house down the street just sold for $180,000, but does not realize those owners carried back financing at 6.5 percent and included $15,000 worth of personal property in the transaction. Although you can simply adopt the approach, "I'll give you $155,000. That's my top offer. Take it or leave it," it's far more effective for you to first set the reference points on which you and the seller can agree. Get the seller to accept a reference point that's favorable to your offer and you're 80 percent of the way home.

THE PURCHASE OFFER CONTRACT

A sample of a purchase offer contract is shown in Figure 8.1. Although there's no such thing as a "standard" purchase contract, this contract shows some of the more important issues that should be addressed by buyers and sellers when they or their Realtors (or lawyers) are putting their agreement in writing. However, no printed contract will necessarily include every issue that you may want to cover. So our discussion includes several items not directly referred to in this form contract.

Date: _____, 19____

Received from _____ the sum
of _____ dollars ($_____) in the form of [ ] cash [ ]
note [ ] check to be deposited and presented for payment upon acceptance of this offer, to secure and apply toward the purchase of the following described property: _____

_____
commonly known as _____
for the purchase price of _____ dollars ($ _____)
subject to conditions, restrictions, reservations, and rights-of-way now on
record, if any.

Balance of the purchase price is to be paid as follows:

_____
_____
_____
_____
_____
_____
_____
_____

It is hereby agreed:
1. That in the event the Buyer shall fail to complete the purchase as herein
provided, the amount paid herewith may at the option of the Seller, be re-
tained as the consideration for execution of this agreement.
2. That an escrow is to be opened with _____ or other designated escrow agent, who will be instructed to prorate current taxes, insurance, rents, sewer-use fees, and interest (if any) of subject property
to _____ unless otherwise provided herein. The amount of
bond assessments, if any, which is a lien or assessed against said property
to become a lien, shall be [ ] paid by Seller, or [ ] assumed by the Buyer
(check one).
3. That escrow is to close on or before _____, and possession of premises shall be given on _____.
4. That certain items of personal property, attached hereto as Exhibit "A,"
are included in the total purchase price as shown above and are to remain
with the property.
5. That final vesting to be: _____

_____
and that evidence of this title to be in the form of owner's policy of title insurance furnished by _____ and paid for by

Figure 8.1   Deposit Receipt and Offer to Purchase

Figure 8.1   *(Continued)*

the Seller. Escrow fees are customarily charged in the State of
_____ and are to be divided equally between Buyer and
Seller, unless otherwise stated. In the event of the cancellation and/or default of this contract, the defaulting party shall be liable for all fees or
charges incurred when that party is otherwise obligated to perform under
this contract.

6. That this payment of earnest money is made subject to the approval of
the Seller and unless so approved and communicated to the Buyer by
(date-time) _____ and subsequently delivered, the return of
the money, upon demand by the Buyer, shall cancel this agreement without damages to the undersigned. In the event of a dispute between the
parties regarding the disposition of the monies paid pursuant to this contract, the broker of the designated escrow agent holding said monies shall
retain possession of such funds without liability and shall not be obligated
to dispose of those funds until there is an agreement between the parties,
or by court order to do so.

7. That the terms written in this Offer and Receipt constitute the entire
contract between the Buyer and Seller and that no oral statements made by
the broker relative to this transaction shall be construed to be part of this
transaction unless incorporated in writing herein.

8. That we will carry out and fulfill the terms and conditions as specified
herein. If either party fails to do so, he or she agrees to pay the expenses
of enforcing this agreement, including reasonable attorney fees.

9. That Buyer and Seller will give notice to the broker if any changes are
made to this agreement.

By: _____ Agent/Broker

I agree to purchase the above-described property on the terms and conditions herein stated:

_____ (Buyer)
_____ (Buyer)

Seller

I agree to sell the above-described property on the terms and conditions
herein stated, and agree to pay the above-signed broker as commission
$_____, or one-half of the deposit should same be forfeited
by purchaser, provided said amount shall not exceed the full amount of
said commission.

_____ (Seller)
_____ (Seller)

Executed this _____, day of _____,
19_____, at _____ AM/PM.

Names of the Parties

Your agreement should name all parties to the transaction. It is especially important that all owners (sellers) are named and are immediately available to sign off on your offer as soon as agreement has been reached. Be wary of negotiating with a seller whose spouse or partners do not actively join in the negotiations. If they do not agree to sign, you have no deal.

Also, some sellers will maintain that their co-owners will go along with whatever they say. Yet, after you have committed, the seller will come back and claim, "Gee, I'm terribly sorry, but now my partner refuses to sign. He thinks I'm giving the property away. He wants another $25,000, but I've told him I can't renege and change the terms. But he insists. So I'll tell you what, if you can agree to another $10,000, I'll go back to my partner and do my best to convince him to get on board. I'm really sorry, but sometimes my partner gets obstinate and there's little I can do to reason with him."

This ploy is one of the oldest tricks in the book. But it often works. So sellers (and buyers) continue to use it. Just don't be surprised when you have it pulled on you if you've proceeded to negotiate in good faith with someone who doesn't have the legal authority to carry out the agreement.

Property Description

The subject property should be identified by street address and legal description. As an extra precaution, you are normally advised to walk the boundaries of the property with reference to a survey or a plot plan. By walking the boundaries you can note specifically whether there appear to be any encroachments, and you can make sure the size lot(s) you think you're buying is (are) actually the size lot(s) you're getting. Especially where a subject site borders a vacant lot or field, a creek, or other unclear delineation, you can't just assume the lot lines run where they appear to run.

Building Description

Usually, your real estate agreement only needs to identify the lot, not the building. That's because the legal definition of real estate (the surface of the earth) includes all structures permanently attached to the land.

However, if the seller has represented to you that the buildings are of a specific size or are built of certain materials, or of a certain historic date or design, then those features you deem critical (whatever they are) could be written into the property description. In Berkeley, California, buyers sued the sellers of a gracious old home because the sellers had (mistakenly) told the buyers that the home had been designed by Julia Morgan, a famous Bay Area architect of the early 1900s. The buyers claimed that they had not just agreed to buy a house on a specific site. Rather, they had contracted to buy a Julia Morgan house. Without the Julia Morgan imprimatur, the buyers believed they were entitled to damages.

So, if you think you're buying a prewar brownstone, or maybe the house where Grover Cleveland was raised, write it into your agreement. Let the sellers know exactly what you expect to receive in all its critical details. Should your expectations (the seller's representations) prove incorrect, you may have legal recourse for contract recision, damages, or both.

Personal Property

Although the legal definition of real estate applies to land and buildings, it does not necessarily include the personal property that may constitute part of your agreement with the sellers. (Generally, the term personal property refers to any items that are not "permanently" attached to a building or the land.) For example, say the sellers of a fourplex provide window air conditioners, miniblinds, ranges, refrigerators, and ceiling fans for their tenants. If you offer to buy that property, you should expressly list these items in your written purchase contract.

While it's true that some courts have broadened the concept of real estate to include personal property that is "adapted for use" with a specific property, you definitely do not want to count on litigation to force the sellers to convey the personal property that you believed was supposed to be included in the sale. So, to leave no doubt, write it out. Go through every unit of the property and list every item that the sellers might plausibly maintain was not a part of your agreement because it was their "personal property" and therefore not included with the sale of the real estate.

This listing of personal property serves another purpose as well. It requires the sellers to clearly point out what personal property belongs to them and what belongs to the tenant. New property owners who do not obtain an accurate list of the sellers' personal property may later find themselves in dispute with tenants when the tenants claim, "That refrigerator is ours. That junk icebox the landlord provided was carted off to the dump two years ago. We bought this refrigerator from Betty's parents." To be doubly safe, then, ask the tenants to sign off on any list of personal property that you and the sellers prepare.

Price and Financing

When you prepare your offer, make sure you spell out precisely the purchase price of the property and the terms of the financing. List the amounts payable, how payable, when payable, and the interest rate(s). Leave nothing that could not be interpreted easily by a disinterested third party. Leave nothing to be decided at some later date—"Seller agrees to carry back $20,000 on mutually agreeable terms"—does not meet the contractual requirements of specificity.

If you are planning to arrange new financing or even if you are assuming the sellers' mortgage, this same advice holds: Don't leave the amount and terms of financing open to question. Several years ago, I agreed to purchase a property and assume the seller's mortgage. However, just prior to closing, the lender pointed out that they intended to increase the interest rate to the market level.

Fortunately, my contract with the sellers specified the assumption would go forward at the same rate that the sellers were paying. So, rather than lose the sale and risk a lawsuit, the sellers had to buy down the mortgage interest rate to its current level from that rate the lender otherwise would have increased it. Similarly, if you agree to arrange new financing, you want the maximum terms spelled out (e.g., 9 percent, 25 years, 20 percent down). Then, if it turns out that (in good faith) the best loan you can find is at 9.75 percent, 20 years, 25 percent down, you need not complete the purchase and you are entitled to a return of your earnest money deposit.

Earnest Money Deposit

Contrary to popular belief, the validity of your purchase offer does not in any way depend on the amount of your earnest money deposit, or for that matter, whether you've even submitted a deposit. Earnest money is nothing more than your good faith showing that you intend to complete your purchase as agreed. More than anything else, you should choose your deposit amount as part of your negotiation strategy.

Large deposits tend to signal to the sellers that you are a serious buyer. Some investors use large deposits to offset their lowball offers.

Such tactic says to the sellers, "I agree that I may not be offering you as much as you think your property is worth, but you can count on me to buy your property. This large deposit proves that I mean what I say. Wouldn't you rather go for a sure thing now rather than wait for a better offer that may never come along?"

On the other hand, a small deposit communicates that you're financially weak, or maybe that you are simply trying to cheaply tie up the property while you mull over other options. If that is your intent, then use a low or no deposit purchase offer. Generally, though, smart sellers won't accept contracts that don't appear legitimate.

To a certain extent, whether your deposit will be seen as large or small, serious or trifling, depends on local custom. Therefore, gauge the impression you will make with the size of your deposit by the amounts local sellers and realty agents think reasonable for the type of transaction you're entering.

Essentially, just remember that a relatively low deposit reduces your credibility and a relatively high deposit enhances your credibility. Perhaps the best of both worlds is to employ a low deposit strategy and rely on other factors to support your credibility as a buyer (ownership of multiple properties, credit records, net worth, man of integrity). But this trick is difficult to pull off. As a rule, few things speak louder than money.

Quality of Title

Our discussion here can't go into all of the legal intricacies that surround the issue of title quality. For that, you need a local attorney or title insurer. However, recognize that the contract form that is used to write up your purchase agreement will specify the title guarantees and exceptions that will govern your transaction. So make sure you know what these are before you sign your name. This precaution is especially necessary when you buy properties through foreclosure, tax sales, auctions, probate, and other sales where the previous owner in possession of the property is not signing the deed.

Probate judges, sheriffs, and bank officials may not be willing or able to fully warrant title in the same way that the previous owners could. As noted earlier, you can partially overcome this potential quality of title problem by purchasing title insurance. But like all types of insurance, title policies list a variety of limits, exceptions, and conditions. They do not cover everything. Although a title policy offers good protection, you (or your attorney) still must identify any important title risks that remain for you to assume.

Property Condition

Your offer to purchase generally should address the issue of property condition in two ways. First, whenever possible, ask the sellers to complete a property disclosure statement that lists every conceivable problem or defect that now or ever has affected the property or the neighborhood (see Chapter 5). In addition, you want to know what efforts the sellers, previous property owners, or neighbors have implemented to solve the problem. ("Oh yes, we kept blowing fuses, so we just rewired around the fuse box. Now we never have any problems." Or maybe, "Well, there was a crack house down the street, but the Neighborhood Watch group got the police to close it down.") The more you can get the sellers to tell you about the property and the neighborhood, the better you can accurately determine the property's market value.

Second, while you can learn a great deal from he sellers, you can't learn everything you need. Remember, sellers are required to disclose only what they know. As added protection, include a property inspection contingency in your offer that permits you to have the property checked out by one or more specialists who can verify the condition of the plumbing, HVAC, electrical system, roofing, and foundation.

Generally, you can specify in your contingency that repair costs should not exceed some stipulated amount. Ideally, the sellers should bear these expenses, but if you've negotiated a bargain price, then you might assume responsibility. If the estimated repair costs go far beyond your specified amount, your contingency clause should give you the right to terminate the purchase agreement and obtain a refund of your earnest money deposit.

Preclosing Property Damage (Casualty Clause)

Most purchase agreements require the sellers to deliver a subject property to the buyer on the date of closing (or the date of possession) in essentially the same condition as it stood on the date the purchase agreement was signed. Consequently if the property suffers damage (fire, earthquake, vandalism, hurricane, flood) after the purchase contract has been signed, but prior to closing, the sellers must repair the property at their expense. Alternatively, in the event of damage, the sellers may be allowed to terminate your purchase agreement and return the earnest money deposit to you.

However, two points are in order here. First, don't assume the sellers retain responsibility for the property. For example, the purchase contracts of HUD, VA, and Fannie Mae shift this responsibility to their buyers. So, always read your contract language and know what you are agreeing to. Also, if you do assume the risk of preclosing property damage, check with your insurance agent. See if you can secure coverage to protect against property losses during this interim period.

Second, be careful about accepting contract language that gives sellers the right to return your earnest money and terminate the purchase agreement should they find themselves unwilling or unable to repair any property damage. Say you drive a very hard bargain and get the sellers to agree to a price of $235,000. After accepting your offer, they begin to entertain second thoughts. Then along comes another offer at $255,000. Mysteriously, the property suffers a $7,500 fire. Now what will the sellers do?

They may drag their feet on repairs and claim problems settling with their insurer. Then, because they "can't" restore the property to its previous condition in time to meet the scheduled closing date, they cancel your contract and return your deposit. The sellers effectively used the casualty clause to shut you out of your bargain.

To avoid this potential difficulty, cancellation of the contract should be at your option, not the option of the sellers. In addition, the contract could either impose financial penalties on the sellers for failure to repair; or it could simply give you an escrow repair credit to compensate for the amount of the damage.

If you're using bank financing, the bank may refuse to close your loan until the damage has been satisfactorily repaired. That puts you in a Catch-22. You can't repair the property until you close your loan. Yet, the lender won't close your loan until after you've made the repairs. This type of problem doesn't occur often, but if you can anticipate the possibility (risk) ahead of time, you and your attorney can draft a casualty clause that adequately protects your interests.

Closing (Settlement) Costs

Most real estate transactions involve thousands of dollars in closing costs. Title insurance, appraisal, mortgage points, buy-down fees, application fees, lender mandated repairs, lawyers' fees, assumption fees, recording fees, transfer taxes, document stamps, survey, property inspections, escrow fees, real estate brokerage fees, and other expenses can quickly add up to a fair-sized amount of money. So who pays each of these costs? You or the sellers? Local custom frequently dictates. But negotiation can override custom. If the sellers won't drop their price as low as you'd like, shift your emphasis to settlement costs.

Quite often, sellers who won't budge $2,500 from their quoted price will agree to pay that much or more for those settlement costs that traditionally are borne by buyers. (Indeed, a 3-2-1 interest rate buy-down that costs the sellers $5,500 can often prove more advantageous to you than will a $5,500 reduction in price. A reduced interest rate will improve your cash flow and allow you to qualify for a larger mortgage.) When it can work to your benefit, let the sellers have the last word on price. But as a trade-off, insist that they pay all (or most) of the costs of settlement.

Closing/Possession Date(s)

In addition to closing costs, your purchase offer should set a time frame for the date(s) of settlement and possession. When sellers (or buyers) place great importance on a quick (delayed) closing date, that date can play a valuable role in the negotiation process. Perhaps because of a need for ready cash, the sellers might trade off a lower price for a fast settlement. Or maybe for tax reasons, the sellers may prefer to delay settlement for 6 months or more.

Likewise for the date of settlement. The sellers might want a fast closing, but they also may want to keep possession of the property (especially if it's their home) for some period that extends beyond the settlement date. Maybe their new home isn't yet completed; or perhaps they would like to postpone moving until after their children finish out the school term. Their reasons vary, but as a smart negotiator, you should feel the sellers out on their closing/possession preferences. Then use this information to shape your offer. If you're willing to meet the sellers' needs on this issue, they may be more inclined to meet your requests on price or terms.

Leases

If you are buying a property that is occupied by tenants, before you write up your offer, make sure you examine each of their leases. Especially investigate these issues:

1. *Rent levels.* How much do the tenants pay in rents? Are any tenants in arrears? Have any tenants prepaid? How long have the current rent levels been in effect?

2. *Concessions.* Did the tenants receive any concessions for signing their leases such as 1 month free rent, a new 12-speed

bicycle, or any other inducements that would lower the effective amount of rents the tenants are paying? Conversely, are any tenants paying high rents because of a "friendly" agreement with the sellers to help them improve the numbers in the income statement they show prospective buyers.

3. *Utilities.* Do the leases require the tenants to pay all their own utilities? If not, which utilities are the owners obligated to provide?

4. *Yard care, snow removal, other services.* Whose responsibility is it to provide yard care, snow removal, or other necessary services such as small repairs within the rental units? Who pays for garbage and trash pickup? Do the leases obligate the sellers to provide laundry facilities, off-street parking, a clubhouse, exercise room, child-care center, or commuter transportation?

5. *Furniture and appliances.* Check the leases to determine whether the owners are required to provide tenants with furniture or appliances? If so, which ones, what quality, and who is responsible for maintenance, repairs, and replacement?

6. *Duration.* What term is remaining on each of the leases? Do the tenants have the option to renew? If renewed, does the lease (or rent control laws) limit the amount of rent increase that you can impose?

7. *Security deposits.* How much money has the owner collected from the tenants in security deposits? Have any tenants prepaid their last month's rent? Do the sellers have an inspection sheet on file that shows the condition of each of the units at the time the tenants moved in? Have the tenants signed those inspection sheets?

8. *Tenant confirmation.* Whenever feasible, ask the tenants to confirm the terms of the lease as the sellers have represented them. Make sure the seller (or their property manager) have not entered into any side agreements with tenants that would modify or override the terms of the lease. Also, check to learn whether the sellers have orally promised any of the tenants any special services, rent relief, or other dispensations.

When you buy a rental property, you generally must comply with the leases and other agreements that the previous owners have entered into with their tenants. These leases will not only affect the amounts of your rental income and operating expenses, they any also affect your plans for tenant removal, renovation, or property conversion (e.g., converting rentals into condominiums). You own the property, but since the tenants were there first, their leasehold rights may trump your rights of ownership.

Before you write an offer to buy a property occupied by tenants, thoroughly investigate tenant rights and owner obligations. The value of the property is linked directly to the terms of its leases. (As a property owner, your rights to manage the property as you choose are also governed by a variety of laws, rules, and regulations. We discuss these restrictions in Chapter 9.)

Contingency Clauses

Most investors condition their purchase offers with a financing contingency and a variety of inspection contingencies. If the investor can't get financing on the terms specified, or if the condition of the property doesn't meet the investors' standards (as written into the purchase contract), the deal may be called off and the investors are entitled to a return of their earnest money.

Other Contingencies

In addition to the financing and inspection contingencies, though, you may want to condition your purchase offer on any of a number of other issues.

For example, if you plan extensive renovations to the property, you could include a permit contingency. Then, if government doesn't approve your plans, you could pull out of the purchase without penalty. Similarly, you could include contingencies for government approval in any other area where your plans are subject to regulatory review (e.g., converting apartments to condominiums, rehab with rent increases, increasing (decreasing) the number of rental units, eliminating on-site parking, asbestos removal, etc.).

Other types of contingencies may pertain to attorney review, the sale of another property, raising funds from coinvestors, market value appraisal, or even some type of market study (feasibility analysis). Indeed, as a buyer, you can condition your purchase on anything you want ranging from the approval of Uncle Harry to an eclipse of the sun.

Contingencies and Negotiation Strategy

Even though you can condition your offer on anything you want, that doesn't mean the sellers are bound to accept it. They may tell you, "No way are we going to pull our property off the market for several months while you try to put together a syndication deal. Come back and talk to us after you've raised the money." In other words, the more you restrict your offer with contingencies, the less likely the sellers will sign it. On the other hand, a clean "no strings attached" offer may gain the sellers' approval even if your price or terms don't meet their expectation.

When given a choice, sellers prefer firm offers. This means you should choose your contingencies carefully. Consider them as part of your overall negotiating strategy. Combine a large earnest money deposit with an offer that looks certain to close and you may find that your sellers will yield their demands on other important contract issues.

Default Clause

Your contract default clause should spell out what happens if you or the sellers fail to carry through the terms of your purchase agreement. Generally, these clauses should deal with at least four critical areas:

1. Method of resolution.

2. Damages.

3. Specific performance.

4. Who bears the expenses.

Method of Resolution. Although most people think lawsuit when another party breaches an agreement, other options you should consider include mediation and arbitration.

If you pursue a lawsuit, you will almost certainly lose even if a court's decision goes in your favor: You will spend tens of thousands of dollars in legal fees; you will see truth and justice perverted beyond recognition; you will encounter lawyers whose dishonesty and incompetence are exceeded only by their arrogance; you will expose yourself and your private life to public view through intrusive discovery procedures that permit lawyers to question you (admissions, interrogatories, depositions) in minute detail about anything that could *in any way* be related to your character or the issues being litigated; the litigation process, itself, can require you to live through years of anxious uncertainty; and even winning verdicts may be overturned on appeal for purely technical reasons, which then starts the trial process all over again.

Make no mistake about it, lawsuits enrich lawyers, judges, and a myriad of expert witnesses, jury consultants, court reporters, legal secretaries, and photocopying services. They do little to settle disputes in a fair, timely, efficient, and cost-effective manner.

Although mediation and arbitration also have their drawbacks, they are less costly, less adversarial, more timely, and more likely to emphasize substance over procedure. Go out and talk to people who have tried to seek redress through litigation. Then decide for yourself whether your purchase contract should instead prescribe mediation and arbitration as the preferred method of dispute resolution.

Damages. Generally, a party who breaches a real estate contract may be held liable for either compensatory damages or liquidated damages. In theory, compensatory damages are supposed to make the innocent party financially whole. In other words, compensatory damages measure the economic loss you've suffered because the other party didn't live up to their part of the bargain. Translating the theory of compensatory damages into an actual dollar amount is subject to a great deal of legal argument. Because of this indefinite calculation, no one can predict ahead of time how much money a jury might award, nor whether an appellate court will uphold that amount.

To overcome this legal wrangling over how much you (or the sellers) have lost because of the other party's breach, some contracts specify an amount called *liquidated damages.* For example, in the event of buyer default, many real estate contracts permit sellers to retain the earnest money deposit as liquidated damages.

We can't go into all the specific pros and cons of compensatory versus liquidated damages. But as a rule, we favor liquidated damage clauses because (properly written) they reduce ambiguity, and in the case of buyer default, they generally limit liability to a relatively tolerable level (the amount of the earnest money deposit). Nevertheless, if you can locate an experienced real estate attorney who is both competent and trustworthy, you should discuss this issue with him or her. At a minimum, make sure you understand the type of damage clause included in your purchase offer. The more you can use this clause to limit your liability, the better off you will be.

NOTE: *In some states, and in some types of contract cases, winning litigants also may recover damages for emotional distress, but this is seldom the general rule. Similarly, in cases of fraud or other egregious behavior, many states permit awards for punitive damages. In contrast to compensatory damages, punitive damages are intended to punish the losing party for "antisocial" or particularly reprehensible conduct. Again, these issues involve technical interpretations of statutes and case law in light of the facts of a particular transaction.*

Specific Performance.   In addition to a claim for damages, some real estate purchase contracts (or contract laws) give buyers (and less frequently sellers) the right to seek specific performance. This means that through legal proceedings (arbitration, lawsuit), you could force defaulting property owners to sell you their property on the terms written into your purchase contract. Generally, you would pursue this remedy when only a specific property might serve your purposes (e.g., to force the agreed sale of the vacant lot next door to your apartment building so that you can comply with the city's off-street parking requirements).

Who Bears the Expenses?   Whether you pursue mediation, arbitration, or litigation, the dispute resolution process can easily run up thousand of dollars in costs and expenses. Therefore, you could look to your purchase offer contract to see what it says about who pays. Although today we hear a great deal about the benefits of "loser pays" types of laws and contract terms, don't accept such a contract clause without due consideration.

In the first place, you must realize that lawyers lose many cases where their clients are in the right. Lawyers may fail to prepare; they may err in tactics or strategy; or perhaps, key witnesses may come across poorly on the witness stand. In addition, the other side may lie in a convincing and unshakable manner. Even in the best of cases, victory is not assured.

Second, if the other side has far more money power than you, they can hire the best and most expensive counsel to overwhelm and intimidate you and your counsel. With such firepower against you, even if you are willing to face the risk of losing your case, you may not be willing or able to face the opponents' legal expenses of say $50,000 or $100,000 (yes, even small-time litigation can easily run up fees of this size if someone has the money to pay them). Thus, regardless of the merits of your case, the potential (even if unlikely) burden of having to bear the other side's expenses may force you to accept a quite unfavorable settlement.

Again, as in all legal matters, our purpose is to inform not advise. Your purchase contract will include many important clauses that will govern the relationship between you and the sellers. We want you to be aware of these contract provisions before you sign your offer. Only then can you and your counsel rewrite, amend, or strike out unacceptable language. Once you and the sellers commit, you're both bound to the extent of the law. To protect yourself, read through and fashion your offer so you know and understand the full nature of your agreement.

SUMMARY

To a certain extent, good buys are not just found, they are created. Regardless of the sellers' original asking price and terms, smart investors frequently can use astute negotiating to sort through the sellers' real needs and emotions and fashion an agreement that gives both parties a win-win agreement.

Although all negotiations are somewhat personal and situation-specific, in general, you can improve you bargaining skills if you adopt these 15 negotiation pointers:

1. Begin your negotiating on common ground. Look for sources of agreement and common interest.

2. Keep the sellers' needs and feelings constantly in view.

3. Learn to defuse potential blowups and always leave something on the table for the other party to feel good about.

4. Distinguish rhetoric from reality. Don't let words needlessly block a fruitful path of negotiating possibilities.

5. Question the seller, but don't interrogate or cross-examine. Often, it's not what you say, but how you say it that's most critical.

6. Never demand; always explain. Give sound and credible reasons to support your offer.

7. Never reject without due consideration. Show empathy for the sellers' position (even if you believe they're way off base).

8. Keep criticisms of the property as objective as possible. Don't insult the seller's tastes or judgement.

9. "Take it or leave it" demands seldom work. Leave room in your offers and counteroffers for give and take, even if it's on relatively minor issues.

10. Learn the realities of the negotiation situation (e.g., type of market, sellers' motives, other buyers' offers, other available properties).

11. Never appear eager to accept a seller's offer or counteroffer. Make the seller work for your concessions.

12. Beware of making oral concessions to a seller's inquiries. "Let's see it in writing" is generally a good response to a seller's oral counteroffer.

13. Keep negotiating risks in mind. Don't push for all you can get. Don't unnecessarily delay your responses.

14. Stockpile information early. Learn as much as you can before negotiations get hot and heavy.

15. Control the reference points of the negotiation. Try to set the standards for evaluating price, terms, and other contract provisions.

Although purchase offer negotiations tend to place primary emphasis on price and terms, don't forget your contract also will include many other critical details. As a minimum, make sure you have adequately provided for the following 14 areas of concern:

1. Does the contract include the names and signatures of all buyers and sellers?

2. Are the site boundaries accurately delineated?

3. Are the building and other site improvements adequately identified and described?

4. Does the contract or contract addendum list all personal property and fixtures included in the sales price? Should you ask the sellers to prepare a separate bill of sale for these items? Does the seller hold clear title to all the personal property that is to be conveyed?

5. Have the sales price and terms of financing been spelled out so precisely that a disinterested third party could unambiguously interpret the agreement? Should the contract include a financing contingency clause?

6. What is the amount of the earnest money deposit? Under what conditions shall it be returned to the buyers?

7. What types of deed must the sellers use to convey title to the property? Is the title free of encumbrances? If not, what liens, easements, encroachments, or other encumbrances cloud the title? Is the title insurable? What exceptions apply?

8. What is the condition of the property? Have you obtained adequate seller disclosures and professional inspections? Have you negotiated an escrow credit for repairs?

9. Who is responsible for repairing preclosing casualty losses? Under what condition can the buyer (seller) terminate the sales contract as the result of preclosing casualty losses?

10. What share of the settlement costs are borne respectively by the buyers and sellers?

11. What are the date(s) of closing and possession?

12. Have you examined all the leases that apply to the rental units currently occupied by tenants? Has the present owner of the property entered into side agreements with any of the tenants? Have you confirmed with the tenants the rental information provided by the sellers?

13. How many contingency clauses have you included in your offer? Are your contingencies consistent with the negotiation strategy you have adopted?

14. What methods of dispute resolution are provided by your offer? What types of default remedies are available to you and the sellers?

When you enter into negotiations with a seller, keep in mind that you are not negotiating price and terms per se. You are negotiating an agreement that includes many other issues. As a result, you can incorporate a full spectrum of trade-offs and compromises into your negotiations. So if you run into what seems to be a negotiating impasse, don't give up. Just shift your focus. Keep trying to discover some combination of ingredients that will give you and the sellers a win-win agreement.

9 PROPERTY MANAGEMENT: ONE PERSON'S DILEMMA IS ANOTHER'S GOLD MINE

In many cases, real estate is for sale because of improper management skills, which often cause the novice landlord unwarranted headaches and needless frustration. Vacancies, late-paying tenants, vandalism, lack of money to pay the bills on time, all of these items of nuisance push many landlords to sell their properties when it really wasn't necessary. Whatever the case, these negative aspects present a great opportunity for the shrewd investor who has the skills to overcome such problems.

I acquired most of my own property management experience when I worked as a resident manager of a 363-apartment unit. My employer owned and operated 28 similar projects throughout the country, and each property was a syndicated partnership operating profitably with less than 2 percent vacancy nationally. This company operated efficiently (the national average vacancy rate at the time was 5 percent) because it stayed on top of things. Proper maintenance, rent collection, advertising, and so on—all of these functions ran like a precision-made Swiss watch.

The company had its own property management book, in excess of 900 pages, which specifically directed the manager of each project on handling just about any situation that arose. From this experience, I have written a chapter of guidelines to assist anyone in managing residential-income property. It is hardly as thorough as a 900-page text; however, I have tried to present the highlights from what I absorbed. If you own or manage, or plan to own or manage, any form of residential real estate, you would be wise to learn these property management skills. By doing so, you can convert an abused, underrented, high-turnover property into an easy-to-operate, money-making gold mine.

PROPERTY MANAGEMENT COMPANIES

Professional real estate management companies have the responsibility to operate the building, pay all the expenses, keep it rented, maintain it, and send the owner a monthly report of their activities, along with a check for any proceeds. Management companies charge anywhere from 5 to 10 percent of the gross collected rents for their services, depending on the size and character of the building being managed.

If you own one rental, or many individual rentals, it would probably be smart to manage them yourself. However, if you plan to be an absentee landlord and live too far from your rentals to manage them yourself, then you should consider hiring a management company.

Like any other business, property management companies have their share of professionally run companies as well as incompetently run ones; but for the most part, they earn their fees. However, the incompetent companies not only operate inefficiently, but in so doing they also cheat the owners of deserving profits. Just to mention a few larcenous schemes that crooked property managers can use to bilk unsuspecting property owners: invoicing the owner for repair expenses that do not exist; renting out a vacant unit while collecting the rent and declaring to the owner that the unit is still vacant; and charging owners excessive amounts for painting or repairs and keeping the overcharge.

Putting property management into the hands of a professional firm can cost you 10 percent of the gross collected rents and maybe a lot more. No one can operate your properties as efficiently as you can, because you have an important investment to protect and nurture. Besides, if you don't have to, why turn the responsibility of operating your properties over to someone else and take the risk of being ripped off by less than competent managers? If you take the time to learn the skills required to efficiently manage your own properties—and these skills are included in this book—it won't be necessary to hire a management company. In conclusion, about the only time I would consider hiring a management company would be in the event I was no longer physically capable to oversee my properties or when I had to relocate to another area and it was no longer practical to manage them myself.

FURNISHED VERSUS UNFURNISHED UNITS

Generally speaking, if you are renting single-family homes, it will be to your advantage to keep your units unfurnished. If you do supply furniture, of course, you can charge more in rent. However, it is then your responsibility to maintain and insure it from theft and fire damage. The major disadvantage of supplying furniture to your tenants is that it creates more turnover. A rented home completely furnished makes it very easy for tenants to get up and move away. On the other hand, a rented home where the tenants supply their own furnishings requires much more of an effort to move into and out of. Invariably, once tenants take the time, effort, and expense to move all their belongings into a home, they are likely to stay awhile.

On the other hand, certain types of rental units require furniture to maintain a high occupancy rate. If you happen to own single or studio apartments that tend to thrive on more transient clientele, then supplying adequate furnishings would be to your advantage.

APPLIANCES

Items such as refrigerators, washers, and dryers are expensive to purchase and maintain, but offering them as an amenity with your rental unit adds saleability to your rental. It has been my experience that buying these appliances at bargain prices as part of the purchase of the entire property is a wise investment. The responsibility of maintenance and repair of such appliances can mostly be turned over to your tenants by inserting the "no-hassle $100 deductible repair clause" into your rental agreement. This particular clause states that "the first $100 in repair of the rented property, including appliances, is the tenant's responsibility" (more on the no-hassle clause later in this chapter).

If you own a multiunit apartment building with nine or more rental units, you have to consider whether to supply a laundry facility with coin-operated washers and dryers, and whether you should buy or lease the equipment. In smaller buildings, eight rental units or less, supplying washers and dryers would not be economically practical because usage would not pay for the cost to run the machines.

Should you buy the coin-operated equipment, they would probably pay for themselves within two years. That's the good part. However, you have to maintain the equipment and be responsible for acts of vandalism and the unauthorized removal of coins from your machines.

On the other hand, you could lease your laundry equipment from a reputable rental company. This way the leasing company would be responsible for supplying and maintaining the equipment while at the same time collecting coins from the machines. The owner would be responsible for paying the utilities. Often, when you lease laundry equipment, the leasing company retains 60 percent of the gross receipts and remits the remaining 40 percent to the owner. Precautionary measures can be taken so that a responsible person oversees the removal of coins from the rented equipment to help eliminate the temptation of skimming from the coin boxes.

UTILITIES AND TRASH REMOVAL

Tenants who rent single-family residences or condominiums usually have the responsibility to pay for the utilities and trash removal. Most apartment buildings, especially the later models, have separate meters for gas and electricity consumption, and the respective companies bill the individual tenants; however, the owner of the building is responsible for paying the water bill. When separate meters are not available for gas and electricity, the owner must add the cost of these items to the rent. Furthermore, trash removal from multiunit buildings is best paid for by the owner so as to maintain a cleaner building and avoid friction with the tenants as to whose responsibility it is.

MAINTENANCE AND REPAIR TIPS

As an owner of rental property, it is often wise to look more like a hard-working maintenance person when you approach your property than like a chauffeur-driven Rockefeller. You'll find that being discreet will get you your rents faster and will help to deter tenants' petty complaints.

You must keep vacancy rates at a minimum to maintain a maximum income level throughout the operation of all your properties. By adequately maintaining your units and keeping your present tenants satisfied within reason, you can reduce their desire to move elsewhere. Of course, you have no control over a situation when a good paying tenant is requested by his employer to relocate to another city. But you can retain good tenants by properly preserving your buildings. It begins by being reasonable about your tenants' complaints and requests.

It is the owner's responsibility to keep everything in working order (except if you have a "no-hassle" $100 deductible, tenant-pays clause in your lease), and at the same time the tenant should be responsible for not misusing the rental property. Painting, carpet shampooing, and plumbing stoppages are the owner's responsibility, but only when the tenant is giving reasonable care to the property. When a tenant continues to pour grease down the kitchen drain, or allows the kids to plug up the toilet with small toys, the tenant becomes responsible for the costs of repair instead of the owner.

Usually a year elapses before a tenant might begin making requests for any refurbishment of the unit, assuming the unit was in tip-top shape initially. A wall or two may require a new coat of paint, old carpeting may need replacing, or possibly only a carpet cleaning is requested. Whatever the case, at this point you cannot ignore a tenant's request to have something done or you may lose a good paying tenant. If your tenant moves out because you wouldn't paint the kitchen, it will cost you much more than a meager paint job. Not only will you have to prepare the unit for a new tenant, but you will probably experience an extended vacancy loss. Therefore, instead of spending a few dollars for a kitchen paint job, you could spend much more by re-renting the unit to a new tenant. Refurbishing the entire unit for a new tenant could cost $500 or more, plus the additional expense of lost revenue with a vacant unit.

It is essential to the profitability of your total operation—whether it is merely a single rental home or numerous apartment buildings—that you preserve and maintain your properties. By doing so you will not only keep quality tenants satisfied, but your occupancy rate and related profits will be kept at a maximum level as well. Then your properties will reflect their maximum value until they are eventually sold.

When I first started in the rental real estate business, the only experience I had in repairing things was high school Shop 101, which basically taught me how to tighten loose screws and sand wood. As a novice investor, I hired most of the required repair work out to those who knew what they were doing. This was a business expense I did not enjoy paying; so I would watch these professionals and ask plenty of questions. What I didn't learn by watching, I learned by reading, and eventually I learned to do most of the repairs myself. (I recommend the Reader's Digest *Complete Do-It-Yourself Manual*.)

Sweat equity essentially is hard work you do yourself to increase the value of the property. You could hire the repair work out to a professional, but that decision is based on whether you have adequate repair funds available. If you decide to hire a contractor, follow these guidelines:

1. Discuss the job you want done with at least two contractors and get written bids for the work.

2. Talk to your neighbors and ask them if they can recommend someone. Good craftspeople build their business on their reputation, so satisfied customers will be your best guide.

3. Get at least three references from the contractor and check them out. Call each reference and ask whether there were any problems; if there were, were they corrected? Also inquire into whether there were extra charges and whether the work was completed on time.

4. Make sure all work complies with applicable government regulations and permitting requirements.

PAINTING THE INTERIOR

Latex paints are recommended for painting the interior because they are easy to apply, can be thinned and cleaned up with water, dry quickly, and have little or no odor. Flat latex paint is best for interior walls and ceilings. Semigloss or enamel finishes are preferred on woodwork, such as doors, window trim, and baseboards. Semigloss is also preferred on walls of bathrooms and kitchens because it will absorb more scrubbing and abuse than flat paints.

Dark colors tend to make rooms appear smaller. Light colors make rooms appear spacious and airy and will more aptly suit most furniture schemes. Recommended is an off-white color like antique white or beige. If you keep all your rentals painted in one standard color, you'll work more efficiently and avoid the waste of partly filled cans of paint in varied colors.

Careless painting wastes time and makes your investment look messy. Proper preparation is necessary to do a good quality job that will endure over the years. You can save money by purchasing your paint in five-gallon cans instead of single gallons. Start by covering everything with plastic drop cloths to protect the furniture and floor. Next, wash the walls and woodwork with soap and water. (Paint adheres better to a clean, nonglossy finish.) Fill all the cracks and holes by spackling. Let dry and then sand to a smooth finish. Remove all fixtures, electrical plates, and switch covers from surfaces to be painted.

Also cover with masking tape such items as door knobs and glass not meant to be painted. Then apply paint to the ceiling first, then the walls, and finish up with the trim and semigloss work.

PREVENTIVE MAINTENANCE

Owning and operating rental property can at times have its annoyances and headaches. Nevertheless, most of these nuisances can be overcome by keeping up with preventive maintenance and informing your tenants of certain guidelines they should follow.

Stopped-up drains are probably a renter or homeowner's biggest headache. The remedy is to install drain strainers (similar to a screen) in your bathtubs and bathroom sinks. This inexpensive device traps hair and large material before it can start collecting in your pipes. A common cause of drain stoppage is children's toys blocking the drain. If you rent to people with children, inform them of the reason for the drain strainer and request that their children refrain from putting small toys in toilets and bathtubs. Bear in mind the old saying, "An ounce of prevention is worth a pound of cure."

SHOWING AND RENTING VACANT UNITS

This section discusses a step-by-step procedure of taking a vacant unit through all the necessary steps to fill it with a good, qualified, paying tenant. While your particular available unit might be the greatest rental in the city, a vacant house or apartment will remain unoccupied indefinitely if the public doesn't know it is available. On the other hand, if you rent the unit to an undesirable, nonpaying deadbeat, you will soon wish the unit were vacant! The surest way to financial suicide, or at least a migraine, is to continually rent to people who won't pay. There are enough qualified prospects to fill your vacant unit; all you have to do is advertise for them and then properly qualify them.

Advertising

Prospecting for tenants is best accomplished through the vacancy signs and classified advertising in your local newspaper. Vacancy signs must be precise and to the point, qualifying the prospective tenant to a certain degree. For example, "Vacancy, 1-Bedroom, quiet and spacious," or "Vacancy, 2-Bedroom, great building for kids." By stating certain facts about the available unit, you will eliminate a lot of unqualified prospects who are looking for something you don't have. Your signs should be legible and large enough so they can easily be seen from a passing vehicle. Erect your vacancy signs on either side of your building, or post them on the lawn near the busiest street for maximum exposure.

Classified advertising should also be precise and qualifying to eliminate unnecessary calls from unqualified people. The four basic principles of good advertising are "AIDA" ATTENTION: Your headline should attract specific prospects. INTEREST: You should expand the headline and offer a benefit to prospects that makes them read the rest of the ad. DESIRE: With good descriptive copy, make prospects want what you have to offer. ACTION: Ask for action by making it easy for prospects to respond to your offer.

ATTENTION . . . Could be a heading like "Newly Decorated," or "Large 3-Bedroom." The purpose of the attention heading is to get the reader to distinguish your ad from the numerous other ads in the same column. Another example would be "Free Rent for One Month." (This type of ad might be used in a rental market already oversupplied with available units. Free rent would definitely get more attention than the other ads in the same column.)

INTEREST . . . To develop interest, you should offer a benefit such as "2 fireplaces," or "Newly Carpeted," or "Great Ocean View" to entice the reader to finish reading the balance of your advertisement.

DESIRE . . . This will precisely describe what you have to offer. Like "2-Bedroom, children friendly, $675," or "1-Bedroom, small units, pool, $550."

ACTION . . . Can be simply a phone number for prospects to call with inquiries.

Classified advertising is printed under specific headings so there is no need to duplicate information that is already available. In other words, it is not necessary to state that your apartment is unfurnished when your ad is running under the column "Unfurnished Apartments," or stating that your house is downtown when your ad is running under a column denoting specific areas in your city.

Begin your ad with the location, then the type of unit. For example:

NEAR DOWNTOWN . . . 2-bedroom, 2-bath, patio and large fenced yard, children and pets welcome. $870.
Call 555-1212.

By beginning your ad with the location you qualify people right from the start. People look for rentals usually based on areas they want to live in. Anyone looking for a two bedroom in the downtown area will respond to this ad; anyone looking for a three bedroom in a different area will look elsewhere.

After a full description, including any particular features, close the ad with the amount of rent you're charging and a phone number. The amount of rent is important because you again qualify the prospect. If you're charging more for rent than a prospect can afford to pay, the person won't bother to call.

The following was a sample advertisement that proved very effective. It ran in my local newspaper under the section Unfurnished Condominiums For Rent:

> RENT WITH OPTION TO BUY . . . Spring Mt. & Jones, 3-Bedroom, 2-Bath, neat & clean, beautifully landscaped and decorated, w/tennis cts, pool & Jacuzzi. $1,095. Call 555-1212.

Showing the Vacant Unit

At this point, your advertisement is running in the local paper and your vacancy signs are strategically located on the available unit. Now it is imperative that the vacant unit be ready to be shown, which means it should be neat and clean throughout. If by chance you are renting an occupied unit that the occupants will be moving out of shortly, then inform the occupants of your intentions. Request that they keep the unit tidy so that you can show the unit to prospects.

While you're showing the unit, begin pointing out features of the unit, such as storage, cabinets, view, and so on. Do not bring up what you might consider to be negative, because what may be a negative aspect to some may not be to others. Furthermore, you should know the square footage of the available unit.

The prospects, if they are interested in the unit, will usually begin by asking questions concerning schools (What are they? What are their reputations?), transportation (Do you know the bus schedules?), shopping, and so on—questions that you should be prepared to answer. If you do not know about the schools in the area, for example, find out what they are.

Renting the Unit

Assume your prospective tenants have seen the unit and have decided to rent it. What do you do now? First, get as much of a deposit as you can and *do not accept a check for a deposit* without first calling the bank for a verification of funds. Or, accept only cash or a money order for the deposit, and try to get at least $500 or more. Anything less could tempt your prospects into not upholding their obligation should they find something they preferred before moving into your rental.

After receiving the deposit and giving your prospects a receipt, have them complete the Rental Application Form. (See Rental Application Form on page 219.) Be sure your prospects fill out the application completely, because you will use this information later to determine whether you will accept them as tenants. Once they have completed the application, check for omissions, and if there are none, notify your tenants that you will phone them once you make a decision on their application.

QUALIFYING THE PROSPECTIVE TENANT

From the Rental Application Form, you now have to determine whether it would be wise to accept your new applicants as tenants. Essentially what you are looking for are applicants who will take good care of the premises, pay their rent on time, and not be a nuisance. Bear in mind that you are about to develop a long-term business relationship with these people, and you do not need the headaches associated with people who won't, or don't, have the capability to pay their rent on time. Once tenants have gained possession of your rental unit and decide not to pay the rent and you want them removed, you must do it by "due process of law." Lawful actions to evict a deadbeat will only bring a judgment for rent monies, court costs, and moving fees. Cases that go to court will undoubtedly require 30 days or more to remedy. The costs involved, plus additional loss of rent, can be very expensive to an owner when this professional deadbeat moves in to your property.

The best way to avoid this money-losing situation is to check on your prospect's history-of-paying habits. Telephone a local credit agency and find out what they require to do a credit check for you. If the prospects have no credit, then inquire into their rent-paying habits with their past two landlords. Occasionally, I will ask prospective tenants if I can see their credit cards. If in fact they have active Visa or MasterCard accounts, that is usually a sign of good credit. Be sure you check the expiration date when you're inspecting credit cards.

Your next concern is whether your future tenants will properly care for your investment while they're living in it. About the only way you can determine that is by calling the previous landlord and inquiring into their living habits. Incidentally, through my past 20 years of land-lording experience, I have observed certain habits of human nature which may assist novice landlords. It has been my experience that people who take good care of their vehicle will in most cases, take good care of the home they live in. Conversely, people who drive a dirty, ill-maintained car in almost every case have dirty and messy homes and won't take good care of your property. This observation will also usually hold true for kids. If the children of the family are reasonably well dressed in clean clothes, it would be a good assumption on your part that the parents will also care for other things, such as your investment. So, when your prospective tenants arrive at your available unit, check out the condition of the car and the children, if any. Later, if you have any doubts about renting to them, let your observations assist in making your decision.

Finally, it is necessary to financially qualify your prospects on their ability to pay the rent. The guidelines for rent qualification are as follows: The monthly rent should not exceed 25 percent of the tenant's gross monthly income. However, if he has no consumer debt (i.e., car loans and credit card payments), then he can afford up to 33 percent of his gross monthly income. Spouse income can be included, but not overtime pay. For example, a prospect who grosses $3,000 per month and has certain consumer debt, usually cannot afford to pay more than $750 per month in rent ($3,000 × 25%). A person with no consumer debt could typically afford one-third of $3,000, or $1,000 per month in rent. Of course, in high rent areas of the country, you may have to relax these general income ratios.

RENTING CONSIDERATIONS

Generally speaking, the more at risk you are, the more you should require in deposits. You are more at risk when the family you rent to has children or pets, such as dogs and cats. Usually, the security deposit on an unfurnished home can be from 75 to 100 percent of the first month's rent. This amount may be adjusted upward for each person or pet in the household. A security deposit is a refundable deposit. Any damage done by the tenants, if any, is deducted from the deposit; the balance is sent to them within 30 days from move-out.

Another necessary deposit is the nonrefundable cleaning deposit. (Certain states prohibit nonrefundable cleaning deposits therefore check your local statutes regarding this matter.) The cleaning deposit is normally priced in the range of $75 to $125, depending on the size and value of the rental. Before your tenants move in, be sure to inform them that the security and cleaning deposits cannot be applied to the last month's rent when they vacate the premises, and that the security deposit will be held until after the unit is vacated with proper notice and has been inspected and found to be in reasonably good condition.

Separate deposits should be required for certain keys, such as key cards (for parking in secured condominium complexes and for tennis courts, etc.). Usually $10 is adequate for keys and $25 each for a key card.

THE MOVE-IN

Before your tenants move in and take over residency of your rental unit, certain items have to be taken care of. All monies owed to you have to be paid in advance in cash, money order, or verified check. This includes the first month's rent (or first and last if it's a long-term lease), and all deposits, including security, cleaning, and key deposits. Be sure the rental agreement is signed and that there is one copy available for the tenant. Also be sure the tenant has one set of keys, plus information on offices to call for the turn-on of all utilities. Finally, inform them that you expect the rent to be paid on time, that there is a three-day grace period, but after that a late fee will be charged (see Chapter 10 for lease provisions in forms).

RENT COLLECTION

Remember, your investment in real estate is a money-making enterprise, not a downtown mission run on charity. Investors who yield to delinquent or nonpaying deadbeats are courting financial disaster. Therefore, be firm with your collection policies and inform your new tenants at the time of move-in what you expect of them. However, you can be flexible. All rents do not have to be paid on the first day of the month. Under certain circumstances, some people might receive their paychecks on the tenth of the month or the fifteenth. If this is the case, make their rent due on a date to coincide with their payday.

After all move-in fees have been paid in cash or verified funds, you can then have a policy of accepting checks for the monthly rent payments. This policy is fine, unless you receive a bad check, and once you do, then your policy should be to accept only cash or money orders from that individual. Check bouncers are a habitual bunch. If you continue to accept checks after one has bounced, you can be assured that more rubber checks will eventually bounce out of your bank account.

Rent checks should be mailed directly to an address of your choice. Once a tenant has established a good payment history with you, more lenient allowances can be made when unforeseen circumstances occur, such as the loss of employment, illness, or death in the family. Whatever the case, definite commitments must be made as to when the debt will be paid and must be immediately followed up on if not.

Resident Manager—Rent-Collection Policy

The following are recommended procedures in the event you have a resident manager living on the premises of your multiunit building. Rent collection should always be in the form of checks or money orders. Absolutely no cash should be accepted. (An exception can be made in the case of emergency or when someone is extremely late in paying the rent.) By having a policy of only accepting checks or money orders, you will eliminate the temptation of the resident manager to borrow small amounts of cash and you will alleviate the risk of the rent monies being stolen.

Each month's rent receipts can be deposited by the resident manager. To do this, order a rubber stamp from the printer, then the manager can stamp the back of the rent checks (For Deposit Only . . .), then deposit them in your bank account.

Rent receipts should be provided to the tenant. Therefore, it is necessary to furnish the manager with a receipt pad in triplicate. One copy of a rent receipt can then be available for the tenant, one for the manager, and one copy for the owner's records.

Delinquent Sheet

A delinquent sheet is essentially a list of overdue tenants.

The resident manager uses the delinquent sheet in rent collection. Assume that all the rents of a particular building are due on the first day of the month. The delinquent sheet has the name of each tenant on it, with a comment section next to the tenant's name so the manager can make notes. As each tenant pays the rent, the name is crossed off the list. Let's say Mrs. Jones in apartment 102 tells the manager that she will pay the rent on the third. The manager would then make a note to that effect on the delinquent list. If a three-day notice was issued, or if an eviction notice was issued to a tenant, this would also be noted. The delinquent sheet is a tool used in record keeping that allows an immediate report on the current rent status.

Eviction Procedure (Nonpayment of Rent)

The following procedure is common in many states for the lawful eviction of a tenant for nonpayment of rent:

1. The tenant in default is served with a Three-Day Notice to Pay Rent or Quit the Premises. To ensure proper legal procedure, the person serving the notice should be the marshal, not the landlord, owner, or resident manager.
2. An Unlawful Detainer is filed with the municipal court clerk, and a Summons is issued.
3. The tenant is served with a Summons and a Complaint.
4. The tenant has the legal right to file against the Complaint, pleading his or her case. In that event, a trial is held.
5. The default of tenant is taken and given to the owner.
6. The court issues a Writ of Possession.
7. The marshal receives the Writ of Possession.
8. The marshal evicts the tenant.

CHOOSING THE RESIDENT MANAGER

Whether you own a building with 4 units, 20 units, or 50 units or more, you may find it desirable to have a resident manager live on the premises. An owner who has a competent manager on the property is relieved of many time-consuming, day-to-day operations and responsibilities.

The typical resident manager team is a husband and wife, with one spouse handling the management responsibilities and the other spouse doing the maintenance. Ideally, one of them would be working a full-time job elsewhere while the other would look after your building. The following are the chief qualities you should look for in a management team, in their order of importance:

1. Honesty.
2. Eagerness and willingness to do the job properly.

3. Ability to accept responsibility.

4. One member of the team who is handy at minor repairs.

5. Pleasant personalities, along with the willingness of one team member to stay at home and assist in the overall operation of the property.

6. Experience.

It is primarily the manager's responsibility to collect rent, show vacancies, and keep the common grounds clean. When team members can handle minor repair work and mow the lawn, you can eliminate the need to always call a professional repair person or hire a lawn maintenance service.

It is very important that the resident manager be on the job to show vacancies and keep order around the building. A would-be manager, who has many outside commitments, is not a good prospect, while a parent with young children tends to be at home more and will be available to deal with tenants' problems.

What you pay the management team depends on the size of the building being managed. Managing a 20-unit building typically would be free rent. For a smaller building, like a fourplex or sixplex, a 25 percent reduction in rental rate would be typical. Buildings larger than 20 units usually involve free rent plus a cash salary. For competitive salaries look in your local newspaper in the classified section under the column "Property Managers Wanted" (or a similar heading).

Supervising the Resident Manager

Duties of the resident manager must be fully explained at the beginning of the owner-employee relationship. Be sure the managers know exactly what is expected of them. Remember, the more responsibility you as owner can delegate to the managers, the more time you will have to pursue other matters.

Monthly reports submitted to the owner are necessary for efficient accounting and ready reference. These reports include a summary of rents (income) collected, a delinquency sheet, and bank deposits made (optional, depending on whether it is the manager or the owner who makes the deposit).

Each entry on the summary of rents (income) collected should include apartment number, rent paid date and due date, amount paid, and type of income (rent, cleaning fee, key deposit, or security deposit). One copy of the rent receipt is also kept on file by the manager, and the tenant receives the third copy, if requested.

Major expenditures, such as replacing carpet or a water heater, should be billed directly to the owner. In fact, it will be helpful if the owner can establish charge accounts with various suppliers. This will reduce the temptation of the manager to pad expense bills or receive kickbacks from salespeople.

Once a qualified and responsible management team is operating your building, you'll find that an occasional monthly supervisory visit is all that is required of your time. Major decisions, such as expensive repairs or recarpeting can be accomplished on such visits. In addition, you can make an inspection of the premises during these visits. Thus, the job of landlording can be enriched by responsible managers, thereby avoiding the headaches and hassles many amateur owners experience through slipshod management practices.

BUDGETING

The successful operation of a multiunit building depends on having a carefully planned budget, then sticking to it without exception. The budget is basically financial planning for the upcoming years. Projections of all income and expenses are made to obtain an overall view of the building's financial well-being. If owners do not properly plan income and expenses, financial suicide is inevitable. Allocations for certain replacement items over the years have to be budgeted and paid for when they need replacing. What happens when owners do not plan properly is deferred maintenance. That, in turn, causes vacancies, which, in turn, causes loss of income and further deferred maintenance and eventual loss in value.

Good budgeting not only encompasses the planning of income and expenses but also the future replacement of capital items, such as carpeting, roofs, pool equipment, and furniture. These items are very costly, but through properly planned budgets, they can easily be replaced when needed. Thus, a contingency fund should be set aside and held in reserve to replace these items when needed. For example, carpeting usually has to be replaced every several years, on average. New carpeting in today's market for a one-bedroom apartment will cost about $700 and with proper care could last five to seven years. Therefore, $100 to $150 per year per apartment (about $8 to $12 per month) should be set aside in a contingency fund to replace carpeting. Similarly, a replacement reserve fund must be set up for items such as window coverings, roofing, furniture, and appliances.

The best way to budget these items is to estimate total outlay for all future capital expenditures, maintaining the fund for each item in a savings account to use when the money is required. For example, you determine that the cost of a new roof is $3,200, and it will last for 20 years. Therefore, divide the total cost by the total number of months and the result is the amount that should be budgeted each month ($3,200 ÷ 240 months = $13.33 per month allocation for a replacement reserve for roofing).

Expense items, such as property taxes and hazard insurance, also have to be budgeted. Taxes and insurance frequently are paid out of an impound account which is already part of your monthly payment. If this is the case, it won't be necessary for you to pay separately the taxes and insurance premium because the holder of the first mortgage will pay these from the impound account. If the first note holder is not paying the taxes and insurance, then it will be necessary for you to arrange these items in your budget. Property taxes are projected at $\frac{1}{12}$ of the annual tax bill per month. Be sure to allow for a future increase by the assessor. Hazard insurance is likewise $\frac{1}{12}$ of the annual insurance premium.

As a rule of thumb, 5 percent of gross collected rents is usually an adequate amount to be budgeted for replacement reserves. However, this amount would have to be increased if your building had additional equipment, such as an elevator, heated pool, or Jacuzzi.

KEEPING RECORDS

Proper record-keeping procedures are necessary so the information will be accessible when needed, especially when income tax time arrives or in the event the IRS decides to audit your income tax return. Keeping records can be accomplished very simply when your investments are single-family homes. All you need is a separate 9″ × 12″ envelope for each home, properly labeled, while keeping all records and expense items inside the envelope. All income collected can be noted on the outside of the envelope, along with addresses of note holders, balance owing on the notes, and initial cost of the property. At the end of each year, a new envelope can be started for the upcoming year.

Multiunit buildings require a little more elaborate record-keeping systems, with a separate set of records for each building. Make up file folders and label them "General Records," "Tenant Records," and "Receipts and Expenses." In the General Records folder retain such information as escrow papers, insurance policies, taxes, notes, and deeds. In the Tenant Records folder, maintain all rental applications, rental agreements, and any other data pertaining to your tenants. All tenant information should be kept for credit rating purposes and landlord inquiries for at least one year after tenants move out. In the Receipts and Expenses folder, retain paid receipts for all expenses related to the building and copies of all rent receipts. Later the expense items can be arranged by category for income tax purposes. At the end of the tax year, this envelope should be stored separately for at least three years, in case the IRS decides to audit.

Cardex

A tenant record, or cardex, is a 5.5″ × 8″ card used by the owner or manager. Whenever a tenant makes payment, it is recorded on the cardex (see Chapter 10 for sample of cardex). A separate cardex is maintained on each rental unit. It is a ready reference of all monies paid and due, plus other important tenant information. If you are computer proficient, you may prefer to keep your records using a property management software package. However, the essential record-keeping principles will remain the same.

Journal of Income and Expenses

A separate journal is required for each multiunit building for which you will post all relevant income and expense data monthly (see Figure 9.1). It includes sections on income, expenses, loans, and depreciation, and it allows you ready access to all current data relating to income and expense. The first section denotes rental and laundry income for each unit for the entire year, and the second section is for posting expenses. All those receipts you have been keeping in a file folder are recorded here monthly. Anything you do not have receipts for can be recorded from your checking account record. Examples of the Monthly Income and Expense and Payment Record appear on page 215.

Once you have completed an entire page on the Expense and Payment Record, total each column and bring the balance forward to the next sheet, then start posting your latest entries. After you have posted your last expenditure for the year, total the last sheet and you'll have your annual expenses for each category of your building.

Be careful not to post on your expense record such capital items as carpeting or a new roof. These are depreciable items, not expenses.

Depreciation Records

Depreciable items are property or equipment having an extended useful life and considered to be improvements to the property. Some

Monthly Income Record   Page # _____
Address _____
Year _____

Unit	Jan	Feb	Mar	Apr	May	Jun	Jul	Aug	Sep	Oct	Nov	Dec
1	650	650	650	650	650							
2	600	600	600	600	600							
3	550	550	550	550	550							
4	400	400	400	400	400							
5	550	550	550	550	550							
6	650	650	650	650	650							
7												
8												
Tot.	3400	3400	3400	3400	3400							

Expense and Payment Record
Address _____ **Year** _____ **Page #** _____

Date	Paid To	Paid For	Total Paid	Mortgage Principal	Mortgage Interest	Tax	Ins.	Mgt.	Repairs & Maint.
1. 1/1	bank	1st mort	1520	245.60	1274.40	240	90		
2. 1/1	Smith	2nd	125	92.40	32.60				
3. 1/3	hdwr.	pts.	19.60						
4. 1/7	water	water	156.71						
5. 1/8	muni ct	evict	221						
6. 2/1	bank	1st mort	1520	248.12	1271.88	240	90		
7.									

Figure 9.1 Income and Expenses Journal

examples are: Carpeting, elevators, new linoleum, roof replacement, swimming pool. Each of these items must be depreciated on a separate depreciation record form (see depreciation methods in Chapter 13).

The following is a depreciation record used for the building itself (a similar depreciation record can be used for capital improvements):

Location and Description of Capital Improvement:
4200 Dexter Road: 8-Unit Apartment Building

Date acquired:	Jan. 96
New or used:	Used
Cost or value:	$320,000
Land value:	$40,000
Salvage value:	0
Depreciable basis:	$280,000
Method of depreciation:	straight-line
Useful life:	27.5 years

	Year	Prior Deprec.	Deprec. Balance	% Year Held	Deprec. This Yr.
1.	1996	0	280,000	100	10,182
2.	1997	10,182	269,818	100	10,182
3.	1998	20,364	259,636	100	10,182
4.					

Annual Statement of Income

This statement brings together all relative income and expense for the year and shows the net profit or loss. Notice how depreciation, not an out-of-pocket expense, is deducted last for tax purposes. This is the actual "tax-shelter" benefit of owning income-producing real estate. Notice also, that this statement of taxable income differs from the income statement used for purposes of valuation. For valuation, neither interest nor depreciation is deducted. (See Chapter 3.) The bottom line in the following example is the net profit or loss reported to the Internal Revenue Service.

SUMMARY

Property management can be a truly rewarding experience or it can be a burdensome daily chore. I have offered you a concise, yet thorough, guide for total property management to assist you at making decisions

Annual Statement of Taxable Income Example
Location: 4200 Dexter Road   Year: 1996

Income		
Rent	$28,471	
Other (laundry)	629	
Total income	29,100	$29,100
Expenses		
Interest	8,410	
Taxes	4,800	
Utilities	1,812	
Service, repairs	321	
Pest control	120	
Insurance	850	
Management	1,800	
Total expenses	18,113	18,113
Net income (before depreciation)		10,987
Less depreciation		10,182
Net income (or loss) for tax purposes		$ 805

and to help you avoid costly pitfalls. Foremost among these guidelines is properly screening your prospective tenants, thereby helping to ensure you will have good-paying tenants who will properly care for your investment. And don't forget the importance of the "no-hassle" clause written into your rental agreement. This will eliminate 90 percent of the late-night phone calls by your tenants requesting repairs. These simple procedures will help to make your investment a truly efficient, successful, and profitable experience.

Overall, always keep in mind that the quality of your property management will determine whether your investment will increase in value. Through effective management, you can work to reduce expenses, increase rents, decrease vacancies, and boost the property's net operating income (NOI). As your NOI climbs higher and higher, so will the value of your property.

10 USEFUL FORMS

The forms in this chapter are for your use as you see fit, including duplication of each page on any type of photocopy equipment.

APPLICATION TO RENT

Everyone needs a place to live, but for your own financial health you must select your tenants carefully. You have a lot invested, both in effort and money, so why in the world would you rent to a nonpaying deadbeat or a malicious tenant? Yet, time after time, inexperienced property owners rent out their valuable properties without taking the time to properly qualify prospective tenants. Remember, you are essentially loaning your property to someone for that person's use for a considerable period. A business relationship is about to develop, and if you rent to someone who habitually pays late and isn't capable of taking good care of your property, you're in for a lot of headaches.

You can overcome most of the problems frequently encountered by novice landlords by properly qualifying your prospective renters. Good-paying tenants who will take care of your property are a valuable asset. Here is some sound advice to assist you in judging whether or not your prospective tenants have the good character and capability of meeting the terms of your rental agreement.

After your prospect has completed filling out the rental application (Figure 10.1), review it carefully. Make sure everything is legible and complete. Make sure the name is correct, because later on if Jim Jones skips the premises, he will be easier to trace with his complete name of James Anthony Jones. If more than one person will occupy the

Name _____ Home Phone _____ Work Phone _____

Spouse/Roommate Name _____ Work Ph. _____

Unit to be occupied by _____ Adults and _____ Children and _____ Pets

Present Address _____ City _____ State _____ Zip _____

Current Landlord/Mgr's Name _____ Phone _____

Why are you leaving? _____

Previous Address _____ City _____ State _____ Zip _____

Landlord/Mgr's Name _____ Phone _____

Applicant's Birth Date _____ Soc. Sec. # _____ Driv. Lic _____

Applicant's Employer _____ Position _____ How long _____

Applicant's Employer's Address _____ Gross monthly pay _____

Spouse/Roommate's Employer _____ Gross monthly pay _____

Credit References: Bank _____ Account # _____ Type _____

Other Active Reference _____ Account # _____

Spouse/Roommate Credit Ref. _____ Account # _____

In an emergency contact: _____ Phone _____

Address _____ City _____ State _____ Zip _____

List all motor vehicles, including RVs, to be kept at the dwelling unit. Include make, model, year, and license plate # for each.

Vehicle #1 _____   Vehicle #2 _____

License _____   License _____

Vehicle #3 _____

License _____

    I (we) declare that the above information is correct and I (we) give my (our) permission for any reporting agency to release my credit file to undersigned property owner solely for the purposes of entering into a rental agreement. I (we) further authorize the owner or his agent to verify the above information including but not limited to contacting creditors, both listed herein or not, and present or former landlords.

    Dated _____, 19_____   Applicant _____

                                                      Applicant _____

Figure 10.1 Application to Rent

premises, get the names of all adults and make each individually responsible for rent payments.

Employment information is also very important. You definitely want to qualify the prospect on his ability to pay rent. As noted earlier, a range of 25 percent to 33 percent of gross monthly income can safely be paid in rent. If your prospect qualifies by salary, then at a more appropriate time you should verify employment. A phone call to the employer is sufficient.

Credit References

This information will be supplied by a local credit bureau, if it is necessary. What I usually do is, after the prospect has completed the rental application, I ask to see the person's credit cards. If, in fact, he or she has active, up-to-date cards (which have not expired), that satisfies any doubts I may have about creditworthiness. Just the fact that the prospect has acquired Visa, MasterCard, or Sears credit cards is usually a good indication of creditworthiness. One final credit check would be to call either the last, or second-from-last listed landlord and inquire into the applicant's character and rent-paying habits.

Spouse/Roommate (Part of Rental Application)

You will have added protection by having the spouse or roommate sign all the documents of the Rental Agreement. This way both parties are individually responsible, and it may be easier to locate one of the tenants if the other skips.

Discrimination Laws

As a landlord you cannot, according to the law, refuse to rent to people because of their race, creed, color, national origin, sex, handicap, religion, or family status. This doesn't mean, however, that you are obligated to rent to anyone just because they have a fistful of money. In particular for a multiunit building, you should have certain standard of behavior to induce harmony in your building. However, you may not segregate your buildings on the basis of designated categories such as "swinging singles" or "households with children." Therefore, your standards should be set in terms of acceptable conduct, not personal characteristics.

INVENTORY OF FURNISHINGS

This form (Figure 10.2) should accompany the lease for each individual unit. It essentially identifies items such as the refrigerator, stove, couch, etc., and denotes their current condition. In a claim for damages, the owner can seek compensation (excluding reasonable wear and tear) from the security/cleaning deposits. The tenants, however, may try to counter that the damage was there prior to move-in. Except in cases of gross negligent damage, a defense of "the damage was there before we moved in" is difficult to overcome. That's why you need proper documentation.

At the time of move-in, ask the tenants to go through the unit room by room with you. Have the tenants fill out the inventory and mark any comments and return the form to you. If comments cannot be made in the space provided, tell your tenants to make any additional comments on the reverse side of this form and note "See reverse side."

CARDEX

A tenant record, or cardex, is a 5.5" × 8" card used by the owner or manager (Figure 10.3). It is a ready reference of all monies paid and due, plus other important tenant information, since every payment is recorded on the cardex.

NOTICE OF CHANGE IN TERMS OF RENTAL AGREEMENT

This form (Figure 10.4) is used to change the rental rate. Usually, 30 days are required for a suitable notice before increasing the rental rate. Specific rental rates are found in the initial rental agreement. However, once the original term of the agreement expires, the landlord has the option of increasing the rental rate.

REMINDERS TO PAY RENT

Delinquency by your tenants should not be tolerated. Effective property owners should predictably react immediately to nonpayment of rent when it is due. Slow-paying tenants usually will react to this predictability and make the rent a high priority on their list of payments.

Rental unit address _____

Tenant _____ Inventory date _____ , 19____

Room	Item	Comments	Condition at Move-out

Tenant agrees that the above information is an accurate inventory and description and assumes responsibility for these items in the dwelling unit as of _____ , 19_____ .

Move-in   Move-out

_____ Date _____   _____ Date _____

_____ Date _____   _____ Date _____

Figure 10.2   Inventory of Furnishings

Figure 10.3 Cardex

Date _____

To _____ , Tenant in possession of _____

_____ .

[ ] Certified mail
[ ] Hand delivered
[ ] Regular mail

You are hereby notified that the terms of tenancy under which you occupy the above address are to be changed as follows:

Effective _____ , 19_____ , your rent will be increased by $_____ per month for a total of $_____ each month.

_____
Property Owner/Manager

Figure 10.4   Notice of Change in Terms of Rental Agreement

Normally, there is a three-day grace period after the rent due date. If the rent is not received within three days of due date, action has to be taken (Figure 10.5). Collection experts agree that a first notice be sent within three days of the due date and a second notice after five days (Figure 10.6). In the event your slow-paying tenant has a history of continued delinquency, a Three-Day Notice to Pay or Quit the Premises could be used in favor of the second notice.

To _____   Date _____

_____

Just a reminder that your rent was past due on _____ . According to the terms of your Rental Agreement, rent more than _____ days past due requires a late charge payment of $_____ . We would appreciate your prompt payment.

Thank you,

_____
Property Owner/Manager

Figure 10.5   Three-Day Reminder to Pay Rent

To _____   Date _____

_____

    Your rent is now past due as of _____ . As of this date, the past-due rent and late charges total $_____ .

    Please settle this account or our legal options will have to be considered. Therefore we ask that you remedy this matter immediately.

Thank you,

_____
Property Owner/Manager

Figure 10.6   Five-Day Reminder to Pay Rent

NOTICE TO PAY RENT OR QUIT THE PREMISES

This form (Figure 10.7) is the three-day pay or quit initiated by the landlord and issued to the tenant in default. Essentially, the tenant has three days from date of this notice to pay all monies in default or move out of the premises. This form is to be issued to the tenant only after the landlord has attempted to obtain the amount owed through other means, such as the three- and five-day reminder notices. Note: Caution should be taken in this matter of the Pay or Quit Notice because laws vary substantially on this matter throughout the country. This particular form may not conform to the laws in some states where new landlord/tenant statues have been enacted. If this is the case, the property owner should seek the appropriate form at a reputable legal stationery store or consult with an attorney.

NOTICE OF ABANDONED PROPERTY

Abandoned personal property that the tenant left behind for whatever reason (which in most cases is of little or no value) has to be disposed of according to the prevailing laws within your particular state. If you carelessly dispose of abandoned property, whether it has value or not, you could leave yourself open to a legal suit or a malicious ex-tenant seeking revenge.

    Abandoned-property statutes can vary substantially from state to state. Junked or abandoned cars frequently are left behind also but are

To _____   Date _____
_____   [ ] Delivered by Marshal
                                         [ ] Certified mail # ____
                                         [ ] Hand delivered

You are hereby notified that the rent for the period _____,
19_____, to _____, 19_____, is now past due. As of this date,
the total sum owing including late charges is $_____. Unless this
sum is received within three days of this dated notice, you will be required
to vacate and surrender the premises.

If it becomes necessary to proceed with legal action for the non-pay-
ment of rent or to obtain possession of the premises, as per the terms of
the Rental Agreement, you will be liable for recovery of our reasonable attorney fees and expenses. You will also be liable for any additional rent for
the time you are in possession of the premises.

_____
Property Owner/Manager

Figure 10.7   Notice to Pay Rent or Quit the Premises

treated differently. If you should be faced with an abandoned junker
on your property, it is best to call your local Department of Motor Vehicles and find out the best way to dispose of it. Junkyards are usually
not allowed to accept vehicles unless the car has a valid signed-off certificate of title.

Most states require proof that an effort was made to contact the
rightful owner of the property. Therefore, in most cases, this notice
(Figure 10.8) should be sufficient and should be sent to the rightful
owner of the abandoned property at the person's last known address.
Caution: If there is obvious substantial value to the property in question, or if you are not familiar with local statutes regarding this matter,
please consult with a qualified attorney.

To _____   Date _____

Address _____

    When you vacated the rented unit located at _____
you left the following described property on the premises:_____
_____
_____ .

    You are hereby informed that unless you claim and remove the
above-described property before _____ , 19_____ , it will
be thrown away, given to charity, or sold in a manner prescribed by law. If
sold, the proceeds will be used to cover the cost of the sale, then to cover
any sums due, and any remaining balance will be forwarded to you.
    Please take care of this matter immediately.

                                            _____
                                            Property Owner/Manager

Figure 10.8   Notice of Abandoned Property

1. This Lease made this _____ day of _____ , 19_____ ,
by and between _____ ,
hereinafter called Landlord, and _____ ,
hereinafter called Tenant.

2. *Description:* The Landlord, in consideration of the rents to be paid
and the covenants and agreements to be performed by the Tenant,
does lease to the Tenant the following premises located in the City
of _____ , County of _____ , State
of _____ , commonly known as _____
_____ .

3. *Terms:* For the term of _____ (months/years) beginning on _____ , 19_____ , and ending
on _____ , 19_____ .
                                            (Continued)

Figure 10.9   Rental-Agreement Residential Lease

Figure 10.9 *(Continued)*

4. *Rent:* Tenant shall pay Landlord, as rent for said premises, the sum of _____ dollars ($_____) per month payable in advance on the first day of each month at Landlord's address above or other place as Landlord may designate in writing. Tenant agrees to pay a $25 late fee if rent is not paid within five days of due date.

5. *Security Deposit:* Landlord acknowledges the receipt of _____ _____ dollars ($_____), which he is to retain as security for the faithful performance of the provisions of this Lease. If Tenant fails to pay rent, or defaults with respect to any provision of this Lease, Landlord may use the security deposit to cure the default or compensate Landlord for all damages sustained by Landlord. Tenant shall immediately on demand reimburse Landlord the sum equal to that portion of security deposit expended by Landlord so as to maintain the security deposit in the sum initially deposited. If Tenant performs all obligations under this Lease, the security deposit, or that portion that was not previously applied by Landlord, shall be returned to Tenant within 15 days after the expiration of this Lease, or after Tenant has vacated the premises.

6. *Possession:* It is understood that if the Tenant is unable to enter into and occupy the leased premises at the time provided, by reason of the said premises not being ready for occupancy, or by reason of holding over of any previous tenant, the Landlord shall not be liable in damage to the Tenant, but during the period the Tenant is unable to occupy said premises, the rental shall be abated and the Landlord is to be the sole judge as to when the premises are ready for occupancy.

7. *Use:* Tenant agrees that the leased premises during the term of this Lease shall be used and occupied by _____ adults and _____ children, and _____ animals, and for no purpose whatsoever other than a residence, without the written consent of the Landlord, and that Tenant will not use the premises for any purpose in violation of any law, municipal ordinance, or regulation, and upon breach of this provision the Landlord may at his option terminate this Lease and repossess the leased premises.

8. *Utilities:* Tenant will pay charges for all water supplied to the premises and pay for all gas, heat, electricity, and other services supplied to the premises, except as provided: _____.

Figure 10.9 *(Continued)*

9. *Repairs and Maintenance:* The Landlord shall at his expense, except for the first $100 in cost which the Tenant pays, keep and maintain the exterior walls, roof, electrical wiring, heating and air-conditioning system, water heater, built-in appliances, and water lines in good condition and repair, except where damage has been caused by negligence or abuse of the Tenant, in which case Tenant shall repair same at his expense.

Tenant agrees that the premises are now in good condition and shall maintain the premises and appliances in the manner in which they were received, reasonable wear and tear excepted.

The _____ agrees to maintain landscaping and swimming pool (if any). Tenant agrees to adequately water the yard and landscaping.

10. *Alterations and Additions:* The Tenant shall not make any alterations, additions, or improvements to the leased premises without the Landlord's written consent. All alterations, additions, or improvements made by either of the parties, except movable furniture, shall be the property of the Landlord and shall remain with the premises at the termination of this Lease.

11. *Assignment:* The Tenant will not assign or transfer this lease or sublet the leased premises without the written consent of the Landlord.

12. *Default:* If the Tenant abandons or vacates the premises before the end of the term of this lease, or if default shall be made by the tenant in the payment of rent, or if the Tenant fails to perform any of the Tenant's agreements in this lease, then and in each and every instance of such abandonment or default, the Tenant's right to enter said premises shall be suspended, and the Landlord may at his option enter the premises and remove and exclude the Tenant from the premises.

13. *Entry by Landlord:* Tenant shall allow the Landlord or his agents to enter the premises at all reasonable times and upon reasonable notice for the purpose of inspecting or maintaining the premises or to show it to prospective tenants or purchasers .

14. *Attorney's Fees:* The Tenant agrees to pay all costs, expenses, and reasonable attorney's fees including obtaining advice of counsel incurred by Landlord in enforcing by legal action or otherwise any of Landlord's rights under this lease or under any law of this state.

(Continued)

Figure 10.9   *(Continued)*

15. *Holding Over:* If Tenant, with the Landlord's consent, remains in possession of the premises after expiration of the term of this lease, such possession will be deemed a month-to-month tenancy at a rental equal to the last monthly rental, and upon all the provisions of this lease applicable to such a month-to-month tenancy.

The parties have executed this Lease on the date first above written.

Landlord	Tenant
By: _____	By: _____
	By: _____

PERSONAL FINANCIAL STATEMENT
(MONTHLY INCOME AND EXPENSES)

MONTHLY INCOME:
    Gross wages   _____
    Rental income   _____
        Property "A"   _____
        Property "B"   _____
    Interest income   _____
    Mortgage income   _____
    Other income   _____
TOTAL MONTHLY INCOME: ===========

MONTHLY EXPENSES:
    Rent   _____
    Real estate loans   _____
        Property "A"   _____
        Property "B"   _____
    Vehicle loan   _____
    Furniture   _____
    Personal loans   _____
    Alimony or child support   _____
    Other   _____
TOTAL MONTHLY EXPENSES: ===========

Figure 10.9   *(Continued)*

BALANCE SHEET (OPTIONAL)

ASSETS:
  Cash on hand   _____
  Cash in bank   _____
  Car (vehicle)   _____
  Life insurance (cash value)   _____
  Real estate: _____
    Property "A"   _____
    Property "B"   _____
  Stocks and bonds   _____
  Mortgages (owed to you)   _____
  Accounts receivable   _____
  Household furniture   _____
  Other personal property   _____
TOTAL ASSETS: _____

LIABILITIES:
  Personal loans   _____
  Vehicle   _____
  Total real estate indebtedness   _____
  Other (furniture, etc.)   _____
TOTAL LIABILITIES: _____

TOTAL NET WORTH: _____

11 OTHER PROFITABLE INVESTMENT TECHNIQUES

Most real estate investors purchase income properties to lease up and hold for income and appreciation. With effective property management, this strategy will almost certainly yield large returns. Over time, as you pay down your mortgage balance and gradually increase your rents, you will build hundreds of thousands of dollars of property wealth. Using this approach, even ownership of just four or five single-family, middle-class houses can push your net worth close to (or above) the million-dollar mark within a period of 20 years.

However, in addition to this long-term buy, manage, and hold investment strategy, some real estate investors favor other investment techniques that can yield quicker profits. Included among these techniques are lease-options, the "6-month rollover," property conversions, TICs, master leases, and "contract flipping." Although these techniques may not work in all markets at all times, in the right situation, any one of them can result in extraordinary returns within a relatively short time frame. So, stay alert for these opportunities.

LEASE-OPTION: THE REAL MONEY MAKER

A lease with an option to purchase (lease-option) is a lease or a month-to-month rental agreement in which the tenant has a leasehold interest in the property with an option to purchase it. The option to purchase is a separate part of the agreement that specifies the price and terms of the sales contract. Under a typical lease-option agreement, the owner (optionor) of a home would give the tenant (optionee) the option to purchase the rented home at a specified price, within a set period, and for an option fee (consideration).

Lease-option is not a new concept. In fact, owners of real property have been optioning their properties for ages, but the use of options on residential property is relatively new. The use of an option, by itself, without a lease, is very useful among land speculators. For example, a knowledgeable land speculator with inside information on future land use could tie up a large land parcel with an option to buy, then sell the option at a later date to a developer. Let's say that our knowledgeable speculator has inside information on the construction of a major thoroughfare or freeway. He could obtain an option, instead of purchasing a large parcel of undeveloped land from an uninformed owner at a bargain price, then later sell the option for a substantial profit to a developer once the construction of the highway commences.

I stumbled on the lease-option concept out of pure necessity. I had a property in downtown Las Vegas that was experiencing more tenant-turnover than I could reasonably tolerate. So I experimented with the property during a vacancy and proceeded to run an ad in the paper offering "rent with option to buy."

The results from the rent-with-option-to-buy advertisement were overwhelming. I must have received ten times the calls I normally would have taken in under a "rental-only" situation. Within a week I had a qualified lease-option tenant residing in the property at a monthly rate $140 higher than the rental rate.

As time passed, I discovered other benefits the lease-option method had over simply renting out my properties. Besides the additional income, I noted that my lease-option tenants took better care of the occupied property than the renters. Further, the holder of an option who fails to exercise it within the term of the agreement forfeits all option fees already paid. Moreover, the benefits of those great low-interest rate assumable loans now came into play, since because of this favorable financing I could wrap the existing loans with seller financing and a higher overriding interest rate and make a profit on the differential.

To illustrate the moneymaking potential of lease-options, I will go through an example based on an actual experience I had with one of my properties. Although the interest rates then were different than they are now, the basic principles still apply. The secret to earning large profits from this technique involves five steps:

1. Locate a bargain-price fixer whose value can be substantially increased through improvements.

2. Preferably, purchase the property with a below-market, low interest rate mortgage assumption, or alternatively, purchase the property using new assumable financing such as FHA 203(b), FHA 203(k), VA, or an assumable ARM.

3. Move into the property and complete your repairs and renovations—this step is only necessary when your financing requires owner occupancy.

4. After completing the renovations, locate lease-option tenants.

5. Eventually sell the property to the tenants using a seller-financed wraparound mortgage; or if the current tenants leave without executing their option to buy, locate another lease-option tenant and repeat the process until one of your tenants goes ahead with the purchase.

There's nothing absolute about these five steps. You might decide to develop your own system that differs in some respects. Nevertheless, using essentially this approach, here's how the numbers worked for me (McLean) in my first lease-option investment:

Purchase price:	$96,000
Down payment	10,000
Cost to renovate	1,200
Total investment	$11,200

Lease-option tenant paid $1,075 per month, which included option fee. Of the $1,075, rent was $850 and $225 was the option fee. Expenses on the property were as follows:

First loan (assumable) payable at $400 per month at 9%	$400
Second loan (assumable) payable at $485 per month at 9%	485
Property taxes at $60 per month	60
Insurance at $30 per month	30
Total expenses	$975

Income on the preceding example is as follows: rent at $850, option fee of $225 for a total of $1,075. See the following:

Gross rent and option fee	$1,075
Less total expenses	975
Monthly cash flow	100
Plus equity buildup at $230 per month	230
Net monthly income	330
Net annual income ($330 × 12)	$3,960

Now we can calculate return on investment (yield). Return on investment is the total cash investment (down payment plus fix-up cost) divided into net annual income including equity buildup. Therefore:

$$\frac{\text{Net annual income of \$3,960}}{\text{Total investment of \$11,200}} = \text{Return on investment}$$

$$\text{Return on investment} = 35.36\%$$

Return on investment is 35.36 percent, based on the period of time before the tenant exercises the option to purchase. Now observe the terms of the option agreement. Remember the purchase price was $96,000; however the tenant has the option to purchase at a specified price and term. The following is the illustrated option-purchase agreement.

Option-purchase price		$115,000
Less: one year of option fees		
($225 × 12) = $2,700	$2,700	
Less: $2,300 cash to exercise		
the option	2,300	
Total down payment	5,000	5,000
Balance seller financed by 11.5%		
wraparound mortgage		$110,000

Under terms of the option, the contract price is $115,000 less down payment (option fees + cash) of $5,000, and the balance to be paid over 20 years at 11.5 percent on a wraparound mortgage. See the following example:

Balance financed at 11.5% on a		
wraparound mortgage		$110,000
Payment on wrap including		
principal & interest	$1,173	
Taxes	60	
Insurance	30	
Total monthly payment	$1,263	

Once the tenant exercises the option, he will pay the seller $1,263 (less $90 taxes and insurance paid elsewhere) in monthly payment for 20 years. Now we can examine the results after the option is exercised.

Monthly payment including principal, interest, taxes and insurance		$1,263
Less taxes and insurance paid elsewhere		90
Total amount paid to seller		$1,173
The following items are what the seller continues to pay on (seller pays)		
Existing first mortgage	$400	
Existing second mortgage	485	
Total seller payment	$885	885
Cash flow to seller		288
Plus equity buildup ($230 per month) as the existing loans pay down		230
Net before income taxes		$518

From the preceding example, the seller will net $518 per month on the initial $10,000 investment plus $1,200 in renovation costs for a total investment of $11,200. Now we can examine return on investment as follows:

Total investment	$11,200
Net income ($518 × 12 months)	6,216

To determine return on investment, divide net income by the total investment which equals the yield or return on investment:

$6,216 ÷ $11,200 = 55.50% yield (Note that this yield will increase more because of the input of the $2,300 down payment, which you will see in a later example.)

Figure 11.1 is a simplified illustration of the mechanics of the lease-option.

Figure 11.2 shows what occurs when the lease-option tenant exercises the option to buy.

As shown in Figure 11.2, the seller continues to pay on existing loans only at $885 per month. Taxes and insurance of $90 are now paid by the buyer. The buyer pays the seller $1,173 per month on the new

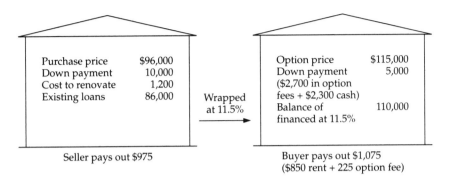

Purchase price	$96,000		Option price	$115,000
Down payment	10,000		Down payment	5,000
Cost to renovate	1,200		($2,700 in option	
Existing loans	86,000	Wrapped	fees + $2,300 cash)	
		at 11.5%	Balance of	110,000
			financed at 11.5%	

Seller pays out $975

Buyer pays out $1,075
($850 rent + 225 option fee)

Figure 11.1   Lease-Option Example (prior to Exercising Option)

wraparound mortgage at 11.5 percent for 20 years. The differential in monthly payments is $288 ($1,173 − $885), which represents the cash flow to the seller. When you add equity buildup of $230, the result is $518 in net income per month before income taxes.

Comparing return on investment, notice that the yield before the option is exercised is 35.36 percent as opposed to 55.50 percent after the option was exercised. Before I go any further, it is necessary to adjust the 55.50 percent notation, because in order to have the tenant exercise the option, an additional $2,300 cash payment was paid, which increases the net income figure. Therefore, net income will be adjusted

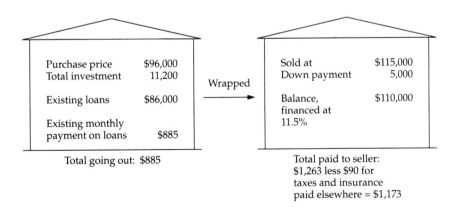

Purchase price	$96,000		Sold at	$115,000
Total investment	11,200	Wrapped	Down payment	5,000
Existing loans	$86,000		Balance,	$110,000
			financed at	
Existing monthly			11.5%	
payment on loans	$885			

Total going out: $885

Total paid to seller:
$1,263 less $90 for
taxes and insurance
paid elsewhere = $1,173

Figure 11.2   Lease-Option Example (after Exercising Option)

upward to $8,516 ($6,216 + $2,300). Now we can calculate the actual return on investment, which will be substantially higher because of $2,300 added to net income after option is exercised:

Total investment	$11,200
Net income of $518 × 12 months + $2300	= $ 8,516
Return on investment = Net income divided by total investment ($8,516 ÷ $11,200)	= 76.04%

Now in the final comparison of return on investment, note that the first year yield is more than twice the yield realized before the option was exercised (76.04% compared with 35.36%). This substantial differential is due to a number of factors. First, remember earlier in the text we discussed the importance of low-interest rate assumable loans? Well, here in the lease-option the value of these beneficial loans truly blossoms. A primary reason for their having such a profitable yield is that these low-interest loans are wrapped by a substantially higher loan. Second, the property is sold at a price $19,000 more than what was paid for it ($115,000 versus $96,000). And, third, when the option to purchase was exercised, the seller received $2,300 cash, which substantially added to the first year income.

As you can see, the lease-option method can be a lucrative tool in real estate investment. It often has a broad market because many potential home buyers like the idea of making their down payment on the installment plan (paying option fees that apply toward the purchase of the home). You would be surprised at how many potential home buyers earn enough income to afford to buy a home, but don't have an adequate down payment to purchase it under other methods of financing.

Figure 11.3 shows a sample Option-to-Purchase Agreement. For the purpose of simplicity, the option is kept separate from the lease for reasons to be discussed later. I also include the advertisement that ran in the *Las Vegas Review Journal* so you can personally get a feel for the property in this example.

Rent with Option to Buy—Valley View & Warm Springs. Beautiful mini-ranch on half-acre zoned for horses with view of strip. 3 bedrooms & 2.5 baths beautifully decorated with oak floors & large country kitchen, den, fireplace & formal dining. Small orchard & covered patio, 2 car garage plus washer & dryer, frig & much more. $1,075. Call 555-1212.

This option is made and entered into this 1st day of April, 19xx, by and between Andy Seller, hereinafter called Landlord (owner), and Fred Buyer, hereinafter called Tenant.

Subject property is a single-family residence located at 3750 Arby, Las Vegas, Nevada 89107.

Landlord hereby agrees to grant an option to purchase to Tenant based on the following terms and conditions: Provided that Tenant shall not then be in default of leased property, Tenant to have option to purchase subject property at a price of $115,000 for one year beginning April 1, 19xx, and expiring March 31, 19xx.

Tenant agrees to pay a monthly option fee of $225 during the term of the option which will be applied toward the purchase price. Tenant further agrees to pay a down payment, including paid option fees, of $5,000 to exercise this option. Tenant agrees to finance the balance owing of $110,000 secured by a wrap-around mortgage in favor of Landowner at 11.5% per annum for 20 years at $1,173.08 per month.

Tenant agrees further to pay all taxes, insurance, and mortgage payments into a trust account for disbursement to all parties concerned and pay for such a trust account.

Tenant also agrees to purchase subject property in "as is" condition.

Landlord agrees to have all loans, taxes, and insurance current at time of execution of this agreement.

Both Landlord and Tenant agree to split all normal closing costs, except Tenant is to pay for title insurance.

Landlord further agrees to apply all security deposits and cleaning fees under the lease agreement toward down payment upon execution of this agreement.

The parties hereto have executed this option on this date first above written:

By _____ Landlord   By _____ Tenant

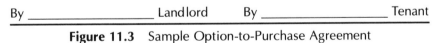

Figure 11.3   Sample Option-to-Purchase Agreement

Important Note about Lease-Option

Under a lease-option agreement it is important to maintain a month-to-month tenancy instead of a fixed-term rental agreement because the tenant could decide not to exercise the option, and in so doing would cease making option payments. The tenant would have the right to occupy the premises under a long-term rental agreement but would not be obligated to pay the option fee. (Of course, the tenant would no longer have the benefit of purchasing the house under the option agreement.) For example, assume that a tenant has a one-year lease with an option to purchase the property, in which case he pays rent plus an option fee. One month into the term of the lease he decides not to exercise the option and ceases making option payments; nevertheless he continues making rental payments only while occupying the premises over the entire term of the lease. In doing so, he has substantially reduced the income flow from the property and you're stuck with him as a tenant only for the full term of the lease.

You can avoid this potential problem simply by maintaining month-to-month rental agreements which are related to an option to purchase. Then, if your tenant decides not to exercise the option, you won't be bound to the terms of a long-term lease agreement, and you could initiate efforts to move him out in 30 days. Then replace him with someone who plans to eventually purchase the property.

Put Everything in Writing

The exact terms of the option must be spelled out in the option. This way there will be no doubt or further negotiation. Both the buyer and seller will know exactly whose responsibility it is to do what, and for how much.

An option to purchase can be as creative as the buyer and seller want it to be; however, it should be kept relatively simple to avoid any misunderstandings. Should by chance your tenant require a longer term on the option, you then essentially have two methods of determining the selling price for those periods. After the first year, you could set the option price at the existing price plus the consumer price index. Another method is to arbitrarily fix a selling price at which the tenant can buy the property during a specific term, such as $100,000 after one year, $110,000 after two years, and $120,000 after three years.

Advantages of Lease-Option

The lease-option concept is a very marketable technique, especially to potential home buyers who lack sufficient down-payment funds. Under a lease-option, the down payment can be paid on the installment plan through option fees. Your primary market then, is prospective home buyers who earn an adequate income to afford such housing, but lack a sufficient down payment to purchase a home under traditional financing methods.

Advantages to you, the seller, are tremendous when compared with renting or selling the property outright. First of all you save a sales commission—and on a $100,000 sale, that's $6,000 in saving. The second advantage is that while the tenant is in the option period, it is likely he will take better care of the property than he would under a rental-only occupancy. Furthermore, should the tenant not exercise the option, he would then forfeit all option fees already paid to you. In addition, certain tax advantages exist, that is, option fees are not taxable until the option is exercised, and selling on installment receives preferential tax treatment. Finally, under lease-option you profit from existing low-interest rate loans because when you sell, the existing loans are wrapped at a higher rate of interest, which generates a greater yield on investment.

Structuring the Option Agreement

The option agreement between you and your tenant can be as creative as the two parties involved want it to be; however, it should be precise, yet simple, to avoid misunderstandings between the parties. Be sure everything is in writing, leaving absolutely nothing to further negotiation.

Certain items, which in many cases might be considered unclear, such as the disposition of prepaid deposits and appliances (washer, dryer, and refrigerator), should be spelled out in the option agreement. For instance, both the cleaning and security deposit, which has been prepaid, can be applied toward the down payment as part of the agreement. And, the exact disposition of all appliances must be spelled out. In other words, if the appliances are to be included in the selling price, say so in the agreement; otherwise spell out the price you require for such items in the agreement.

Another consideration you have to make is what rate of interest to charge the buyer on the wraparound mortgage? It makes good business sense to be fair and reasonable. Bear in mind that you will be competing with conventional lenders, because you are, in effect, acting as a conventional lender when you wrap existing loans, which in reality is creating a new loan. Then, as a rule of thumb, charge a rate of interest comparable to what conventional lenders are charging. But, remember, you do not charge loan origination fees! This means substantial savings to the prospective buyer. This is an important selling feature that deserves further attention. Conventional lenders have a variety of incidental charges that are added to the cost of originating a new loan. Remember the credit report at $50, appraisal at $300, 1 to 2 percent of the loan proceeds in points, plus the inconvenience and time to complete the required paperwork? Therefore, remind your potential buyers of the convenience and cost-savings benefits they receive under the lease-option technique.

Finally, as part of your "tools of the trade," it will be necessary for you to purchase a book that covers interest rates and associated monthly loan payments. It is essentially a book of tables to calculate monthly loan payments for specific term and interest rate. Contemporary Books of Chicago publishes "Payment Tables for Monthly Mortgage Loans," and similar books are available in most bookstores. (If you're skilled in finance, you could use instead an electronic calculator or computer spreadsheet.)

SIX-MONTH ROLLOVER 100 PERCENT FINANCED

This investment technique is ideal for the investor who can raise $50,000 to $100,000 in ready-cash working capital. It involves paying cash for property, quickly renovating it, then reselling at a profit wherein you recoup the entire investment on the sale. The ready-cash working capital can either be generated from your own funds, a partnership, or from a private or institutional lender. The principle behind this technique is that a cash purchase commands a bargain price, especially when the seller is motivated to sell.

For example, let's say you have located a particular property which, if purchased for $67,000 cash and renovated, could be sold within 6 months for $100,000. For the benefit of this example, we will presume that you have a lender that will lend you $75,000 for 6 months.

The finance cost is calculated as follows: A financial institution or private lender might fund such a loan, including renovation costs, at 10 percent interest plus 2 points. The loan proceeds consist of $72,000, of which $67,000 represents the purchase price while $5,000 is the cost of renovation. Therefore, interest on $72,000 for 6 months is $3,600 plus 2 points at a cost of $1,440 for a total cost of $5,040. Although this cost to finance at first glance may seem excessive, this investment technique supports a high finance cost because of a great net profit, especially considering this technique was used without any of your own funds.

If by chance you were fortunate enough to possess enough ready cash to use the Six-Month Rollover technique without borrowing the required working capital, then obviously you'd be that much farther ahead because you save $5,040 in finance charges.

Six-Month Rollover 100 Percent Financed

Purchase price		$ 67,000
Less the following expenses to acquire & renovate:		
Closing costs	$ 500	
Cost to renovate	5,000	
Cost to finance	5,040	
Tax and insurance (6 months)	300	
Utilities (6 months)	200	
Total expenses	$11,040	
Total expenses and purchase price		78,040
Property is sold for $100,000		100,000
Less the following selling expenses:		
Sales commission (6%)	$ 6,000	
Closing costs	500	
Total expenses and purchase price	78,040	
Total overall expense	84,540	84,540
Net profit before taxes		$ 15,460

The sales commission is another variable cost which was included in the analysis. Due to the short period of time involved in this technique, I usually find it necessary to pay a commission to procure a quick sale. However, if you can make a sale without the services of an agent, you would earn yourself an additional $6,000.

Ingredients of the Short-Term Rollover

The key to this investment technique, assuming the working capital is to be borrowed, is to have a lender tentatively arranged for such a transaction. Then, as soon as you find a property in which you wish to invest, you would make an offer contingent upon acquiring sufficient financing. If your offer is accepted, it would then be analyzed by your lender. Should the lender agree, then you're in business; if not, your offer would then be nullified because of the financing contingency inserted into your offer to purchase.

To profit from this technique, certain rules must be applied and only certain properties qualify. You can use this rule of thumb when purchasing a property: If you buy it at no more than two-thirds of its selling price after it's fixed up, you made a good deal. In the preceding example, the purchase price was $67,000 which is two-thirds the selling price of $100,000. If you purchased a home for $80,000, the selling price would have to be $120,000 to incorporate the two-thirds ratio.

Properties which best qualify are those that have a substantial amount of equity and the seller is unwilling to carry back a note; they require much renovation, yet are sound in structure and overall construction. A large amount of equity means that the seller, has in most cases, owned the property for an extended period. Since he bought the property for substantially less many years ago and is unwilling to carry a note or renovate the property, he would be inclined to sell at a bargain price in order to be totally cashed out of the property.

Let's detail this method again just to illustrate exactly what happens. To begin with, you may need a lender who will advance the entire proceeds, including renovation capital. You purchase the property using the loan proceeds to pay all existing loans in full and to pay the seller cash for his equity. The lender will then create a new first mortgage on the subject property. (You could perhaps use an FHA 203(k) mortgage for the acquisition and repairs. However, the drawback here is that an FHA 203(k) loan may take 4 to 8 weeks to close.) With the additional renovation capital, you refurbish the property, then sell at a substantial profit. When the property is sold, you pay off the lender with a new first mortgage, and you earn the differential, which is the profit.

In conclusion, when you purchase a property and intend to sell it within one year, you can earn substantial savings on title insurance. Some title companies will allow you to pay an additional retainer of say, $50, which will be the total cost of title insurance when you sell. The cost of such a policy without the retainer is approximately $500, so you can save $450 by paying in advance for the retainer when you purchase the property.

CONVERSIONS

Apartments with new life as condominiums. . . . Gas stations now operating as retail outlets (Seven-Elevens). . . . Old homes converted to office space. . . . What was once farm acreage is now a sprawling urban shopping center. These phenomena are examples of changing usage of both land and buildings brought about by a city's growth and change.

An oversupply of gas stations throughout the city serves as an example. Because of overwhelming competition among these service stations, the more unprofitable ones shut down and remain vacant, while others are converted to needed parking lots and retail outlets.

Conversions provide boundless opportunities for the creative investor. Converting an old house located in the downtown area can be very profitable, because office space sometimes rents at twice the rental rate of housing, and in certain areas of the country it is even more.

Several years ago, when I worked for Wolverine Development in Lansing, Michigan, the company was involved with investing in strategic corner locations in the path of the city's outward growth. We would purchase single-family homes on a potentially good corner location, with the long-term intention of converting it to a more profitable rental use. This method had a great advantage over investing in similarly located vacant land because improved property can generate income and be depreciated.

Converting land use and its buildings is like turning straw into gold. But how can you take advantage of these changes in land use? Begin by obtaining an overall zoning map from your city's planning department. Each area of the city has a particular zoning (residential, multiunit, agricultural, commercial, and industrial) limiting its land use. A good conversion prospect would be a residential home already located within a commercial zone. If the property you wish to convert is located in a residential zone, it would require a change in zoning for you to accomplish your objective. Applying for a variance or zoning change normally entails much time and effort. The simplest properties to convert are those that are adjacent to the zoning you wish to convert to. If you're interested in pursuing this matter, check with your local planning department and inquire into the necessary procedure.

Condominium Conversion

To convert an apartment building into individual condominium units, ideally, you should purchase the apartments inexpensively enough so that each unit will easily convert to a saleable condo. Because of legal procedures and incidental costs to convert, not to mention the time and effort, as much as a two-to-one rule of thumb is sometimes required. A large markup is necessary so as to cover the marketing, renovation, and attorney costs incurred plus the risk and talent necessary to make such a conversion.

You must also consider the legal procedures necessary to accomplish condominium conversion. First, the city has to approve the change in use. You will be required to submit plans explaining exactly how you intend to make the conversion. Should the city consider your plans adequate, it will approve the conversion. If not, certain changes, such as additional parking or bathrooms, may be needed before you get permission from the city.

Before going ahead with plans for a condo conversion, analyze the local area to determine what comparable condos are selling for. If you can purchase an apartment building at a low enough price, then renovate and sell the converted units and earn a profit while absorbing time and costs to convert, then by all means go ahead with your plans.

To illustrate how you might calculate the potential profits of converting rental apartments into individually owned condominium units, here's an example for a 16-unit building:

Acquisition price	$480,000
Rehab @ $7,500 per unit	120,000
Attorney fees (condo document preparation, government permitting process, sales contract preparation, closing document review)	40,000
Marketing costs (advertising, sales commissions)	45,000
Mortgage interest (12-month renovation and sellout)	50,000
Incidentals (architect, interior design, landscaping, government permits)	35,000
Total costs	$770,000
Cost per unit	$ 48,125

In this example, the investor paid $480,000 ($30,000 per unit) to acquire this 16-unit rental property. And after all costs of conversion, his total investment increased to $770,000 ($48,125 per unit). But these figures haven't yet considered profits. If the investor wants to net around $10,000 per unit, he will need to sell the units at a price approaching $60,000 each.

Although the figures in this example may be considered "typical," they are by no means absolute. Every item from acquisition cost to incidentals is subject to wide variance depending on the local market, the specific property to be acquired, the amount of planned renovation, the degree of complexity of the condo conversion laws and procedures, and the marketing strategy to be adopted. Therefore, to decide whether such a project is feasible in your area, you need to research rental properties, condo prices, and conversion laws. Do some scratch pad feasibility calculations. Then, if preliminary estimates look promising, talk with an investor, contractor, attorney, or real estate consultant experienced in the conversion process. With the knowledge gained from these talks (and perhaps some follow-up research), you can decide whether this investment technique offers you enough profit potential to compensate for its risks.

Tenants in Common (TICs)

In some parts of the country, oppressive rent control and condo conversion laws make it almost impossible to convert rental apartments into condominiums even though such conversions would be very profitable. However, innovative real estate investors and entrepreneurs have found several ways to circumvent these restrictive regulations. In Berkeley, California (also commonly known as the People's Republic of Berkeley), and other left-wing-dominated cities in the San Francisco Bay Area, innovative investors have pioneered a conversion concept called TIC.

The term TIC (pronounced T-I-C) stands for tenant-in-common and is a popular form of joint ownership that's been given a unique twist to create sort of a hybrid property—something between, say, a co-op and a condominium.

As the plan typically works in the Bay Area, an investor (or group of investors) locates an older 4-unit rental house that due to rent controls has a depressed market value of say $300,000 ($75,000 per unit). As individual condo units, the apartments would sell for $145,000 each, for a total building value of $580,000; however, restrictive conversion laws eliminate this possibility.

But here's where creativity counts. Investors buy the property. Then they advertise for four households (individuals, married couple, partners, friends, families) who would like to own one of the individual units. Once found, they sell them pro rata shares of ownership in the total building at a price of say $130,000 each (if the units are of unequal quality, the pro rata division would charge some owners more and others less). Next, the respective joint owners enter into long-term leases for "their" units with all the other owners.

Although in a legal sense, all of the households jointly own the entire building; in a practical sense, each becomes the proprietor of a specific unit. Later, if one of the co-owners wishes to sell their share of the building, they can do so. The purchaser pays the seller the value of his interest and obtains leasehold right to his unit.

In addition to circumventing restrictive condo conversion laws, TICs have another advantage: Organizing a TIC is much simpler and less costly than the legal documentation and government permitting that is typically required when condo conversions are allowed. In fact, since with a TIC all you are doing is selling a building to a groups of co-owners, no special laws apply.

Although the TIC concept in rental properties has primarily been implemented as a response to excessive government, it need not be limited to that use. Even if you don't live in a "People's Republic" you might explore this investment technique in your area. Because a TIC is far easier to structure than a condo conversion, it might be a good way for you to gain experience in "buying wholesale" and "selling retail." Your greatest obstacles will be finding a lawyer who can give you competent legal counsel and explain the concept to potential buyers and building co-owners.

To learn more about the TIC concept, consider taking a tax-deductible trip to the San Francisco Bay Area and talk to investors, unit owners, and attorneys who have firsthand experience with these types of properties. Maybe you can pioneer the concept in your area.

Converting Apartments to Office Space

Office space may rent for twice the rental rate of comparable apartment rental space. Just from this observation it would appear profitable to convert apartments to office space. But before you go ahead with such a conversion, consider these important questions:

- Is the property you wish to convert within a commercial zone? If not, can it easily be changed to the proper zoning?
- What is the current vacancy rate for office space in the area of the subject property? If too much space is already available, it would be unwise to convert.
- Do you have adequate parking for office space? The city may require one parking space for every 250–500 square feet of rentable office space.
- How much will it cost to convert? Could you borrow the money to finance such a conversion? And, finally, will the cost, legal procedures, and time and effort be worth the eventual profit you will realize?

Study the situation carefully. Thoroughly analyze the finances of the projected conversion. Keep in tune with the requirements given, and if you can convert and finance at a reasonable cost and still earn a substantial profit, then go ahead with your plans.

MASTER LEASES

To make money in real estate, you need control over a property. The most common way to obtain this control is through purchase and ownership. Some investors, though, don't buy their properties—at least not right away. Instead, they master-lease them.

For example, say you locate a 12-unit apartment building that is poorly managed and needs upgrading. You could offer to buy the property, but you don't have the financial power to arrange new financing and the owner doesn't want to sell the property using a land contract or purchase money mortgage. At the present time, the property is barely producing enough cash flow to pay expenses, property taxes, and mortgage payments. The owner wants to turn this money pit into a moneymaker, but lacks the will to invest the necessary time, effort, money, and talent.

The solution: You could master-lease the entire 12-unit building and guarantee the owner a steady no-hassle monthly income. In return, you obtain the right to upgrade the building and property management to increase its net operating income (NOI).

Generally, a master lease gives you possession of the property for a period of 5 to 15 years and an option to buy at a prearranged price. During the period of your lease, you would be able to pocket the difference between what you pay to operate the property including lease payments to the owner and the amounts you collect from the individual tenants who live in each of the apartments. Here's how the before-and-after numbers might look:

Before/Owner Management

Gross potential income @ $500 per unit	$72,000
Vacancy losses @ 15%	10,800
Effective gross income	$61,200
Expenses	
Utilities	14,400
Maintenance	8,360
Advertising	2,770
Insurance	3,110
Property taxes	6,888
Miscellaneous (evictions, attorney fees, bad debts, vandalism, pest control, bookkeeping, etc.)	5,000
Total expenses	40,528
Net operating income	20,672
Mortgage payments	19,791
Before-tax cash flow	$ 881

After/Your Management

Gross potential income @ $575 per unit	$82,800
Vacancy losses @ 4%	3,312
Effective gross income	$79,488
Expenses	
Utilities	2,230
Maintenance and upkeep	13,200
Advertising	670
Insurance	2,630
Property taxes	7,300
Miscellaneous	2,500
Total expenses	28,530
Net operating income	50,958
Leasehold payments to owner	25,000
Before-tax cash flow (to you)	$25,958

How did you manage such a spectacular turnaround? (1) You upgraded the property and implemented a thorough maintenance and upkeep program; (2) with a more attractive property and a more attentive management, you were able to attract and retain high quality tenants; (3) you individually metered the apartment units to reduce your utilities; (4) you raised rents to reflect the more appealing condition of the property and the more pleasant ambience created by higher quality, neighbor-considerate, rule-abiding tenants; (5) you shopped for lower cost property and liability insurance coverage; and (6) by reducing turnover and encouraging word-of-mouth tenant referrals, you cut out most of your advertising expense.

Not only did your property turnaround increase the NOI, correspondingly, higher NOI and lower risk, more attractive apartments lead to a much higher building value. This means that if you exercised your option to buy, you could probably arrange 100 percent financing to pay off the owner, yet still give the lender a 70 to 80 percent loan-to-value ratio as measured against the property's higher value. In lieu of buying the property, you might also consider selling your leasehold and option rights to another investor. Given the much better NOI that you've created, these rights should command a substantial price. In effect, an investor would be paying you for the right to earn $25,958 per year (plus future increases) for the remaining term of your master lease, and the right to buy the property at a now bargain price.

As you can see from the example, a properly structured master lease with option to buy can create significant profit opportunities for investor-entrepreneurs who are willing to tackle turning a poorly managed, run-down property into an attractive, effectively operated apartment building.

CONTRACT FLIPPING

Generally, when you sign a contract to buy or option a property, you may later assign that contract to another investor. This technique, which is called contract flipping, offers significant profit opportunities with relatively little up-front cash investment.

Let's say that a developer announces plans to build a luxury hi-rise condominium project with units priced from $225,000 up to $775,000. However, the units won't be ready for occupancy for 18 months. In the meantime, though, buyers can reserve a unit with a deposit of $5,000. You pick a choice view unit priced at $500,000 and give the developer $5,000 of earnest money. During the construction period, this project receives rave reviews and wonderful publicity. Buyers are now signing up on waiting lists. The value of your reserved unit jumps up to $550,000. Yet, your purchase contract gives you the right to buy it at a mere $500,000. What do you do? If you want a quick $45,000 profit, "flip" your contract. Assign your right to buy this unit for a payment of $50,000. You've just made a nine-fold return on your original investment.

Of course, if this new project receives bad reviews, if mortgage interest rates skyrocket, or if the local economy goes into the tank, the market prices of these units could fall and you may have to forfeit your $5,000 deposit. So, in a sense, contract flipping is more like speculating than investing.

On the other hand, though, you need not limit use of this technique to projects under construction. Some savvy investors scout the market for bargain-priced existing properties, place the seller under contract with a small deposit, and then locate another investor who will pay them a fee (premium) for the right to step into their shoes and buy the property on the favorable terms they've previously negotiated. Although any type of contract flipping has its risks, for investors who are skilled in spotting underpriced properties, this technique can yield high returns in short time periods.

SUMMARY

Buy, manage, and hold for increased rents and property appreciation is a time-tested, effective way to build wealth in real estate. As an alternative strategy, however, you might buy, fix up, and resell your properties using a lease-option purchase contract. Under the right market conditions, this technique can increase your returns in three ways: (1) The option price you offer your tenants should exceed the price you paid for the property plus the amounts you paid for improvements; (2) during the rental period, your rent collections and option fee monies will exceed the monthly income you would receive from a straight rental; and (3) when you can sell the property by wrapping lower rate financing with higher rate seller financing, you will earn a monthly income with virtually no management effort and very little of your own capital investment remaining in the property. Once you develop a system that will work in your market, the lease-option investment technique can prove to be a real moneymaker.

In addition to lease-option, other alternative investment strategies include the 6-month rollover, property conversions, TICs, master leases, and contract flipping. Although each of these techniques involves various risks and requires a degree of specialized expertise and market knowledge, in the right circumstances, any one of them can pay off with high profits.

Overall, the basic theme of this chapter is that you need not wait passively for your real estate returns to be generated by market forces outside your control. Through creativity, knowledge, and alertness to opportunity, you can generate returns that substantially beat the market. As we pointed out at the beginning of this book, this explains why most people can do far better in real estate than in the stock market. In the stock market, you buy and *hope* prices go up. But you have no control over the results. In contrast, with real estate, you can use your mind, your market knowledge, and your entrepreneurial talents to create a strategy that can produce good returns in whatever type of market you're currently experiencing.

12 SELLING YOUR PROPERTY

At some point, regardless of your specific investment strategy, you will probably want to sell (or exchange, see Chapter 13) one or more of your properties. When that time comes, you must decide whether to sell the property yourself or employ a real estate professional. In making this decision, you should not only think about the amount of the sales commission that you will have to pay an agent, but also the services that agent can provide.

AGENT SERVICES

Selling a property involves time, money, effort, and expertise. Investors who are not willing to fulfill these obligations are not likely to sell their own property successfully.

Because most investors would rather delegate these activities, the real estate brokerage business exists to provide service to sellers. The full range of services that an agent can provide to a seller are too numerous to mention here, but some of the more important ones include:

- The agent works full time for the seller to find buyers for his property. He is not just available after work, on certain evenings, or on Sunday afternoons.
- The agent can rely on sources other than newspaper advertisements to supply a majority of his prospects. He gets them from referrals by past customers, financial institutions, hotels and motels, educational institutions, other professionals such as lawyers and insurance agents, company personnel departments,

builders, other types of advertising, canvassing, and "For Sale" signs.

- The agent can provide sellers with an appraisal showing the fair market value of their properties. This appraisal is based on what similar houses have *sold* for, not what their *asking prices* may have been.

- The agent can give helpful pointers on how sellers should prepare their properties to improve their value and encourage a quick sale.

- The agent can calculate how much sellers will "net" from a sale after all expenses have been paid, including any balance on a mortgage, taxes, or other liens.

- The agent can show the property to its best advantage and bring out those features that appeal to each specific prospective buyer. Remember that agents get to know their customer's needs so that they can show only those properties in which the buyer is likely to have an interest.

- The agent in performing these services which will facilitate the sale, frees the sellers' time for other endeavors.

- The agent can aid sellers in finding their next property and set up a Section 1031 exchange to save on taxes (see Chapter 13).

- The agent can help negotiate the sale and give advice concerning the pros and cons of each offer.

- The agent can help a buyer overcome obstacles to buying the sellers' property, such as obtaining financing, selling an existing property, working an exchange, or getting finances in order.

- The agent can follow up on prospects who have shown an interest in a property.

- The agent can exact from buyers their true objections to a property, so that sellers can attempt to overcome them. Usually buyers will be more direct with an agent than a property owner.

- The agent can prequalify the prospect and help sellers avoid wasting time accepting an offer from buyers who cannot put together the financial resources to close the sale.

- The agent can handle any details and questions about selling a property that a seller may have from the time of listing to after the closing.

- A majority of buyers rely on agents to help them find properties (see Chapter 5). Therefore, by-owner sellers may miss that large number of buyers who want the services that top agents typically provide.

Obstacles to "By Owner" Sales

Although many factors may account for an investor's difficulty in selling a property, the following items are most common:

- An emotional involvement with the property such that buyer criticism results in arguments between the buyer and the owner.
- An unwillingness to price the property in line with its market value.
- A failure to remain available during the evening hours and on weekends waiting for buyers to call or come by.
- An inability to help potential buyers to understand or secure financing of the property.
- An overdependence on newspaper advertising to bring buyers to the property.
- A personality or emotional makeup that does not lend itself well to direct negotiations with buyers.
- An inability to attend to the technical and practical problems associated with selling and buying a property.

Cost of Brokerage Services

Instead of focusing on the agent's commission, property owners should primarily be concerned with what they will "net" from a sale after paying off all necessary mortgages, liens, closing expenses, and selling fees. In effect, the real cost of the brokerage service is the difference between what a seller would "net" if he employed an agent and the net amount he would receive if he chose to sell the property himself.

On the surface it might appear that the difference in "net" between using an agent and selling "By Owner" would be the amount of the real estate sales commission. However, this situation would result only if "all other things were equal." In practice, though, they seldom are.

To obtain a better picture of what this net difference might be, you should consider four separate items: (1) the selling price of the property, (2) selling expenses incurred by the owner, (3) federal income tax law, and (4) opportunity costs.

Selling Price. As mentioned in Chapter 5, the selling price of a property by owner is usually less than that of a similar property sold through an agent. This fact then, reduces the difference in nets by the amount that the price by owner is less than the agent's price.

Selling Expenses. The selling expenses when using an agent are fixed fairly closely by the amount of the sales commission, which may range between 3 and 10 percent depending on the type of property and the type of listing. (Types of listings are discussed later in this chapter.) When an owner sells a property, the amount spent out of pocket on selling expenses varies directly with the length of time the property is on the market.

In some cases, an owner may get lucky and have to spend only $500 to $1,000 out of pocket, and in other instances that amount may go much higher and the owner still not be successful. The difference in net is further reduced by the amounts a by-owner seller must spend out of pocket for such things as advertising, signs, telephone, additional legal costs, appraisal fees, and other miscellaneous amounts.

Federal Income Tax. As discussed in Chapter 13, out-of-pocket selling expenses may be deducted in calculating the capital gain resulting from the sale of a property. Therefore, even if out-of-pocket expenses of a by-owner seller are less than those incurred by a seller who uses an agent, the sum is less than the absolute dollar difference between these amounts because of the resulting tax deduction. Again, this will reduce the difference in nets between the by-owner seller and agent seller.

Opportunity Costs. Opportunity costs are costs incurred by a by-owner seller for the time, effort, and aggravation that selling a property entails such as the cost of the time wasted staying around hoping for appointments that may or may not show and to answer a telephone that may or may not ring.

The method of calculating the true cost of the brokerage service is illustrated in the following example: Assume that a property can be sold by an agent for $100,000 with a 6 percent sales commission. A by-owner seller can get a price of $97,500 with selling expenses of $1,000. Moreover, assume the seller is in a 35 percent marginal tax bracket. In addition, the closing costs and mortgage balance that will have to be paid by the seller regardless of how he sells the house equal $65,000. The nets of each case are computed as follows:

	By-Owner Seller	Agent Seller
Sales price	$97,500	$100,000
Mortgage and closing	− 65,000	− 65,000
Selling expenses after tax break	− 650	− 3,900
	(1,000 × .65)	(.65 × .06 × 100,000)
Opportunities costs imputed	− 750	0
Net under each method	31,100	31,100
Difference in nets	0	

As you can see, based on the figures in this example, even though the seller who employed a real estate agent to sell his property paid an after-tax sales commission of $3,900, his net of $31,100 equaled the net realized by the by-owner seller.

Although no one can predict ahead of time what the different net amounts might be to any specific seller, this example is certainly not an atypical case. And probably only in unusual instances would the net received in a by-owner sale exceed the net received in an agent sale by any substantial amount when all appropriate items are considered. The basic point is that the true cost of the brokerage services to a seller can be a positive (benefit) amount and even in a worst-case scenario, it will seldom come close to approaching the nominal dollar amount of the sales commission.

In her book *Housewise,* real estate investor Suzanne Brangham points out, "Frequently—about once a day—someone asks me why I don't get a real estate license and avoid paying someone else the commission on each property I handle. My answer to this is that I don't want to *sell* real estate—I want to invest in it and renovate it . . . more importantly, if I did try to sell my own properties, I'd lose some of the most valuable assets in this business—the agents I work with. Good agents know what properties are selling for, which areas are strong, and which neighborhoods are getting hot. They know what's gone up in value and which areas may be coming down."

In other words, Suzanne is saying that the agents she works with don't cost her money. Instead, the information, knowledge, and services they provide help her make money. Of course, only you can figure out the sales strategy that's best for you to pursue. But whatever you decide, make sure you consider all of the potential costs and benefits of going it alone versus using an agent. Don't naively believe that you can simply "sell the property yourself and save the commission."

LISTING AGREEMENTS

A listing contract is the employment agreement between a seller of a property and the real estate brokerage firm. The three most common types of listing contracts are (1) open listing; (2) exclusive agency; and (3) exclusive right to sell. Under the first two types of listing agreements, owners retain the right to sell their property themselves without paying a brokerage commission. Under the exclusive right to sell listing agreement the owners agree to pay as long as a sale takes place within a stated time.

There is no one best listing contract for all sellers. It mainly depends on whether you want to retain the right to sell your property yourself, or hire one or a number of brokers. Each type contract has advantages and disadvantages.

Many good agents though, will hesitate to accept an open or exclusive listing. These agent prefer an exclusive right-to-sell agreement. They want to protect the time and money that they will invest in their efforts to sell your property. Unless, you have a good reason to retain the right-to-sell your own property, it is recommended that you do give the agent an exclusive right-to-sell agreement.

If you sign an exclusive right-to-sell contract, make sure, though, that the brokerage firm will allow you to terminate the agreement in good faith at anytime with *no further obligation* to that broker. Otherwise you could be prohibited from listing your property with another broker or selling it yourself until after the date that the original listing agreement would have expired.

Note that the preceding advice stresses "termination in good faith." You should have a justifiable cause for canceling. For example, a case where a sales agent of the broker made unauthorized disclosures to buyers would be good cause to terminate. Most reputable brokers will permit cancellations of this nature.

In addition to the termination clause, you should examine a listing contract on the following points:

- *A written contract.* That the contract should be in writing cannot be stressed too highly. The listing agreement is a legal contract and common sense dictates that any agreement under which one party is to pay a commission to another party should be in writing to clearly define the responsibilities and obligations of each party.

- *Identification.* The property must be identified. This does not necessarily mean a full legal description, but one sufficiently clear to avoid confusion or misunderstanding. "Acreage in Aiken County" is not an adequate description. A number of cases are in court records where an insufficient property identification caused a misunderstanding between a buyer and seller as to what property was actually sold (bought).

- *Sales price.* Both the price and terms of the sale should be stated. A broker should not accept a listing at an inflated selling price merely to obtain the listing in hopes of renegotiating the price before the listing runs out. This procedure is unfair and misleading to the seller.

- *Commission.* This is a negotiable fee and may be any amount both parties agree to. It may be a fixed dollar amount or a percentage of the sales price or a combination of both. "Net listings" in which the commission is all money above a given net amount are prohibited by law in most states. If an offer is submitted substantially below the listing price, some brokers will accept a lower commission than stated in the listing contract to help the sale go through. It is illegal for real estate trade associations to set commission rates that member firms must charge.

- *Signatures.* All owners of the property should sign the contract. It is a good policy for both a husband and wife to sign even though the property is in one name only. The broker should sign also as he or she is a party to the contract and must be obligated to perform specific duties to the seller. A salesperson may not sign the listing contract unless authorized to do so by the employing broker.

- *Expiration date.* A definite expiration date should be stated in the listing agreement. A typical listing period for a house or small income property is 90 days, although 120 days may not be unreasonable. A listing contract for more than 120 days should not be signed except in unusual circumstances. Listing contracts for larger income properties may reasonably run a little longer, say 120 days to 180 days, with renewal if the agent seems to be doing a good job of promoting the property.

- *Type of listing.* The listing contract must clearly state and define the type listing it is. An "exclusive right to sell" listing must clearly state that it is such a listing and must contain a statement of the seller's obligation to pay a commission no matter who sells the property.

- *Delivery of copy.* Most state laws require an agent to *immediately* give a copy of any listing contract to the parties who have signed it.

- *Automatic renewal.* The listing contract should not contain an automatic renewal clause. These clauses frequently provide that if an owner does not notify the listing broker in writing at least 10 days before expiration of the intention to cancel the contract, it is automatically renewed for 60 or 90 days. Most courts will not enforce these clauses.

- *Cancellation of contract.* Either the owner or the real estate broker may cancel a listing contract at any time prior to the execution of a contract of sale with a buyer who is ready, willing, and able to purchase at the listed price. If an owner cancels the listing contract *without cause* before the agent has found a purchaser and before expiration of the listing contract, the broker can sue the owner for any loss or damage that he may have sustained because of the cancellation. However, as a practical matter, most brokers allow cancellation by a client at any time without obligation as long as no buyer has been located. However, sometimes, even though you are allowed to terminate the listing, you will be prohibited from listing with another brokerage firm until the time the listing would otherwise have expired.

    If a real estate broker fails to perform as agreed in the listing contract, or cancels the contract before its expiration, the owner may recover from the broker the loss (if any) sustained by reason of the agent's default or cancellation. As a practical matter, though, no compensable damage would have occurred.

- *Personal property.* The listing contract should clearly identify personal property that will be included in the sale. Drapes, carpets, window air conditioning units, appliances, and even shrubs are examples of items that often cause disputes between buyer, seller, and broker, when it is unclear whether they are to remain the property of the seller or the tenants.

- *Offers.* Real estate brokers may not refuse to forward a bona fide offer because they are not satisfied with it or believe that the seller will reject it. They must present all written offers for consideration by the seller. They cannot hold one back in favor of another or until an offer in possession of the seller has been considered. Brokers cannot assign priorities to offers received. All offers to purchase must be presented promptly to the seller. Once accepted by the seller, the signed acceptance must be promptly delivered to the purchaser. Delay in delivery could allow the purchaser time to withdraw the offer.

- *Earnest money deposit.* A bona fide offer should be accompanied by an earnest money deposit. Many listing contracts provide that on default of the buyer the earnest money is divided equally between the broker and seller. You, however, can change this agreement such that you are entitled to all of it. If the listing contract is silent on this point the forfeited deposit in most states belongs to the seller.

- *Obligations of broker.* Basically, the listing contract obligates the real estate broker to do everything possible to find a buyer for the listed property who is ready, willing, and able to purchase. A broker who advertises and shows a property regularly is thought to be fulfilling that obligation.

- *Earning the commission.* Unless otherwise stated in the listing contract, the real estate agent earns a commission by finding a willing and able buyer for your property. If the buyer can't locate financing, if the property does not pass inspection, or if some other buyer contingency clause isn't met, you want your listing agreement to exempt you from paying a commission. Similarly, you also want a provision that releases you from the obligation to pay a commission if for some reason beyond your control you can't close (e.g., title problem of which you were unaware).

Obligations of the Sales Agent

Although the listing agreement sets forth the basic legal relationship between you and your brokerage firm, you should expect your sales agent to go substantially beyond the bare bones minimum duties spelled out in the listing agreement. More specifically, the listing firm and your agent should:

1. Work actively to *find* buyers for your property, not simply show properties to prospects who come to them.

2. Notify you at least weekly what specific actions they are taking to find a buyer for your property.

3. Place your property on the market at its market value or only slightly above it.

4. When your property has been priced in the right range, agents should not try to talk you into accepting offers substantially less than its listing price.

5. Any undesirable features of your property should have been considered when its market value was estimated; therefore, no need exists for you to reduce your price materially to compensate for any defects.

6. All offers, with no exceptions, should be presented to you as soon as they have been received by the agency; the firm should assist you in preparing your property for sale by suggesting the types of changes that would increase its market value and marketability.

7. No sold sign should be placed on your home until after the sale has closed. Although a "sale pending" sign may be used, the firm should still work to obtain back-up offers on your property.

8. You should be given time to consult an attorney prior to signing anything or be free to insert a clause that the sales contract is subject to your rescission if your attorney later finds it unacceptable. However, in these cases the attorney should be used to check the terms of the contract, not to rewrite it or to change for sake of change and inflating his charges.

9. The sales agent should help the buyer work out the necessary financing for the purchase of your property and should not receive a kickback from the lender (this is done in some areas when certain lenders want to encourage sales agents to bring them mortgage business).

10. Sales agents should not make contract concessions without your express permission (e.g., telling the buyer without your knowledge that you will include the refrigerator and stove in the sale).

11. The sales agent should serve as a good faith negotiator between you and the buyer without coercing you into accepting an unreasonable offer. He also should be able to tell you when the sales contract is signed approximately how much you will net from the sale.

12. The firm should keep you informed about what is happening from the time the contract of sale is signed up to the date of closing.

13. The sales agent should have an accurate closing statement prepared for you accounting for all receipts and expenditures relevant to you.

14. The sales agent should make no unauthorized disclosures to prospects about your personal situation which might harm your strength in negotiating (e.g., that you have to move in three weeks or that you are in need of ready cash for another property that you are buying).

15. The sales agent should learn all of the information about your property that is discussed in Chapter 3.

16. The sales agent should inform you before you sign a sales contract as to the probability that the buyer is financially able to close the transaction.

17. The sales agent should try to get at least a $1,000 or more earnest money deposit; of course, the larger the value of your property the more the agent should obtain. Sometimes it's appropriate for buyers to tender a relatively small earnest money deposit with their offer, but then agree to increase it to 5 or 10% of the purchase price as soon as you accept the offer.

18. Your agent should make all disclosures to you that may be required by your state's agency disclosure laws. In addition, the agent should explain the duties and obligations required of agents by your state's agency statutes, case law, and licensing rules and regulations.

Your Obligations to Your Agent

When you use an agent to sell your property, the selling process becomes a joint effort. Nearly every seasoned sales agent can remember a sale that was lost because an owner failed to use common sense. So, when you employ an agent, your reasonable cooperation with the agent's requests can enhance your chances of a speedy sale.

Specifically, the first thing you should do is to get your property in tip-top shape. Second, you generally should allow the agent to show the property without your interruption and distraction. Would you like your boss looking over your shoulder when you are doing your job?

Third, if you are using an exclusive right-to-sell listing contract, you should refer any prospective buyers to the sales agent. You should let the agent do what you are paying him or her to do.

And fourth, be fair. If the agent has done the job, pay the commission. Don't try to negotiate or make side deals with buyers around an agent you have hired on an exclusive right to sell basis. Owners have the right to sell their own property, but when they use an agent, that relationship should be on a good-faith basis or it should not be entered into.

PREPARE THE PROPERTY FOR TOP DOLLAR

To receive top dollar for your property in the shortest time, you may need to spend time and money getting it ready for sale. Your property should make an immediate favorable impression on prospective buyers. Few things turn buyers off as fast as a property that is not aesthetically pleasing. And yet, many sellers surprisingly ignore even a basic sprucing up of their property before placing it on the market.

This tendency of sellers to let their properties run down works to your advantage as a buyer; but as a seller, you don't want your property's poor condition or appearance to detract from your selling price. Furthermore, a sub-par property draws inferior tenants at lower rent levels. And since buyers of income properties (should) pay close attention to tenant quality and operating income, these deficiencies, too, will contribute to a lower selling price. In other words, putting your property in tip-top condition is not only a sound philosophy of property management, it stands tall as an important part of your sales strategy.

To illustrate the importance of preparing a property for sale, consider this example. Although the property in question was a single-family home, the same principles apply to all types of properties.

Example Some years back, a friend asked me over to see if I could determine why his house would not sell. He had had it on and off the market for over a year with no success. Nevertheless, the home was priced reasonably for its location and physical structure.

When I inspected it, several problems were apparent. The wallpaper in the bedrooms, kitchen, and living room was faded and drab in color. The kitchen floor tile was permanently stained and discolored and two of the bedrooms had tile floors rather than more desirable hardwood or carpeting. The upstairs attic had been converted into a children's bedroom and recreation area; however, because no duct work was available to the upstairs, a gas space heater had been installed.

Overall, it was obvious that prospective buyers recognized that the interior of the house lacked warmth and color and were leery of having children playing unattended near a gas space heater. So I recommended that the owner install light-colored, inexpensive carpeting in the bedrooms and repaper the rooms with an attractive, inexpensive prepasted wallpaper. Also, I suggested that he put new tile in the kitchen and take the space heater out of his attic and replace it with baseboard electric heat. Furthermore, I advised the owner to remove about 60 percent of the overgrown shrubs and plants from his yard because it looked like a jungle.

After four days of work and $837 in expenses for the carpeting and electric heat (including hired installation), paint, wallpaper, tile (which he installed himself), and rental of a chain saw for removal of the bushes and shrubs, the owner again placed the house on the market. It sold 45 days later for $4,000 more than he had previously been asking. This was not a bad return for $837 and four days of work.

The people who owned the house were so close to its shortcomings that they just didn't notice them. The point is that when you try to sell (or rent out) a property you must evaluate it as buyers (or tenants) in the market will view it, not according to your own tastes and what you have grown accustomed to.

Usually, it's best when redecorating to use colors that will blend with about any color of furnishings. A fresh coat or two of off-white paint will add a lot to most rooms. And prospective buyers won't have to worry about refurbishing right after taking possession.

Other Important Areas to Look for Changes

When thinking about how you might economically improve your property, you should look carefully at the following areas because they are important to prospective buyers. Remember, the more problems you can overcome, the fewer the number of criticisms the buyer will be able to raise during your negotiations.

Plumbing.   All the faucets should be checked for leaks and drips. Where washers are needed, they should be replaced. You should not simply tighten the handle down to the extent that the seat is damaged. Persons examining plumbing will frequently turn all the faucets on and off to see if there is any damage in the internal workings. All the drains should also be checked to make sure that they drain quickly. Check the water closets to determine whether the water shuts off automatically as it is supposed to. Toilet seats that are discolored or cracked should be replaced. The perimeters of all bathroom fixtures, showers, and bathtubs should be checked. Any cracks should be repaired with caulking compound, especially where leaks are present. If it is cold outside, you should take care to protect pipes exposed to the weather. Also, stains of previous leaks should be removed. A stain is a dead giveaway to a buyer that you have a plumbing problem.

Electrical System. All electrical outlets should work properly and their locations should be known. A negative feature of many older properties is an insufficient number of outlets to handle today's many new electrical appliances. The fuse or circuit breaker box should be in good working order. Any fluorescent bulbs that are weak or slow in coming on should be replaced or the starters should be replaced if necessary. Burned outlets should be replaced. An outlet should never have a large number of cords plugged in with adapters and extension cords. This suggests insufficient outlets and is also a fire hazard.

Heating and Air Conditioning. The heating and air conditioning system should be in good working order. Nothing would be more negative to a buyer than to walk into a property in the middle of summer and find that the air conditioning is inadequate to cool the home (or that the heating system is inadequate to heat the home properly in the winter). Filters on the furnace and air conditioning equipment should be changed prior to showing the property. Some buyers will inspect the filters. If a very dirty one is found, the person may assume that the filters have not been changed regularly and that the system itself may have received some damage. Clean filters indicate to many buyers that you have taken proper care of the equipment. Also heating and air conditioning duct outlets should be cleaned. If the property has gas heat or a gas water heater, make sure to throw away old matches from previous manual pilot lightings. Failure to do so will indicate trouble in keeping the pilot lit.

Windows. Any cracked or broken windows should be replaced. In addition, broken pulleys and damaged frames and sills should be repaired. All windows that open should lift up and down easily.

Appliances. Appliances such as built-in oven, range, garbage disposal, dishwasher, or refrigerator that are to be included in the sale should function properly. Refrigerators should be kept defrosted and ovens should remain clean while the property is on the market (whenever possible, get your tenants to cooperate with you in keeping their appliances and their living units in neat and clean shape during the sales effort).

Walls and Ceilings.   Walls and ceilings should be attractive. Any cracks in plaster should be repaired. Faded or dark colored walls should be painted or papered. Strive for a bright, cheerful look in the property. To reduce your work, buy prepasted wallpaper and good-quality paint that will cover with just one coat. Paint and wallpaper are probably the two items that will return the most gain relative to their cost. Remember to use color schemes that are attractive to a wide range of buyers (and tenants).

Doors.   Screen or storm doors should be checked for screens that are in need of replacement and springs that are too weak. All interior doors should open and close easily without being too tight or too loose. Doors that are too tight can be planed relatively easily to stop their dragging. Since security is a major factor in many tenants' minds, replacement of worn locks or locks that are easily picked or broken with a sturdier variety can add to the property's desirability. However, don't go overboard in installing too many locks, chains, and bolts. A preponderance of these security devices can make the buyer (tenant) question the safety of the neighborhood.

Landscaping.   Except in special circumstances, property owners who spend thousands of dollars on landscaping are not likely to have their money returned for this expenditure. However, a well-kept yard will add materially to resale potential. Therefore, spend some time getting the yard in shape. The grass should be cut and leaves raked regularly. In addition, dead or unattractive shrubbery should be removed and perhaps replaced with new shrubbery. If time and season permit, planting flowers or installing flower boxes can significantly increase the attractiveness of your property.

Storage Areas.   All storage areas should be cleaned and items of no value thrown away. This job will need to be done anyway before you hand over possession to a buyer and will materially add to the appearance of spaciousness within the storage areas. It is difficult to imagine how roomy a closet, attic, or basement is when that area is crammed to the brim. Spaciousness in closets is a very important factor. Again, here's another area of property preparation where you may need to enlist the cooperation of your tenants.

General Cleaning. Your property should be cleaned from top to bottom. Most buyers want a property that has been well taken care of. Bathrooms and kitchens are especially important. Special efforts to remove stains on sinks, toilet bowls, and bathtubs as well as countertops and cabinet areas can add wonders to the appeal of a property. Potted flowers in bathrooms and kitchens can also add to the appeal. Floors should be scrubbed and carpets vacuumed regularly during the selling period. Clean windows and mirrors are also very important. (One more time, I want to emphasize the need to get your tenants to cooperate in keeping your property in top condition. Moreover, buyers will draw inferences about the quality of your tenants from how neat and clean they maintain their units. If your tenants won't practice tidy housekeeping, consider replacing them with tenants who will honor your requests.)

Safety Factors. While cleaning and repairing your property take special note of anything that might cause someone to stumble, fall, or otherwise be injured. For example, loose carpeting, torn linoleum, loose handrails, and scattered wires and cords can be dangerous. You are responsible for the safety of all the people coming in and out of your property. Also, safety factors help sell a property because buyers want their own tenants to be safe.

Major Improvements and Alterations. In most cases, the amounts you spend on major property improvements cannot be recovered dollar for dollar, although they can give you a substantial marketability edge over the competition. If you consider adding a room, modernizing a bath or kitchen, converting a garage to a recreation room or some similar change, keep the amenities and characteristics comparable with others in the neighborhood (see Chapters 3 and 4).

Compliance Issues

As noted in Chapter 5, real estate law has dramatically shifted from *caveat emptor* (let the buyer beware) to *caveat vendor* (let the seller beware). Consequently, as part of your property preparation, you are encouraged to discuss the issue of seller disclosures with your attorney and your real estate agent. A variety of disclosure laws (which differ by state and city) now apply to property condition (roof, foundation,

HVAC, plumbing and electrical systems, etc.), environmental hazards (lead paint, asbestos, underground storage tanks, water quality, EMFs, radon, etc.), code compliance (zoning, building permits, safety regulations, etc.), location (floodplain, mudslide area, earthquake fault line, excessive crime, nearby landfills, other off-site hazards, etc.), and virtually anything else that might tend to upset someone, at some time, for some reason.

In other words, today no seller is completely safe from dissatisfied buyer claims of seller nondisclosure, misrepresentation, or fraud. Although complaining investors typically are accorded less status under the disclosure laws than homebuyers, you can never be certain how a court will rule. Therefore, when you prepare your property for sale, do it honestly. Don't try to hide, cover up, or disguise any defects or problems. Either bring the problems into compliance with any applicable laws and building regulations or truthfully disclose deficiencies.

"As-Is" Sales Still Require Disclosures

Some property owners know that their buildings have an unsound foundation, a leaky roof, or a no-longer-used underground heating oil tank. In an attempt to get around disclosure, however, they (or their agents) will advertise such properties "as-is." By putting prospective buyers on notice that they must inspect the property for themselves, some sellers think they have fulfilled their legal obligation. But these sellers are mistaken. If you know of a "material defect" in your property, you must disclose it. Otherwise, you run the risk of losing a legal action based on nondisclosure or fraud.

Describing a property as is does not relieve you of the legal responsibility to tell buyers about significant problems that are within your knowledge. So, once again we emphasize that, in selling property, full disclosure is the best policy. If for some reason you can't repair, alleviate, or eliminate a property defect, then make sure you explicitly inform the buyer (preferably in writing, so, if necessary, you can later prove your truthfulness).

ATTRACTING BUYERS

Generally if you have listed your property with a real estate firm, that firm will assume the responsibility of getting the word out about your property. However, don't simply assume that your agent is doing the job that's necessary. Today, most top agents prepare marketing plans for their listed properties. So, get with your agent and decide the best ways to reach prospective buyers. These methods should include:

- Newspaper advertising.
- Word-of-mouth referrals.
- Networking through apartment owners association groups.
- Electronic information highway (Internet, commercial on-line services, Realtors Information Network, MLS, etc.).
- Advertising in specialized investor publications.
- Cold-calling current or prospective real estate investors.

Advertising and Promotion

In advertising circles, the elements of a good advertisement have often been represented by the acronym AIDA: (1) Attention, (2) Interest, (3) Desire, and (4) Action.

Attention. As a first step, advertisements for your property need to grab the attention of prospects. Foremost, you (or your agent) must select the media that best reaches your targeted prospects. In the sale of real estate, this first step is relatively easy because many publications, on-line bulletin boards, and other advertising promotional outlets offer specialized listing sections for income properties. Buyers who are in the market know where to look for properties.

Nevertheless, your ad will be competing with dozens (sometimes hundreds or even thousands) of other ads. So, you must figure out some way to set your ad apart by size, typography, color, illustration, headline, word choice, or other creative techniques. The best way to achieve this goal is to look closely at other ads for similar properties, and then do something different. At this point, you chiefly want to design and position your ad so that it draws the prospect's eye toward it.

Interest. Once you have grabbed the prospect's attention, the next step is to interest him or her in your specific property. To create interest, you should give the prospect concrete information about your property. Avoid cliches like "real moneymaker," "fantastic opportunity," or other abstract grandiose claims that have been touted by others since time immemorial. Stick to the facts and criteria that serious investors will use to judge properties such as gross rent multiplier (GRM), net operating income (NOI), cap rate (R), and property location and description (Westside brick fourplex: three, 2BR, 2 Bth units plus oversized owners' suite).

Desire. As you arouse interest, your ad should also stimulate desire. Make the property sound good relative to other advertised properties. Cite specific facts (not vague claims) that give your rentals a competitive advantage over others. Have you rented your units to good, long-term tenants who take excellent care of the property? Does the building require low-maintenance expense? Are you offering a bargain price, OWC financing, a low-rate assumable mortgage, lease-option, master-lease, or other "easy-to-buy" technique? Does the property offer strong fix-up possibilities, and above-average rate of appreciation, or perhaps condo conversion potential?

Few buyers call every ad. So give them reasons to call about your property. Study other ads. Then, use your ad to highlight your property's competitive advantages, compared with others.

Action. As a final step, tell your prospects what to do. Don't leave the action stage to their imagination. Don't simply list a telephone number. Tell the prospects to call for an appointment, attend an open house, drive by the property, or make an offer. Also, give them a reason to take action now. Although "won't last" is approaching cliche, it still conveys a sense that prospects should not put off until tomorrow what needs to be done today. In some way, you want to convey the message, "those who snooze, lose."

Display Honesty. Although not typically considered a part of AIDA framework, a fifth and critically important element of your advertising is honesty. Too many real estate ads grab attention, create desire, and generate action, but then the property fails to deliver as promised. In fact, some real estate agents explicitly use this tactic to obtain leads. In running ads, their goal is not to sell properties, per se. Rather their ads are designed to get the names of potential buyers and then try to talk them into using the services of that agent to help them locate the type of property that the investors are looking for.

In principle, there's nothing wrong with this approach. But, in practice, if the lead generating ad deceives, misleads, or even over-promises, the prospect not only won't buy the advertised property, he or she will doubt the agent's competence and integrity. So, regardless of whether you are trying to sell a specific property or generate a lead, your advertising should not read in such a way that prospects are destined for disappointment when they inspect and evaluate the actual property. Yes, accent your property's advantageous features or terms of financing. But don't presell a product you can't deliver.

NEGOTIATING THE SALES CONTRACT

In Chapter 8, we've previously discussed this topic from your position as a buyer. Therefore, since the same negotiating strategies and tactics can be employed by sellers, we won't again cover that ground here. Essentially, we will just remind you that in your talks with buyers, you are not negotiating price, you are negotiating an *agreement*. Never let your negotiations center exclusively on price. Too often, this mistake puts buyers and sellers into polar opposites where each one is trying to pull the other into their position.

Instead, remember that your sales agreement will incorporate many issues such as earnest money deposit, closing date, possession date, personal property, lease guarantees, closing costs, prorations, repair escrow, contingencies, terms of financing, type of financing, amount of financing, type of deed, quality of title, casualty risks, and default remedies. Price need not represent the only, nor even the most critical issue.

Most importantly, you want an agreement that closes. No lawyer has ever drafted a contract that was immune to challenge in the courts (either on bona fides or pretense). Sales contracts seldom close because of legal threats. They close because both parties believe they are gaining more than they are giving up. By keeping the other parties' full complement of needs in view along with multidimensional possibilities for give-and-take, you can create a win-win agreement that both you and the other party will gladly honor.

SUMMARY

When the time comes to sell one or more of your properties, you will first have to decide whether to employ a real estate brokerage firm, and if so, what type of listing agreement to enter into. In making this decision, you should consider the services that the realty firm can provide as well as realistically evaluate whether you could put forth the necessary time, effort, and expertise to do it yourself.

Most "For Sale By Owner" sellers try to sell their own properties to "save the commission." But once a full accounting is made for sales price differences, selling expenses, opportunity costs, and tax deductions, these anticipated savings often disappear. In addition, when selling by owner, you forfeit the opportunity to develop a strong relationship with a top agent who can help you discover choice properties to buy. None of these considerations necessarily means you shouldn't try to sell your own property. Some owners do profit by doing so. On the other hand, don't mistakenly believe that this effort will prove cheap or easy.

Generally, as part of the sales process, you should put your property in tip-top condition. Preparing your property for sale not only enables you to impress buyers with the quality of your property, it will help you attract better tenants at higher rents. With better tenants, higher rents, reduced turnover, and stable operating expenses, your property will yield a greater NOI with lower risk. Therefore, as the market capitalizes your NOI with a lower cap rate, your building will show a larger market value. Preparation pays off.

After preparing your property for sale, you (or your agent) will need to attract prospective buyers through advertising and promotion. As a concise guide, you can structure your ads to fit the AIDA framework. Moreover, your ads (and all other communications with prospective buyers) should display forthright honesty. This practice not only will prove effective in turning up real buyers, it will reduce the chance that your buyer will later try to void or rescind the sales contract for reasons of seller nondisclosure, misrepresentation, or fraud.

Toward this same goal of a smooth closing process and a satisfied buyer, your negotiations should search for a win-win sales agreement that considers a full range of topics where price becomes just one of many issues that's open to give-and-take. As an added insight, don't forget that real estate investors are buying the future. Keep their dreams alive with the specific ways that they will make money with your property and the price they pay today will become less important to them. When you *buy*, focus specifically on getting a good price relative to today's prices. When you *sell*, set future profits as the standard and buyers will be more likely to meet your price, especially if in return you give them other terms or concessions that make them feel good about the deal "they've" negotiated.

13 HOW TO REDUCE YOUR TAXES

It is sad commentary today that for many investors taxes have become their largest annual outlay. Income taxes on rental income and capital gains; property taxes; worker's compensation, unemployment, and Social Security taxes for employees; impact fees, special assessments; bond levies; sales taxes; and the "hidden" taxes of rent controls, property regulations, and the out-of-control costs of litigation all add up to hundreds of billions of dollars a year. Although the United States was founded on the twin ideas that people are entitled to both their property and the fruits of their labor, for the most part, governments at all levels (federal, state, and local) have pushed those founding ideas into the dustbin of history.

Consequently, you must do all you can to protect what you earn. Otherwise, you will find yourself working and investing so that others may spend the wealth that you have produced through your sustained efforts and risk taking. That task is becoming more difficult. Not only do present-day governments generally ignore our rights of property and industry, they also ignore the fundamental principle of justice that law should remain simple and stable.

THE RISKS OF CHANGE AND COMPLEXITY

At the founding of the United States of America, Publius (John Jay, Alexander Hamilton, and James Madison) wrote these words in *The Federalist:*

> It will be of little avail to the people that the laws are made by men of their own choice if the laws be so voluminous that they cannot

be read, or so incoherent that they cannot be understood; if they be repeated or revised before they are promulgated, or undergo such incessant changes that no man who knows what the law is today can guess what it will be tomorrow.

Can anything be more contradictory to the preceding principles than the current federal income tax laws (not to mention also the various and ever-changing laws of liability that can wreak havoc on property owners)? At present, the Internal Revenue Code, court cases, regulations, interpretive rulings, and journal commentary take up more than one million pages of text. Moreover, the Internal Revenue Service, the U. S. Department of the Treasury, and Congress change or threaten to change the tax laws on an almost daily basis.

The Risks of Change

Up until December 1986 when the massive Tax Reform Act of 1986 (TRA 1986) was enacted, most real estate investors calculated the anticipated yields from their properties using an after-tax cash flow model based on the then current tax laws. Correspondingly, investors used the discounted net present value (NPV) of these after-tax cash flows to figure the price they should pay for their real estate investments. This pricing technique proved to be a big mistake.

Unlike its policy with prior tax reform measures, with the passage of TRA 1986, Congress failed to grandfather existing property owners. For the first time in our nation's history, Congress forced real estate investors to abandon the existing tax computations that had made their property investments feasible and instead made them pay the new, greatly increased taxes required by TRA 1986. As a result, most income properties immediately lost 20 to 30 percent of their market value and tens of thousands of limited partners in apartment and office building syndication projects were completely wiped out. With thousands of apartment and office buildings now worth less than the balance on their outstanding mortgages, investors *en masse* simply gave their properties back to their lenders.

Although most Americans have been led to believe that the S&L debacle was caused by greed, fraud, and deregulation, in fact, the biggest culprit was TRA 1986. No doubt, the oil bust and oversupply also played a role. But after TRA 1986, investing in rental properties could not prove profitable for most "passive" (see later discussion) investors. Large-scale investment capital disappeared. In its place came the vulture funds who were only willing to pay 20 cents to 50 cents on the dollar for properties. With a massive number of foreclosures for the vultures to feed upon, traditional property transactions became few and far between.

What lessons can you learn from this government-induced fiasco? First and foremost, never invest in real estate using after-tax yields as your investment criterion—unless you also factor in an extra large measure of return to offset the real risk that government will once again apply new unfavorable tax laws *retroactively* to existing property owners. That is why in this book we have emphasized pretax cash flow and valuation techniques.

Second, recognize that the downturn in the prices of apartment buildings were not caused by long-term shortfalls in demand as some analysts have argued. It was excess supply, job losses, and TRA 1986 that combined to turn many real estate investments into losses. However, with the economy now back on track in nearly all parts of the country, apartment vacancy rates falling to 10-year lows, and a more conservative outlook in Washington that realizes the power to tax is the power to destroy, the mid- to long-term outlook for investments in rental housing looks brighter than it has in years.

In the past, many real estate investors didn't really buy properties, they bought *tax shelters.* In the light of frequent tax law changes, this investment strategy proved fraught with risk (even if generally recognized). Today, smart investors are buying into market fundamentals, and those fundamentals seem promising.

The Risks of Complexity

Besides the risks of tax law changes, all investors also face the risks of complexity. Without a doubt, income tax laws are "so voluminous that they can't be read, and so incoherent that they can't be understood."

For example, in recent years, *Money Magazine* has created an income and expense profile for a typical investor and sent the figures to 50 CPAs, tax lawyers, and the IRS. *Money* has asked these tax experts to calculate this hypothetical household's federal income tax liability. Guess what? Among these 50 separately prepared tax returns, no two have ever produced the same answer. In fact, in 1991, the difference between the high and low tax bill was a whopping $66,000. (See *Money,* May, 1996, p. 13.)

What does all of this mean to you? Most importantly, never forget that the constant change and complexity of tax law makes it uncertain and incomprehensible not just to average citizens, but also to tax preparers. This doesn't mean that some parts of the law aren't relatively certain (e.g., the deductibility of mortgage interest paid to finance rental properties, or say the 2-year replacement residence rule). It does mean, though, that in many instances, figuring your tax liability will require judgment calls (e.g., the allocation of property value between land and improvements for purposes of calculating depreciation).

Therefore, you will need to choose whether to take an aggressive stance on matters of judgment to reduce your taxes to the lowest possible level. Or, should you "play it safe?" Pay more, take less than the law *might* allow, and reduce your chance of an audit.

You and your tax advisor can answer this question only after considering your total personal situation in light of current IRS audit standards and the "hot issues" that may flag your return for audit. Nevertheless, before you choose to "play it safe," consider the following points.

Audits Are a Tactic of Intimidation.   "Playing it safe" is exactly what the IRS wants you to do. The IRS operates primarily through intimidation. They want taxpayers to fear an audit. The fewer the number of people who "push the envelope," the more money the IRS collects for the government. However, the lawful role of the IRS is not to raise the maximum amount of revenue. Rather, statutorily, the IRS is charged with enforcing the tax laws. Therefore, as long as you can plausibly support an aggressive position that reduces your taxes, you have little to fear from the audit itself. (Of course, the time, effort, and expense you will incur is a proper consideration.)

You Can Renegotiate Your Assessment.   Even if the audit goes against your position, that doesn't mean you have completely lost. When the IRS assesses you more in taxes, you can renegotiate the amount (based on the facts of your case and applicable tax law, not simply, "I'll give you 50 cents on the dollar") with the examiner, another examiner, or the manager of the IRS office responsible for your audit. In many (if not most) cases, through these renegotiations, you can persuade the IRS to reduce its additional assessments.

You Can Appeal Your Assessment.   Absent a satisfactory resolution at the local level, you can ask the district appeals office to reduce or eliminate the additional assessment. Although theoretically, the appeals office could reopen your file and bring new challenges and even higher assessments, it rarely does so. The prime task of the appeals office is to get cases settled as quickly as possible. As a result, appeals officers acquiesce to lower assessments in more than 50 percent of the cases that come before them.

You Can Litigate Your Assessment. Nevertheless, some cases aren't settled on appeal. But again, you aren't compelled to accept the decision of an appeals officer. You have further appeal possibilities through several different court procedures. Furthermore, because of the large cost of litigating tax cases and the limited number of government lawyers to handle them, few cases actually go to trial.

You Can Represent Yourself without Worry or Large Costs. You may think that audits, appeals, and court litigation will cost you far more than you could possibly save in taxes. While that may be true, it's not necessarily true. Up through the appeals office, you can easily represent yourself as long as you are willing to prepare your case (facts, records, laws) in a way that meets IRS standards. This task is not difficult (see, e.g., the excellent book by tax attorney Fred Daily, *Stand Up to the I.R.S.*, Nolo Press, Berkeley, CA, 1996).

Furthermore, if you move your case from the appeals office to the small claims tax court (tax assessments of less than $10,000 for each year in question), you still can represent yourself without difficulty. However, if you choose to litigate in regular Tax Court or a U. S. District Court, you probably should retain a tax pro to carry on your battle. At that point, your legal expenses will shoot up. Yet, keep in mind, the time, effort, and expenses you incur to win your position shouldn't be measured against the tax savings of just one year. If the issue will also affect your future tax returns (or past returns that are still open to audit), then you've got more at stake than just the initial assessment. Failing to fight for the position you believe is correct could cost you additional taxes over a large number of years.

Relatively Few Returns Are Audited. As a final point here, remember, your aggressive position to minimize income taxes won't be challenged automatically. Even if your return is flagged for attention by IRS computers, that doesn't mean you will be called in for an audit. In recent years, the IRS has scheduled office or field exams for fewer than 1 percent of all tax returns filed. In addition, most returns are not examined in total. Typically, only certain items are questioned as a matter of law or documentation.

This brings us back to where we started this discussion. Because it has the personnel to investigate (not to mention litigate) fewer than 1 percent of all tax returns filed, the IRS realizes that it must appear far more formidable than it actually is. Therefore, don't let the intimidating image of the IRS deter you from minimizing your tax payments. Even in the rare event that the IRS does choose your return for examination, as long as you can plausibly support your positions by citing case law, statutes, or revenue rulings (since these sources of authority frequently contradict each other, select those most favorable to your position) and some reasonable (not perfect) records, you need not fear the audit.

At the very worst, you will have played the game with long odds in your favor. And even though at times the dice may roll against you, over the long run, an aggressive tax position will generally yield far more wins than losses.

"Plausible" Position.   By advising you to consider an aggressive tax position when faced with matters of judgment or ambiguity, we want you to *avoid* paying taxes that you do not owe—not *evade* paying the taxes that you do owe. You should not spend $20,000 to renovate your personal residence and then claim this expense was incurred to upgrade your rental properties. You should not collect your rents in cash so that they will leave no paper trail for the IRS to follow. You should not sell your properties privately on contract so that you can hide your capital gains and interest income from the IRS.

In other words, before you take action to reduce your taxable income (or correspondingly, increase your deductible expenses), verify your position with a tax pro. A "plausible" position is one that can be at least tentatively supported by one or more recognized tax authorities (cases, statutes, regulations, or revenue rulings) and some records (contemporaneous or ex post). In contrast, failing to report rental income or running personal expenses through your rental property accounts does not meet this test. Stretch your interpretation of the facts and law to favor your position and at most you'll end up owing more in taxes (plus interest and maybe some penalties). Purposely misrepresent the facts and you subject yourself to the possibility of criminal prosecution.

Using a Tax Pro

Although you can represent yourself at an audit or appeal, you should consult a tax pro to help you plan your tax strategy, prepare your returns, and, if necessary, prepare for an audit. Too many tax law changes and too much complexity makes it nearly impossible for the great majority of Americans to understand the tax laws.

In the following pages, we discuss some basics of income tax law as they apply to property owners. But use this discussion as a starting point. In addition, we want to emphasize the need to consult a tax pro *before* you buy or sell a property, and *before* you develop your operating budget. Very often how you structure your transactions and how you structure and document your spending will dramatically affect your present and future tax liabilities.

Now to begin our substantive review of federal income tax law, let's look at some ways owning your own home can save you taxes.

HOMEOWNER TAX SAVINGS

Because government policy favors home ownership over renting, homeowners are permitted several great tax-reducing advantages.

Item 1: Deferring Tax on the Sale of a Residence

You can defer tax on the gain from the sale of your home if you meet the following three tests:

1. *Principal residence test.* This test requires that you have used your old house as your principal residence and you now use, or intend to use, your new house as a principal residence. Only one principal residence, for tax deferral purposes, is allowed at any one time. You cannot defer tax on the profitable sale of a principal residence by buying a summer cottage, nor can you defer the tax on the sale of a second home.

2. *Time test.* This test requires that within two years of the sale of your old house you buy, or build, and use your new house as a principal residence.

3. *Investment test.* Generally, this test requires that you buy or build a house equal to, or more than, the price you received from the sale of the old house. If the replacement house costs less, part of the gain is taxed. Tax deferring is mandatory when you qualify under the preceding three tests.

Exchanging houses or trading is considered the same as a sale for tax deferral purposes. If you make an even exchange, or pay additional cash, there is no tax on the trade. However, if you receive cash in the trade for the replacement house, you generally realize a taxable gain.

Item 2: Tax-Free Residence Sale if Age 55 or Older

You can avoid tax on profits up to $125,000 once in a lifetime, if you are 55 or older when you sell or exchange your principal residence. To claim this exclusion, you must: (1) elect to avoid tax; (2) be 55 or older before the date of sale; and (3) for at least three of the five years prior to the sale have owned and occupied the house as your principal residence. You cannot use this exclusion when you sell only a partial interest in the home.

If you and your spouse own the home jointly and file a joint return in the year of the sale, only one of you need meet the age requirement of 55 or older and qualify under ownership and residency requirements three out of the last five years.

Use caution when taking the tax-free election. Because this is a once-in-a-lifetime exclusion, consider using the tax deferral method under Item 1 when the gain from the sale of your home is substantially less than the $125,000 exclusion and you plan to reinvest the proceeds in a replacement home. If, for example, you did qualify for the $125,000 exclusion, and after the sale of your home the gain was only $15,000 and you elected to exclude it, you will have used up the full amount of your once-in-a-lifetime exclusion. You could defer this gain if you buy a replacement house at a cost equal to or more than the sales price of the old house. Then, later when you sell the replacement house without a further home purchase, the election to exclude the gain can then be made.

Refinancing

Generally speaking, the points you pay to refinance your principal residence are not deductible, regardless of how you pay them, if they are not paid in connection with the purchase or improvement of the home. However, the portion of points is deductible if you use a part of the proceeds to make an improvement on your principal residence. The amount apportioned for the improvement can either be deducted in full in the year you pay it, or you may also deduct the apportioned amount over the life of the loan.

Deducting Expenses When Renting Out Part of Your Home

That part of your home you occupy is handled differently for tax purposes from the rented part. Rental income and expenses allocated to the rented part of a property are reported on Schedule E. The expenses allocated to the rental part are deductible, whether or not you itemize personal deductions. Deductions for mortgage interest and property taxes on your personal part of the property are itemized deductions. Repair expenses apportioned to your personal unit are nondeductible personal expenses.

Depreciation after Conversion of Home to Rental.   If you convert your residence to a rental property, you can begin to take the depreciation on the building. The amount of depreciation allowed is based on whichever is lower, the building's fair market value at the time of conversion or the adjusted cost basis (original purchase price plus capital improvements until time of conversion).

Basis to Use on a Sale of Rental.   If you sell and realize a profit, then you use the adjusted cost basis at the time of conversion less depreciation. If you sell and realize a loss, you use the lower of adjusted cost basis or fair market value at the time of conversion, less any accrued depreciation.

RULES FOR VACATION HOMES

The federal income tax law prohibits most homeowners from deducting losses (expenses in excess of income) while renting out a personal vacation home. A vacation home can be a condominium, apartment, single-family house, house trailer, motor home, or house boat. Certain tests are formulated to disallow losses. These tests are based on the days of rental and personal usage. The following tests will determine whether you are allowed losses: (1) If the vacation home is rented for less than 15 days, you cannot deduct expenses allocated to the rental (except for interest and real estate taxes). If you sell and realize a profit on the rental, the profit is not taxable.

(2) If the vacation home is rented for 15 days or more, then you have to determine if your personal use of the home exceeds a 14-day or 10 percent time test (10% of the number of days the home is rented). If it does, then you are considered to have used the home as a residence during the year and rental expenses are deductible only to the extent of gross rental income. Therefore, if gross rental income exceeds expenses, the operating gain is fully taxable.

(3) If you rent the vacation home for 15 days or more, but your rental usage is less than the 14-day/10-percent test, then you are not considered to have made personal use of the residence during the

year. In this case, expenses in excess of gross rental income may be deductible. Previous tax court cases have allowed loss deductions when the owner made little personal use of the vacation home and proved to have bought the house to earn a profitable amount in resale.

INTEREST DEDUCTIONS

Deducting Interest Paid on a Home Mortgage

Tax law places certain limitations on the ability to deduct interest as an expense on a home mortgage. Under the rules, you are allowed to deduct home mortgage interest only up to the original purchase price of the home and the cost of home improvements. Additional amounts, but not more than the fair market value of the home, can be borrowed for educational and medical expenses with the interest still remaining deductible. To qualify, the home has to be used as security for the debt. (In addition, certain limitations apply to home mortgages in excess of $1,000,000 and taxpayers whose adjusted gross income exceeds $108,450.)

To illustrate, say you purchased a home for $80,000, and three years later you added on a den costing $12,000. You are limited in the amount of financing on which interest can be deducted to $92,000. If you borrowed $100,000, the interest on the additional $8,000 loan would not be deductible as home-mortgage interest. Since the additional loan of $8,000 is above the $92,000 limit, it will be treated as personal-consumer interest which is not deductible. On the other hand, if the additional $8,000 was used for medical or educational costs, the interest would then be deductible.

What home improvements qualify to increase the amount you can borrow? Generally, a home improvement is considered to include all expenditures that will add value to your home and last for an extended period, such as, swimming pool, new roof, new patio or deck, siding, built-in appliances, built-in cabinets, alarm system, hot water heater, new sidewalk, replacement windows, insulation, and certain landscaping.

Rules for Business Use of Your Home

To claim a deduction for a home office the office must be used exclusively for an office (the room where your spouse watches television or sews while you work does not qualify) and on a regular basis. The office in the home must be used for: (1) actually meeting patients, clients, or customers (making phone calls to patients or customers won't qualify); or (2) as the primary place of business. Taxpayers can operate more than one business for the purpose of this test; therefore employees can moonlight in another business and claim a home office deduction as long as they qualify under the other tests. In addition, an employee can claim home office deductions if the office is maintained for the convenience of the employer. An unattached structure to the home used in connection with the taxpayer's business will also qualify.

According to tax law, certain deductions are allowed for a home office, such as depreciation, insurance, utilities, and so on, which can offset income realized from that business. These deductions can only be claimed up to the net income of that business.

For example, an employee operates a separate business out of his home as a writer. He earned $4,400 in royalties during the year. His expenses for the year were: postage and office supplies $920; subscriptions $1,280; depreciation on his home office $2,400; utilities $200; and insurance on his home office $90. Deductions for depreciation, insurance, and utilities can only be used to the extent of the net income of the home business determined without these items. See the following:

Royalties		$4,400
Expenses other than home office		
Postage and office supplies	$ 920	
Subscriptions	1,280	
Subtotal	2,200	2,200
Net income before		
home office deductions		$2,200

In the preceding example, this taxpayer's deductions for home office are limited to $2,200. Home-office expenses cannot be used as a tax loss to offset other income. Although he has a total of $2,690 in home-office expenses (depreciation $2,400 + $200 utilities + $90 insurance = $2,690), he is left with $490 in unused deductions that can be carried forward and used against business income in future years.

RULES FOR DEPRECIATION

Depreciation is the percentage reduction in loss of value of an asset over its physical life. It is strictly a bookkeeping entry, which is not an out-of-

Table 13.1   Review of Changes in Depreciation

Old Law	1986 Reforms
Income property is depreciated over 19 years	Residential rentals are depreciated over 27.5 years; commercial rentals 39.5 years
Income property is depreciated either by straight-line or accelerated methods	Only straight-line method of depreciation is allowed on income property
Real estate investments are not subject to "at-risk" rules	Real estate investments are subject to "at-risk" rules
Vehicles are depreciated over 3 years	Vehicles are depreciated over 5 years
Most machinery and equipment is depreciated over 5 years	Most machinery and equipment is depreciated over 7 years
Personal property is depreciated using the 150 percent declining balance method	Personal property is depreciated using the 200 percent declining balance method

pocket expense to the investor. The Tax Reform Act of 1986 has dramatically reduced the benefits of depreciation in a number of ways (see Table 13.1). The number of years a property can be written off has been lengthened from 19 years to 27.5 years, and 39.5 years in certain cases. Also, accelerated methods have been eliminated, thus reducing benefits during the early years of the holding period. And, because of the new lower tax rates, depreciation tax benefits are not worth as much as they were before tax reform.

What Can Be Depreciated?

Many different kinds of property can be depreciated, such as machinery, buildings, vehicles, patents, copyrights, furniture, and equipment. Property is depreciable if it meets all three of these tests:

1. It must be used in business or held for the production of income (e.g., to earn rent or royalty income).
2. It must have a useful life that can be determined, and its useful life must be longer than one year. The useful life of a piece

of property is an estimate of how long you can expect to use it in your business or to earn rent or royalty income.

3. It must be something that wears out, decays, gets used up, becomes obsolete, or loses value from natural causes.

Depreciable property may be tangible (i.e., it can be seen or touched) or intangible. Intangible property includes such items as a copyright or franchise. Depreciable property may be personal or real. Personal property is property, such as machinery and equipment that is not real estate. Real estate is land and generally anything that is erected on, growing on, or attached to land. However, land itself is not depreciable.

Depreciation not only serves the purpose of determining taxable income, but is also the essence of why real estate has been a "tax shelter." Historically, real estate investors have been able to earn substantial net income free of taxes from their properties, and in certain cases while actually showing taxable losses that could be written off against salary income. Thus the tax-shelter benefit of real estate, because the taxable loss (which in reality is actually a net gain, or profit) can shelter salary income from other sources.

Depreciating Buildings.   Now, real property must be written off over much longer periods, with the accelerated methods available under previous rules no longer being available. Therefore, only the straight-line method can be used. However, the mid-month convention still can be used. In addition, the Reform Act rules extended the application of the mid-month convention to include all real property, as opposed to the old rule, which limited certain property.

Under the current law, residential and nonresidential property have different depreciation periods. Residential real estate is depreciated over a 27.5-year period, and nonresidential real estate (commercial real estate such as office buildings and shopping centers) is depreciated over a 39.5-year period. Residential property is defined as a building with 80 percent or more of its rental income derived from dwelling units. A dwelling unit is defined as an apartment or house used to provide living accommodations. This does not include hotels or motels that rent more than half of their capacity on a temporary basis.

Depreciating Certain Land Improvements.   Under the current rules, certain land improvements are depreciated over 15 years using the 150 percent declining-balance method. Conversion to the straight-line method at the time that maximizes deductions is also allowed.

Depreciable land improvements are items such as bridges, roads, sidewalks, and landscaping. Sewer pipes are depreciated over a 20-year period. Buildings and their improvements are not allowed under this method.

Depreciating Equipment and Fixtures—Current Rules.   Personal property, such as vehicles, equipment, or furniture, is generally written off by using the accelerated 200 percent declining-balance method over a 5- or 7-year period. For example, most cars and light trucks will be depreciated over 5 years. Most office furniture, fixtures, and equipment (desks, safes, and certain communication equipment) will be depreciated over 7 years. The half-year convention also applies to personal property. (Note that the accelerated methods of 150 percent and 200 percent declining balance are calculated at one-and-a-half, and twice, respectively, the rate of the straight-line method.) The following example of the declining-balance method illustrates how this method works for five-year property (see Table 13.2).

The 1986 rules permit a switch to the straight-line method when it will provide a larger deduction. In the fifth year, for example, the 200 percent declining balance method would provide a deduction of $830 (40% × $2,074). Switching to the straight-line method in the fifth year provides a deduction of $1,382 ($2,074 of costs not yet written off, divided by the 1.5 years remaining in the depreciation period). The half-year convention causes the depreciation period to be extended to a sixth year.

The calculations for seven-year property and the 150 percent declining-balance method of depreciation are similar, except that under the 150 percent method one-and-a-half times the straight-line method is used (30% instead of 40%) in the depreciation-rate column.

Table 13.2   Example of the 200 Percent Declining-Balance Method

Year	(Declining Balance) Cost—Depreciation	Depreciation Rate	Amount of Depreciation
1	$12,000	40% × .5 (half)	$ 2,400
2	9,600	40	3,840
3	5,760	40	2,304
4	3,456	40	1,382
5	2,074	—	1,382
6	692	—	692
			$12,000

"At-Risk" Rules—Changes since TRA 1986

Under the old law, real estate was exempt from the government's strict "at-risk" rules. The 1986 rules treat real estate the same as other investment activities.

At-risk rules limit the amount of losses you can deduct. Specifically, these losses (deductions) cannot exceed the total of:

- The cash you contribute to the business.
- The adjusted basis of your property contributions to the business.
- The amount you borrowed for the business, but only to the extent you pledge other assets or have personal liability as security for the borrowing.

The exception to this is financing secured only by the property itself, called "qualified nonrecourse financing." To qualify, the nonrecourse financing must be:

- Secured only by the real property.
- Actual debt (not disguised equity similar to convertible debt).
- Obtained from a qualified lender, such as an institutional lender or related party. (If obtained from a related party, such as the seller or the promoter of the investment, the loan is required to be at reasonable market rates similar to those made to unrelated parties.)

RULES FOR PASSIVE LOSSES

A so-called passive activity is any activity that involves the conduct of any trade or business in which you do not materially participate. *Any rental activity will be a passive activity even if you materially participate in it.* A trade or business includes any activity involving research or experimentation and, to the extent provided in the regulations, any activity in connection with a trade or business, or any activity for which a deduction is allowed as an expense for the production of income. You are considered to materially participate if you are involved in the operation of the activity on a regular, continuous, and substantial basis. Participation by your spouse will be considered in determining whether you materially participate. Also, as of 1993, persons who work in real estate such as sales agents, contractors, or developers, are given certain exceptions to the passive loss rules.

For the tax years beginning after 1986, deductions from passive activities may only be used to offset your income from passive activities (see Table 13.3). Any excess deductions result in a "passive-activity loss" and may not be deducted against your other income but may be carried over and applied against passive income in future years. In addition, any allowable credits from passive activity may only be used to offset your tax liability allocable to your passive activities. Any *excess* "passive-activity credit" may not be claimed against your tax liability on your other income but may be carried over and applied against tax on passive-activity income in future years. These rules apply to any individual, estate, trust, closely held C corporation, or personal service corporation.

Certain Passive-Income Losses Can Offset Other Income

As mentioned before, an interest in real estate rental activity, no matter how much you participate, will not be considered an active business. This means that losses from real estate investments are only allowed to offset income and gains from other passive investments. Therefore, real estate losses cannot shelter wage or active business income. However, as noted previously, there is a major exception to this rule to assist moderate-income taxpayers who invest in real estate.

Certain investors can apply passive-income losses to wage earnings or income from an active business. To qualify for this real estate loss exception (up to a maximum of $25,000), the investor must meet both an

Table 13.3 Review of Changes for Passive Losses

Old Law	1986 Law
No limitations on deductions of losses on real estate	Deductible losses on real estate are limited to $25,000, reduced for adjusted gross over $100,000
Losses are deductible regardless of whether you actively participate in managing the property	Losses are not deductible inside the $25,000 cap unless you actively participate in managing the property
Losses from real estate can be used to offset other income sources	Losses in excess of $25,000 can be used only to offset gains from other passive investments

income and participation test. The investor's adjusted gross income must be less than $150,000. The entire $25,000 loss allowance is permitted for taxpayers with adjusted gross income up to $100,000. The $25,000 loss allowance is reduced by 50 percent of the amount by which the adjusted gross income is more than $100,000. Thus, if the adjusted gross income exceeds $150,000, this allowance rule will not apply.

The other requirement to qualify for this loss allowance is that the investor must "actively participate." (This rule is not as stringent as other participation tests, as you will soon see.) To get the benefit of up to $25,000 in tax losses, the investor is required to meet the following two tests:

1. The investor must own at least 10 percent of the value of the activity during the entire year which he or she is the owner.

2. The investor is required to make management decisions or arrange for others to provide such services. It is not necessary for the investor to do certain things directly, such as repairs or approving prospective tenants. The hiring of a repairperson and a rental agent does not violate the participation test; however caution should be taken if you hire a management company to operate the property. The property-management agreement should clearly indicate that the investor is involved in the decision-making process.

Taxpayers in the Real Property Business

As mentioned earlier, in 1993, Congress created a new category called, "taxpayers in the real property business." This category includes (but is not limited to) real estate agents, contractors, property managers, leasing agents, converters, and owners of rental properties. The great advantage of fitting yourself into this category is that you are exempt from the passive loss rules and may use your rental property tax losses to offset the taxable income you receive from any other source including wages, commissions, dividends, interest, and royalties.

However, here's the catch. You must work in a real estate related trade or business at least 750 hours per year, or an average of slightly over 14 hours per week. In addition, more than one-half the personal services you perform each year must fall within the definition of a real property trade or business. In other words, you can't simply go out and get a license to sell real estate and automatically qualify for the preferred tax treatment. Nevertheless, for people who actually do work in real estate, the "hours worked" test won't be difficult to meet.

Furthermore, event if you work as say, a schoolteacher or an auto mechanic, once you begin to build a portfolio of properties, you may be able to meet the "hours worked" test if you can somehow spend at least one half the hours you work each year on your real estate activities. Obviously, to do so you would have to either cut back on the hours you work in your regular job, or almost work a second full-time job with your properties. However, if you are putting a lot of time and effort into fixing up and renovating your properties, you might be able to pull it off. Time spent working evenings and weekends can really add up.

To illustrate why this concept of passive losses can be important, consider the following example. Say you own a portfolio of rental properties worth $2,000,000. Your NOI from these properties is $170,000 a year. Your interest expense equals $148,000 a year and your allowable depreciation totals $60,000. Therefore, your taxable income (loss) from these properties amounts to ($38,000). Here are the figures:

Taxable Income

NOI	$170,000
less	
Interest	148,000
Depreciation	60,000
equals	
Taxable income (loss)	$(38,000)

Before-Tax Cash Flow

NOI	$170,000
Debt service	168,700
BTCF	$ 1,300

As you can see, at present these properties are producing a positive (if barely) cash flow but a negative income for tax purposes. Now the question becomes, what happens to that $38,000 tax loss?

Generally speaking, if the investor earns more than $150,000 per year in a nonrealty trade or business, the investor can only use this tax loss to offset other "passive" income, or carry the loss forward to use in later years (see later discussion). If the investor earns between $100,000 and $150,000 a year, then only a pro rata portion of the first $25,000 of loss may be used to offset other earned income. The remainder is carried forward or used to offset other passive income. The investor who earns from other employment $100,000 or less gets the benefit of a

$25,000 loss immediately and carries $13,000 of loss forward (or applies it to other passive income).

Now, if on the other hand, the investor meets the "real property trade or business" work test, he may immediately use the entire $38,000 loss to offset current earnings. For example, assume the investor is a high-volume real estate sales agent, who before accounting for investment properties, earns a taxable income of $200,000 a year. Because the tax law exempts this sales agent (and many others in real estate related employment) from the passive loss rules, the agent may use the entire $38,000 to offset the $200,000 in earnings from sales commissions. Here are the calculations assuming a 39.6 percent marginal tax rate (MTR):

Investor earnings (taxable)	$200,000
MTR (assumed)	39.6%
Taxes owed without realty losses	$ 79,200

Now, with the special tax loss treatment, here's how the realty "losses" help offset this sales agent's tax liability:

Investor earnings (taxable)	$200,000
Realty tax losses	(− 38,000)
Taxable income	162,000
MTR (assumed)	39.6%
Taxes owed	$ 64,152

By owning income properties and fitting within the "real property trade or business" work test, this sales agent/investor was able to shelter $38,000 of sales commission earnings from federal income taxes, thus reducing the agent's tax bill by $15,048 (79,200 − 64,152). As noted earlier, investors who aren't permitted to use income property tax losses immediately to offset other income may carry these tax losses forward to use in future years.

Passive-Income Losses Are Carried Forward

Those losses the investor couldn't use during one tax year are not lost forever. In fact, they are carried forward as "suspended losses" and used in one of two ways:

1. If the investor has unused losses incurred in prior years and carried forward, he can apply those losses against income or gains in the passive-income category in future years. Under

the old rules, the losses would have been used to shelter income from other sources, just as the real estate agent did in the preceding example. However, under the current rules they will be used to shelter the income in later years for the same or other passive-income investments.

2. Unused suspended losses from prior years can be used to reduce any gain you realize when you sell your investment.

In determining income or loss from an activity, do not consider any (1) gross income from interest, dividends, annuities, or royalties not derived in the ordinary course of a trade or business; (2) expenses (other than interest) that are clearly and directly allocable to such income; (3) interest expense properly allocable to such income; and (4) gain or loss from the disposition of property producing such income or held for investment. Any interest in a passive activity is not treated as property held for investment. In addition, you do not include wages, salaries, professional fees, or other amounts received as compensation for services rendered as income from a passive activity.

Rental Real Estate Activity

An individual will be allowed a deduction for any passive-activity loss or the deduction equivalent of the passive-activity credit for any tax year from rental real estate activities in which he or she actively participated. Not counting the mentioned exception, the amount allowed under this rule cannot be more than $25,000 (or $12,500 for a married individual filing separately). This amount is reduced by 50 percent of the amount by which your adjusted gross income is more than $100,000 ($50,000 for married filing separately). Therefore, if your adjusted gross income exceeds $150,000 ($75,000 for married filing separately), you may not deduct passive losses against your earnings.

NOTE: *As are all discussions in this chapter, the preceding explanation of passive loss rules omits many important technicalities that are far more complex than can fit into this treatment here. But as you can easily see, the complexity of this law not only makes employment of a tax pro essential, it perfectly illustrates how lawmakers have completely abandoned the most elementary notions of justice and common sense.*

ALTERNATIVE MINIMUM TAX (AMT)

Because of the complexities of the AMT, only a brief overview deserves mention here. The subject of the AMT requires a tax pro's attention to enable you to get an understanding of the subject and to learn whether you qualify under the rules of the AMT. Generally, only the wealthiest and the most heavily tax-sheltered taxpayers will run into serious AMT tax liabilities. (For more information on the Alternative Minimum Tax for individuals, including the new rules, see IRS Publication 909, Alternative Minimum Tax.)

CAPITAL GAINS

The treatment of capital gains has traditionally been one of the most important benefits for real estate investors. Before TRA 1986, capital gains rules allowed the taxpayer to exclude 60 percent of the gain realized on the sale of an asset for tax purposes. Now under the new rules, certain capital gains benefits have been repealed, and all gains realized in the sale of an asset are subject to taxation up to a rate as high as 28 percent.

In addition, Congress changed the taxation on installment sales. An installment sale is one in which the seller carries back financing and the buyer pays for the property over an extended term. Under the previous rules, the seller would report a pro rata portion of each payment as a capital gain in the year in which it was received. This technique could be used by sellers to significantly reduce their liability for capital gains taxes both in the year they sold their property and in future years.

A Simplified Installment Sale Example (Old Law)

For example, assume that an about-to-retire executive in the (then) 50 percent tax bracket sold a property and realized a taxable capital gain of $200,000. If this executive accepted all cash in the year of sale, she immediately would have become liable for $100,000 in federal income taxes on that taxable gain (50% × $200,000). However, if instead, she carried back financing for a term of say, 20 years, she would only have to pay a pro rata share of the gain according to how much principal repayment she received each year.

As a second benefit, since this executive was about to retire in a year or two, she anticipated that her marginal tax rate would fall to 25 percent. So, not only would an installment sale help her defer taxes, by subjecting the gain to a lower tax rate, it would also reduce the total amount of taxes she would have to pay. In other words, rather than immediately paying $100,000 in taxes on her capital gain in the year of sale, she would "only" pay around $50,000 (25% × $200,000) and those payments would be spread over 20 years, with the majority not falling due until after year 12. (That's because during the early years of the financing, most of the buyer's monthly payments would go to pay interest. Only during the later years would the seller receive substantial payments toward principal.)

Do Installment Sales Still Make Sense?

Because many sellers liked the idea of paying less taxes over a long period, installment sales gained a strong following. However, after TRA 1986 and several subsequent, more limited tax law changes, some investors have begun to question whether installment sales still make sense for sellers. For example, John Reed writes in his book, *Aggressive Tax Avoidance* (Reed Publishing Co., Danville, CA, 1995) that, "Real estate investors have long regarded installment sales as one of the main tax saving devices available to them . . . [but] I've got news for you . . . installment sales have nothing to do with saving taxes . . . If you want to save taxes when you get rid of a property, *exchange*."

While Reed is certainly correct that exchanging is a great tax-saving technique (see discussion p. 300), he comes down too hard on installment sales. In opposing seller carryback financing (for sellers, not buyers), Reed makes the following good points:

1. *Bracket compression.* In some past tax years, marginal tax rates (MTRs) for investors ranged from a low of 15 percent up to a high of 91 percent. With such a wide range of rates, deferring taxes from high-rate years until lower-rate years could save enormous amounts of taxes. Now, though, providing you have positive taxable income, MTRs for capital gains fall within the relatively narrow range of 15 percent to 28 percent, with a great majority of investors hitting the maximum with or without capital gain income. In other words, whether you pay now or pay later, you're still likely to pay at a rate of 28 percent (not including state income taxes or federal surcharges).

2. *Opportunity costs.* Reed further notes that even if by playing the rate switch game you do save some taxes, you will lose far more by tying up your money in seller financing and having to settle for an 8 to 12 percent return on your money rather than, say, the 20 percent you could earn by reinvesting your after-tax sales proceeds in more real estate.

3. *AMT blackhole.* By electing the installment sale, Reed points out, you expose yourself to the "mind-boggling" calculations of the Alternative Minimum Tax and potential additional tax liability. So, even if the installment sale appears to save you taxes, after bringing in the AMT, not only could you go crazy trying to run the numbers (actually computer software programs are available to ease the pain somewhat), you could end up paying more, not less.

4. *Carryforward losses.* If your property has been producing passive losses that you have had to carry forward (rather than being able to write them off in the years they were generated), now's the time to use them. Rather than elect an installment sale to defer your capital gain taxes, cancel them out with those losses that are hanging in "suspension."

Overall, Reed's points are sound. He deserves credit for forcing investors to look more carefully at whether an installment sale will produce the tax savings that are popularly believed. In another sense, though, Reed doesn't seem to go far enough in his analysis.

Certainly, you want to carefully examine the tax effects of all your decisions *before you make them;* and the installment sale may not yield the tax savings that some believe it will. Nevertheless, you can't let your investment decisions be driven by tax strategy alone. (That's why so many pre-1986 TRA investors ended up with massive real estate losses. Their deals were driven exclusively by tax shelter benefits. After most tax shelters were wiped out by the passive loss rules, the values of those investments collapsed.) Reed alludes to this point in bringing up the issue of opportunity costs. He says, "Why leave your money tied up in OWC financing just to save taxes when you could instead use those sales proceeds to buy more properties and earn much higher returns?"

Here's the Answer

As Robert Bruss frequently points out in his columns, owners should consider OWC financing because it can help them get their properties sold faster and at a higher price. This is especially the case when mortgage lenders are going through one of their tight money phases and are refusing to make investor loans except on onerous terms with rigorous qualifying standards. Therefore, your returns from the installment sale shouldn't be measured simply by tax savings and interest earnings on the buyer's mortgage. You also should ask whether OWC financing will get you a quicker sale and a higher price.

In addition, your interest earnings can prove quite lucrative, especially if you're able to use wraparound financing. Moreover, interest earnings on a buyer mortgage (depending on creditworthiness, amount of down payment, and the quality of the collateral) deserve a lower risk category than does property ownership. And it requires less effort to pull a mortgage check out of the mailbox each month than it does to manage apartments and collect rents.

What's the Bottom Line for Sellers?

That old equivocating answer, "It all depends" applies to installment sales. As John Reed ably points out, the potential tax savings of the installment sale may not loom as large as many sellers anticipate. On the other hand, the benefits of an installment sale extend beyond tax savings. If you have reached the stage in life where you want to enjoy a stable monthly income without the efforts of property ownership, then when compared with long-term bonds at 6 or 7 percent interest, a seller mortgage that earns say 8.5 to 12 percent interest might look pretty good. And if OWC financing helps you get a better price for your property, all the better.

As with all other business decisions, to evaluate the merits of an installment sale, you must consider not only the tax effects, but also your personal situation, your tolerance for risk (not all buyers make their payments), and any other direct or indirect costs and benefits. You should neither accept it nor reject it out of hand. Instead, give it considered thought and work through the numbers with a tax pro and a Realtor experienced in investment properties.

Implications for Buyers

Nothing in the preceding discussion of installment sales is meant to discourage buyers from seeking OWC financing. As a buyer, whether you borrow from a bank or a seller will not change your federal income tax liabilities. However, we will point out once again that if you do agree to pay the seller a higher price in exchange for favorable terms, make sure you include a prepayment discount. If you refinance or sell the property early, you won't want to pay the seller for terms that you end up not using. In addition, when you arrange seller terms, try to negotiate assumable financing that you can pass along to your buyers when you sell (or exchange) the property.

TAX-FREE EXCHANGES

If you own a corporate stock that has had a big run-up in price, you may think that now is the time to sell before the market stalls or turns down. But selling creates a serious problem. Due to federal income tax law, you will lose a big part of your gain to the U.S. Treasury. As a result, many stock market investors hold their stocks long after they should have sold them because they can't bear the thought of immediately throwing away close to one-third of their profits in taxes (possibly more depending on the level of their state and local income taxes).

On the other hand, real estate investors need not face this dilemma. As explained earlier, for many investors the installment sale can help them defer, and perhaps reduce, the amount of their profits they lose to taxes. Just as important, but not nearly as well known, real estate investors can also eliminate or defer their federal income tax liabilities by trading up. These two techniques—installment sales and exchanging—give owners of income properties a substantial tax advantage over investors who choose stocks, bonds, and most other types of real and financial assets.

Exchanges Don't Necessarily Involve Two-Way Trades

Due to lack of knowledge, most real estate investors who have some awareness of tax-free exchanges believe that to use this tax benefit, they must find a seller who will accept one or more of their currently owned properties in trade. While this does represent one way to enter into a tax-free exchange, it does not represent the most commonly used exchange technique. Most exchanges, in fact, actually involve at least three different investors.

The Three-Party Exchange

Three-party exchanges outnumber two-party "trade-in" exchanges because it's usually difficult to find an owner of a property you want who also will want the property you plan to trade up. Although it's sometimes possible to negotiate a two-way trade by convincing an unwilling seller to accept your property and then turn around and sell it, to do so may cause you to spend too much negotiating capital that you could devote to other issues such as a lower price or OWC financing.

Instead, most serious real estate investors arrange a three-party exchange through the following steps: (1) you locate a buyer for the property you want to trade; (2) you locate a property you want to buy;

and (3) you set up an escrow whereby you deed your property to your buyer, the buyer pays his cash to your seller, and your seller conveys his property to you. In effect, no property has really been "exchanged" for another property. Because of this anomaly, John Reed (a leading expert on exchanges) suggests renaming this technique the "interdependent sale and reinvestment" strategy.

Exchanges Are Complex, but Easy

As you might suspect, anything that involves federal tax laws will be entangled in a spider web of rules and regulations, and Section 1031 Exchanges (as they are called in the Internal Revenue Code) do not prove an exception to this norm. However, even though exchange rules are complex, exchange transactions are relatively easy to administer when you work with a pro who is experienced in successfully setting up and carrying out tax-free exchanges.

John Reed says the total extra costs (including attorney fees and escrow charges) of conducting an exchange should run less that $2,000. Professional Publishing Company (now taken over by Dearborn Financial in Chicago) even publishes standard forms (Forms 102.1, 102.2, and 102.3) which may be used to complete the required paperwork according to law. Note, though, even if you use standard forms, that doesn't negate the need to use a tax or realty exchange pro. Moreover, be aware that the great majority of CPAs and real estate attorneys know little about Section 1031 exchanges. So, unless your accountant or lawyer definitely has mastered this area of the law, get a referral for someone who has. (If you live in at least a midsize city, there's probably a property exchange club whose members include investors and commercial realty brokers who will be able to recommend competent and experienced professionals.)

NOTE: *In dealing with accountants and lawyers, they have frequently told me things like, "Oh, you don't want to get involved in something like that," or "That's more trouble than it's worth," or "Sure, I can handle it, no problem." In my younger, inexperienced days I simply accepted such comments without question. "Surely, I can count on the wisdom and good faith of my accountant or lawyer," I told myself. (Okay, those of you who have worked with lawyers and accountants can now stop laughing. I admitted I used to be naive.)*

The points here are twofold: (1) To hide their own ignorance, lawyers and accountants who do not understand an issue will often advise against "getting involved with that" whatever "that" may be, so as not to disclose to you that they really don't know what they are talking about; or (2) depending on how much they need the business (or perhaps they don't want to lose you as a client), accountants and lawyers frequently claim expertise and competence in areas in which they have neither know-how nor experience.

Naturally, either or both of these tendencies can cost you a bundle. (Yes, you can sue for malpractice, and I have. But it's not a recommended course of action.) To reduce the chance of professional error, misinformation, or just plain bad advice, don't let your accountant or attorney bluff you. Pepper them with detailed and specific questions about the issue at hand and their actual experience in successfully dealing with these issues. Whatever you do, don't naively accept the counsel of any professional (lawyer, accountant, real estate agent, medical doctor, etc.). These are people with serious limitations, not demigods. Require them to *earn* your trust and respect through knowledge and performance, not expect it simply because they may place several initials after their name.

Are Tax-Free Exchanges Really "Tax-Free"?

Some people quibble with the term "tax-free" exchange. They say that an exchange doesn't eliminate taxes, it only defers payment to a later date. This view is wrong on four counts:

1. The exchange, itself, is tax-free if you follow the rules (see following section).

2. Whether you must pay taxes at a later date depends on how you divest yourself of the property. If you hold it until death, the property passes into your estate free of any capital gains taxes.

3. As another alternative, you could arrange a sale in a later year in which you have tax losses that you can use to offset the amount of your capital gain.

4. If Americans are sensible enough to elect legislators who understand the importance of productive investment, we may see the capital gains tax abolished (or at least indexed).

In other words, the most important issue for you to consider is that exchanges eliminate capital gains in the year you dispose of your property through trading up. Whether you pay in future years will depend on how savvy you are in developing your tax-avoidance strategies, and the tax law that exists in some future year. By exchanging, you eliminate a definite tax liability in the year of disposition and accept an uncertain and contingent future tax liability. That's a tax trade-off you should always be willing to make.

Section 1031 Exchange Rules

Stated as simply and briefly as possible, Section 1031 tax-free exchanges must comply with five principal rules:

1. *Like-kind exchange.* Here's another source of confusion. The tax law states that only exchanges of "like-kind" properties qualify for the preferred tax treatment. However, "like-kind" doesn't mean fourplex to fourplex, or even apartment building to apartment building as some people believe. The concept is actually much broader and includes "all property [types] held for productive use in a trade or business or for investment." As a matter of law, you are permitted to exchange nearly any type of real estate for any other type of real estate and still arrange your transaction to fall within Section 1031 guidelines.

2. *45-Day rule.* If all parties to an exchange are known and in agreement, you can close all properties simultaneously. Otherwise, you can use a delayed exchange procedure that specifies two time deadlines. One of these is the 45-day rule that says you must identify the property you want to acquire within 45 days after the date of closing with the buyer of your present property (i.e., before midnight of the 44th day).

3. *180-Day closing.* The second time requirement states that you must close on your acquisition property within 180 days of closing the disposition of the property you are "trading up."

4. *Escrow restrictions.* Tax-free exchanges generally require various "exchange" proceeds to be paid into and distributed out of an escrow arrangement. The escrow agent must be completely independent of you (e.g., not your attorney, real estate agent, bank officer, spouse, company's employees, or anyone else who is subject to your exclusive control or directions). Most importantly, you must not be able to withdraw any money from this escrow or otherwise pull out of the exchange agreement prior to the date the escrow agent has scheduled disbursements and property conveyances.

5. *Trading up.* To gain the benefit of a tax-free exchange, you must trade for a property of equal or greater value. Trading down or accepting a cash "boot" exposes you to a liability for capital gains taxes. If because of this tax lability your "seller" doesn't want to trade down or accept a cash sale, then you (or your realty agent) can create a "daisy

chain" of exchange participants until a property owner is found who wants to cash out or trade down real estate holdings and is willing to accept the capital gains tax liability for doing so. (A seller who has planned a total tax strategy may not have to pay any taxes despite realizing taxable income from your specific transaction. Also, since heirs receive properties on a stepped-up basis, they will incur little or no capital gains tax liability unless they sell their inherited property for substantially more that its estimated market value at the time it entered the deceased's estate.)

To keep lawyers and accountants fully employed at absurdly high hourly fees, the tax law embellishes the preceding rules with various details, definitions, regulations, and requirements. So, as noted earlier, the trick is not only to use an experienced exchange pro to guide you *before* you enter into any purchase or sale agreement, but also to keep the exchange process in compliance throughout each step until all closings are completed.

REPORTING RENTAL INCOME AND DEDUCTIONS

Rental income and expenses are reported on Schedule E of your tax return. You report the gross amount received, then deduct such expenses as mortgage interest, property taxes, maintenance costs, and depreciation. The net income is added to your other taxable income. If you realize a loss, you can reduce the amount of your other taxable income within certain limitations (see passive-loss limitation rules discussed earlier).

On the cash basis, you report rental income for the year in which you receive payment.

On the accrual basis, you report rental income for the year in which you are entitled to receive payment. You do not report accrued income if the financial condition of your tenant makes collection doubtful. If you sue for payment, you do not report income until you win a collectible judgment.

Insurance proceeds for loss of rental income because of fire or casualty loss are reported as ordinary income.

Payment by tenant for cancelling a lease or modifying its terms is reported as ordinary income when received. You may deduct expenses realized from the cancellation and any unamortized balance for expenses paid in negotiating the lease.

Security deposits are treated as trust funds and are not reported as income. However, if your tenant breaches the lease agreement, then you are entitled to use the security deposit as rent, at which time you report it as income.

Checklist of Deductions from Rental Income

- *Real estate taxes.* Property taxes are deductible, but special assessments for paving roads, sewers, or other improvements may have to be depreciated or added to the cost of the land.
- *Depreciation.* Be sure to deduct depreciation; it is the tax shelter benefit of real estate ownership.
- *Maintenance expenses.* Repairs, pool service, heating, lighting, water, gas, electricity, telephone, and other service costs.
- *Management expenses.* Include the cost of stationery and postage stamps, or the total cost of a management service.
- *Traveling expenses.* These include travel back and forth from properties for repairs or showing vacancies.
- *Legal expenses.* These include the costs incurred while evicting a tenant. Expenses incurred for negotiating long-term leases are considered capital expenditures and deductible over the term of the lease.
- *Interest expense.* This includes interest on mortgages and other indebtedness related to the property.
- *Advertising expense.* This includes the cost of vacancy signs and newspaper advertising.
- *Insurance expense.* This includes the cost of premiums for fire and casualty loss.

Note the difference between repair expenses and an improvement. Only incidental repair costs and maintenance costs are deductible against rental income. Improvement and replacement costs are treated differently. Improvements or repairs that add value or prolong the life of the property are considered capital improvements and may not be deducted but may be added to the cost basis of the property, and then be depreciated. For example, the cost to repair the roof of a rental property is considered an expense and is deducted against rental income. However, the cost to replace the entire roof is considered an improvement (adds value and prolongs the physical life of the property) and is therefore depreciated over its expected life.

TAX CREDITS

In addition to the property expenses that you are permitted to deduct from your gross income, in some cases, you also may be entitled to reduce your income liability though the use of tax credits. Whereas a tax deduction serves to offset income, a tax credit offsets your actual tax liability.

For example, say you subtract all tax-deductible expenses from your gross income and calculate your taxable income at $40,000. If you are in the 28 percent tax bracket, you would own $11,200 (.28 × 40,000) in income taxes. However, let's assume that you also are entitled to a tax credit of $4,000. Now, after accounting for this credit, your tax liability falls from $11,200 to $7,200 (11,200 − 4,000).

So, how do you get these tax credits? As tax law stands today, tax credits aren't as easy to come by as they once were. Currently, you have five possibilities:

1. *Mortgage credit certificates.* These tax credits are only available to first-time home buyers whose state or local governments are participating in a program Congress created in 1984 and has continued to reauthorize since then. To calculate the amount of this tax credit permitted, you multiply 0.2 times the amount of your annual mortgage interest. If you paid $9,000 in mortgage interest this year, in addition you would receive an $1,800 tax credit (0.2 × 9,000). If your area offers an MCC and you haven't yet invested in your first home, we urge you to get the details on this program as they apply to home buyers where you live (or plan to live).

2. *Low-income housing tax credits.* These tax credits are available to real estate investors who build new or substantially rehabilitate rental housing that is rented to households with low incomes.

3. *Nonresidential rehabs.* Nonresidential rehabilitation tax credits are available to investors who substantially renovate commercial buildings that were originally constructed before 1936.

4. *Certified historic rehabs.* Historical societies in various states have the authority to certify residential and nonresidential buildings as "historically significant." Investors who rehabilitate and restore these structures to meet historical preservation standards are entitled to tax credits.

5. *ADA building modifications.* The Americans with Disabilities Act requires the owners (or lessees) of some existing public or commercial buildings (not including rental housing) to adapt their properties to meet the accessibility and use needs of people who are physically disabled. Meeting the financial burden of these ADA requirements may entitle the owner (lessee) to tax credits to partially offset these expenses.

Although calculating the amount of tax credits available through the mortgage credit certificate program is quite straightforward, the other tax credits cited require the application of complex formulas involving tax credit percentages and the amounts of qualified rehab, renovation, or restoration expenses. For further information the IRS publishes updates from time to time.

In the years prior to TRA 1986, the types of tax credits available to real estate investors were more widely applicable than those under current law—especially the investment tax credit (ITC). So, because more favorable tax laws may return, check periodically to see whether any tax credits you can use have been newly enacted. When available, tax credits can slice thousands off your income taxes.

PROPERTY TAXES

"If you think that your property taxes are too high," writes tax consultant Harry Koemig, "you're probably right! Research shows that nearly half of all properties may be assessed illegally or excessively." While Koenig may overstate the situation somewhat, there's certainly no doubt that millions of property owners pay more in property taxes than they need to. Yet, with just a little attention and planning, you can avoid falling into this trap by taking several precautions:

1. *Check the accuracy of your assessed valuation.* Usually, tax assessors base their tax calculations on a property's market value. Look closely at the assessor's value estimate on your tax bill . Can you find comp sales of similar properties that would support a *lower* value for your property? If so, you may have grounds to request a tax reduction (see Chapter 3 for more details on appraisal techniques).

2. *Compare your purchase price to the assessor's estimate of market value.* Apart from providing comp sales, if you can show the assessor that you recently paid $190,000 for a property that he has appraised at $240,000, you've got a prima facie case for lower taxes.

3. *Look for unequal treatment.* Under the law, assessors must tax properties in a neighborhood in an equal (fair) and uniform manner. This means that you might be able to successfully argue for lower taxes even though the assessor has accurately estimated the market value of your property. How? By showing that the assessor has assigned lower values to similar nearby properties. (All property tax data are publicly available.) If faced with this issue, the assessor will have to cut your taxes because once everyone's tax notices have been sent out, it's not politically feasible (even if lawful) for the assessor to start telling people he's made a mistake and they actually owe more than is stated on their tax bill.

4. *Recognize the difference between assessed value and market value.* Typically, property taxes are based on assessed value, which is calculated as a percentage of market value. If your tax notice shows an assessed value of $80,000 and you know your property's worth $120,000, don't necessarily conclude that you've been underassessed. If tax law sates that assessed values should equal 50 percent of market value, then your assessed value should come in at $60,000 (0.5 × 120,000) not $80,000.

5. *Does your property suffer any negative features that the assessor has not considered?* Even though comp properties may appear similar, are there really significant differences? Does your property abut railroad tracks or a busy, noisy highway? Does it lack a basement, built-in appliances, a desirable floor plan, or off-street parking? Does it have a flat roof? (In some areas, flat roofs reduce value because they tend to leak and are costly to replace.)

6. *Do you or your property qualify for any exemptions?* Most property tax laws grant preferential treatment to various persons or properties. For example, veterans, seniors, blind persons, and hardship cases may be entitled to reduced assessments based on their special status. Similarly, historic properties, properties in areas designated for revitalization, energy-efficient properties, or properties rented to low-income households may be eligible for reduced assessments. Check with your assessor's office to see what exemptions might apply in your city or county.

7. *Verify that your assessment meets all technical requirements specified in the law.* Tax assessors and the legislative bodies that levy property taxes must operate within a set of rules, regulations, laws, and even constitutional requirements. For instance, some technical or procedural requirements may pertain to assessed value ratios, property classification, land-improvements ratio, conducting public hearings,

notice of public hearings, permissible valuation techniques, and allocation of assessed value between real and personal property.

8. *Learn tax assessment laws before you improve or rehabilitate a property.* The property tax laws of every state list the types of property that are taxed and the applicable rates. Once you discover the detailed nature of these laws, you then can develop an improvement strategy that adds value without adding taxes. For an excellent discussion of this topic and numerous case examples, see the book by Steve Carlson, *The Best Home for Less: How to Drastically Reduce Your Taxes, Utility Bills, and Construction Costs When You Build, Remodel, or Redecorate* (Avon Books, New York, 1992, p. 373).

A related issue here is the subject of permits. Some investors contract for remodeling and renovations without securing the appropriate permits. The thought is that the government can't tax what it doesn't know. The danger with this approach, though, is that at some later date the building inspector may discover your unpermitted work. In some cities, that means the inspector can require you to tear out the work and to do it over. This is especially a risk where unpermitted work doesn't meet code requirements. In the past, governments often overlooked unpermitted work and failed to keep their property tax records up to date. But now with computer data banks, buyer prepurchase inspections, and seller disclosure statements, such work is more likely to be discovered. Furthermore, in their unrelenting quest for greater tax revenues, local governments recognize that unreported remodeling and renovations are costing them millions of dollars each year in lost tax revenues.

As a result, the trend throughout the country is toward more thorough property investigations and harsher sanctions. While many city and county governments still lack the personnel, resources, or political will to change their careless practices, don't naively count on these assessment inefficiencies continuing indefinitely.

SUMMARY

Income taxes and property taxes can often take large chunks out of your earnings. To reduce this drain on your livelihood, you can either practice tax evasion or tax avoidance. Tax evasion refers to such illegal schemes as maintaining two sets of books, not reporting rents, overstating expenses, or running personal expense through your property accounts. In contrast, tax avoidance refers to perfectly legal strategies and tactics you can use such as depreciation deductions, tax credits, installment sales, tax-free exchange, and income shifting (e.g., timing of receipts and converting ordinary income into capital gains).

The key to a successful tax evasion plan is to line up trusted and competent property managers who will look after your properties while you are in jail. The key to successful tax avoidance strategies is knowledge and planning. By knowing the law, you can structure your income expenses, and transactions to minimize, if not eliminate, your income tax liabilities. Before you act, ask your accountant three questions: (1) How can I arrange and document this spending to make sure it's tax deductible? (2) How can I structure my receipt of income and capital gains to keep from losing it to the IRS? and (3) Can I arrange this spending or investment to qualify for any allowable tax credits?

Although the income tax law stands as a fact of life (at least for the present), the amount of income tax you pay does not. Through careful planning at the *start* of each year, you will find that you can slice your tax bill at the end of the year by thousands of dollars.

Similarly, all property owners must pay property taxes. But the amount of taxes you pay need not be the amount indicated on your tax statement. Through negotiations with the tax assessor's office or through formal appeal procedures, you may be able to pay less than the sum the assessor originally said you owed. Moreover, by learning the details of property tax laws and assessment practices *before* you remodel or renovate a property, you can make your improvements with an eye toward keeping your assessments down while enhancing the desirability of the property for your tenants.

Although you should never let tax avoidance drive your investment strategy, neither should you develop an investment strategy that fails to explore all available opportunities for tax avoidance. The stakes are too high. With governments' insatiable appetite for more of your money, your best defense is a strong offense. And a strong offense necessitates aggressive tax planning.

14 REAL ESTATE CAN GIVE YOU LIFETIME INCOME

Although owning income property can be profitable and fun, these benefits do not occur without work and effort on your part. We have provided a guide to investing in real estate; however, it is you who must implement the ideas presented in the text. You are required to do the following: Locate the right property to invest in, negotiate with the seller for its purchase, locate tenants, collect rents, handle improvements and repairs, and prepare your income tax returns to reduce or eliminate your tax liabilities.

It is you who must determine whether you can perform these activities. Such responsibilities are the drawbacks of owning income property. Now consider the advantages.

Over periods of 10 to 20 years, real estate, on the average, will appreciate one-and-a-half times the rate of inflation. That's right . . . 1.5 times the rate of inflation. Thus, you have a super hedge against inflation. Real estate cycles come and go. But over the longer run, the price trend has always headed up.

Not only, then, is inflation on your side as a real estate investor, but time is also. As time passes, rents can be increased, which means that the property you initially purchased which may have had little or no cash flow, can later yield positive cash flow from these increases.

Many property owners who have held on to their properties for a long time are able to live off the net rental income. In other words, income property purchased today with a small down payment will unlikely net a large positive cash flow. Yet as time passes, the property appreciates and rents are increased gradually, which over the long term will produce a substantial net income for the owner. Therefore, the longer you own the property, the greater the net income from it becomes. And during the time of ownership you enjoy the tax shelter benefits from the property. In other words, buy income property as soon as you can, then enjoy the income and wealth benefits as you grow older.

Besides the benefits of appreciation, growing income, and tax shelter, you also have a refinancing benefit. You can periodically refinance your holdings as the market value of your properties increases. Every few years you can refinance certain properties, pulling out cash to reinvest in more properties.

Still another method of income production occurs when the owner of real estate decides to sell. After owning property for an extended period, the owner will realize a sizable gain from the sale. He has the option of taking all cash from the gain or of accepting a note for his equity in the property. This is ideal for retirees who quit their jobs, sell their properties, carry the financing on a installment sale, and enjoy the income from those monthly checks.

Variations of how real estate can provide income for its owner are almost boundless. But where will you as an individual be as time goes on? That is entirely up to you. You can either be a landlord or a tenant or a homeowner. As a tenant you are only a tiny cog in the great financial wheels of progress that continues to pay rent (which is income to the landlord) just to have a place to live. Or you can join in the general prosperity that is enjoyed by the deserving people who are owners of property. You can become knowledgeable and experienced about real estate and with careful planning, take control of your own future. Even as a homeowner, you have the privilege at day's end to return to your appreciating investment—to that wonderful parcel of earth which belongs solely to you and has often been called "home, sweet home."

INDEX